The Blackwell Great Minds series gives readers a strong sense of the fundamental views of the great western thinkers and captures the relevance of these figures to the way we think and live today.

Forthcoming

blackwell great minds

edited by Steven Nadler

mill

Wendy Donner and Richard Fumerton

WILEY-BLACKWELL

A John Wiley & Sons, Ltd., Publication

Blackwell Publishing was acquired by John Wiley & Sons in February 2007.
Blackwell's publishing program has been merged with Wiley's global Scientific,
Technical, and Medical business to form Wiley-Blackwell.

Registered Office
John Wiley & Sons Ltd, The Atrium, Southern Gate, Chichester, West Sussex,
PO19 8SQ, United Kingdom

Editorial Offices
350 Main Street, Malden, MA 02148-5020, USA
9600 Garsington Road, Oxford, OX4 2DQ, UK
The Atrium, Southern Gate, Chichester, West Sussex, PO19 8SQ, UK

For details of our global editorial offices, for customer services, and for information
about how to apply for permission to reuse the copyright material in this book
please see our website at www.wiley.com/wiley-blackwell.

The right of Wendy Donner and Richard Fumerton to be identified as the authors
of this work has been asserted in accordance with the Copyright, Designs and
Patents Act 1988.

Library of Congress Cataloging-in-Publication Data

Donner, Wendy, 1948–
    Mill / Wendy Donner and Richard Fumerton ; edited by Steven Nadler.
        p. cm. – (Blackwell great minds)
    Includes bibliographical references and index.
    ISBN 978-1-4051-5087-3 (hardcover : alk. paper) – ISBN 978-1-4051-5088-0
(pbk. : alk. paper)   1. Mill, John Stuart, 1806–1873.   I. Fumerton, Richard A.,
1949–   II. Nadler, Steven M., 1958–   III. Title.

    B1607.D66 2009
    192–dc22

                                                              2008026392

A catalogue record for this book is available from the British Library.

Set in 9.5pt/12.5pt Trump Medieval
by Graphicraft Limited, Hong Kong
Printed in Singapore by Fabulous Printers Pte Ltd

1   2009

To David Lyons and Henry R. West (W. D.)

For my daughter-in-law Meg and my son-in-law David (R. F.)

contents

acknowledgments

Wendy Donner

I have many friends and colleagues to thank for contributing to this work directly or indirectly through their comments, conversation, and scholarship. Thanks are especially due to Kwame Anthony Appiah, Bruce Baum, Elizabeth Brake, D. G. Brown, Grant Cosby, Roger Crisp, Ben Eggleston, Alan Fuchs, Michele Green, John Haldane, the late R. M. Hare, Ellen Haring, David Lyons, Dale Miller, Maria Morales, the late Robert Nozick, Martha Nussbaum, Roger Paden, Ann Robson, the late John M. Robson, Fred Rosen, Alan Ryan, John Skorupski, Piers Stephens, L. W. Sumner , C. L. Ten, Nadia Urbinati, Georgios Varouxakis, Henry R. West, Fred Wilson, May Yoh, and Alex Zakaras.

I would like to express my gratitude to Carleton University for granting me a Faculty of Arts and Social Sciences Research Award in 2005 which allowed me to work on this manuscript during the period of May–December 2005. I am also grateful for receiving a Carleton University SSHRC Institutional Grant in 2005 and a Research Grant from the Vice-President (Research) and Dean of the Faculty of Arts and Social Sciences in 2006. All of these forms of institutional support were enormously helpful to this work. I thank Nick Bellorini and Liz Cremona of Wiley-Blackwell for their valuable work on this project. Copy-editor Claire Creffield has been a pleasure to work with and I thank her for her wonderful expertise and assistance.

I am grateful to Georgios Varouxakis, Philip Schofield, and Paul Kelly for inviting me to deliver a Keynote Address on "John Stuart Mill and Virtue Ethics" at the John Stuart Mill Bicentennial Conference, the ninth conference of the International Society for Utilitarian Studies, hosted by the Bentham Project at University College London in April 2007. Thanks are due to the members of the audience for engaging questions and comments. Thanks are also due to Ann Cudd and Ben Eggleston of the University of Kansas for inviting me to deliver a public lecture (co-sponsored by Philosophy, Women's Studies, and Humanities and Western Civilization) at their university in March 2007.

Richard Fumerton

Let me begin by thanking Wendy Donner for convincing me to be part of this project. Her energy and enthusiasm were critical to its completion. Although we don't always agree on the interpretation of Mill, I also profited greatly from reading Fred Wilson's work on Mill's logic, metaphysics, and epistemology. My interest in the history of philosophy is driven largely by my interest in the philosophical issues various historical figures raise. I first became interested in Mill in the context of my ongoing interest in philosophical problems of perception. And those interests were nurtured initially in undergraduate seminars I took at the University of Toronto with Francis Sparshott and Peter Hess. They continued to grow at Brown under the influence of Roderick Chisholm and Ernest Sosa. I would also like to close by thanking our copy-editor Claire Creffield for her excellent work.

abbreviations

CW   *The Collected Works of John Stuart Mill*, ed. John M. Robson, 33 vols. (Toronto: University of Toronto Press, 1963–91).

EWH   *An Examination of Sir William Hamilton's Philosophy* (London: Longmans, Green, and Company, 1889).

introduction

Biography: John Stuart Mill (1806–1873)

John Stuart Mill was born in London in 1806. His father, James Mill, was a philosopher, economist, and historian, who also held a prominent position in the East India Company. James Mill, along with Jeremy Bentham, was a founding father of a group known as the Philosophical Radicals, of which John Stuart Mill also became a prominent member. The group was known for its enthusiastic endorsement of utilitarianism as a moral and political philosophy, a philosophy they hoped would transform the political shape of the western world. James Mill played a critical role in the intellectual development of his eldest son, John Stuart Mill. John Stuart Mill was pushed very hard – he was taught Greek at the age of three and Latin at the age of eight. His studies in philosophy, economics, and politics, began early, and, under the influence of both his father and Jeremy Bentham, Mill became a committed utilitarian determined to carry on the legacy of his teachers. The pressure of his education and of living up to his father's intellectual expectations took its toll and Mill suffered a "mental crisis" in his early twenties. Mill himself credits his discovery of and interest in poetry, and in particular Wordsworth, with giving his life a kind of balance that made it richer and more fulfilling. Rather than continue a formal education, Mill followed his father in working for the East India Company from 1823 to 1858, a position that allowed him enough flexibility to pursue his intellectual writing.

While Mill is most famous for his more theoretical philosophical and political writings, he was also clearly interested in applying abstract principles. He wrote for the *London Review* which later became the *London and Westminster Review*, eventually becoming its editor. He also successfully ran as a Liberal for parliament in 1865 (representing Westminster and the ideas of the Philosophical Radicals until 1868). He was the Rector of St Andrews University in Scotland from 1865 to 1868. He took an active role in many political causes of his time including the abolitionist and women's suffrage campaigns. Indeed he was the first in parliament to introduce a bill giving women the right to vote. Mill's economic writings advocated a system of workers' cooperatives to improve the condition of the working class.

The dominant (and domineering) influence in Mill's life was almost certainly his father, but Mill himself viewed Harriet Taylor as one of the most important figures in his intellectual development. Mill met Taylor when she was a married woman, and despite her marriage to another man, the two maintained an extraordinarily close relationship for over two decades. Though by almost all accounts the relationship was platonic, it was, nevertheless, highly controversial, straining relations even between Mill and his siblings. When Taylor's husband died, Mill and Taylor were finally able to marry in 1851. Mill viewed Taylor as a collaborator on some of his important work, and in particular with respect to *On Liberty* (published shortly after her death in 1858).

It is difficult to overstate Mill's influence on most of the major areas of philosophy, and in particular on moral, social, and political philosophy. His *On Liberty* remains one of the best-known and widely discussed defenses of liberalism. No discussion of liberty and its fundamental place in a legitimate society is complete without taking into account the views Mill defends in that work. *Utilitarianism* may be the most frequently assigned reading in any standard introductory course on ethics. While it is a defense of the view that the only thing desirable as an end is happiness, Mill makes clear that he is working with an extremely broad conception of pleasure or happiness, one reminiscent of Greek virtue ethics. Mill's *The Subjection of Women* was a work well ahead of its time and remains the classic statement of a liberal feminist philosophy. While Mill's writings on logic, philosophy of language, metaphysics, and epistemology are, perhaps, less influential today, at one time they too dominated the philosophical landscape. Mill's famous methods (called to this day Mill's Methods) to discover causal truth are still a standard part of many informal logic texts. And although it is not clear that Mill endorses the view sometimes attributed to him, his work in the philosophy of language, in particular his view of names, has enjoyed a bit of a renaissance with the advent of so-called direct theories of reference.

In many ways Mill represented the culmination of British empiricism. His *System of Logic* was widely used for a very long time, and it was far more than a book on logic. *A System of Logic* explores fundamental issues in the philosophy of language, the epistemology and metaphysics of causation, the way in which we expand knowledge through inference, and even the analysis of moral judgment. His *Examination of Sir William Hamilton's Philosophy* is anything but a mere critical examination of the view of another important philosopher. It is a systematic attempt to work out the implications of a radical empiricism developed earlier by philosophers like George Berkeley and David Hume. In a way, Mill's work in this area provided a kind of bridge from the British empiricists to the twentieth-century positivists, and the fact that he was godfather to Bertrand Russell, one of the philosophical giants of the next century is, perhaps, a suitable metaphor for Mill's philosophical role. Mill died in Avignon, France, in 1873.

Major Works

A System of Logic, 1843
Principles of Political Economy, 1848
On Liberty, 1859
Utilitarianism, 1861
Considerations on Representative Government, 1861
An Examination of Sir William Hamilton's Philosophy, 1865
The Subjection of Women, 1869
Autobiography, 1873
Three Essays on Religion, 1874

The Collected Works of John Stuart Mill, 1963–91, general editor John M. Robson, contains 33 volumes of Mill's works. Volume 1 contains his literary essays, including "Thoughts on Poetry and its Varieties" (1833), and "Tennyson's Poems" (1835).

Introduction to Part I, Mill's Moral and Political Philosophy

Wendy Donner

John Stuart Mill was a formidable figure of the nineteenth century, a public intellectual, politician, and activist who made enduring contributions to moral, social, and political philosophy as well as to political life.

Mill's philosophy offers a rich, complex, and intriguing version of utilitarianism and liberalism. It is remarkably intricate. It is heavily influenced by and deeply linked to virtue ethics, and one of the aims of the chapters in Part I is to foreground and pay due respect to the elements of virtue ethics and politics in Mill's corpus. In Mill's theory the foundations remain utilitarian, for the development and exercise of the virtues provide the best chance of promoting happiness for all. But the characterization of human happiness is essentially interwoven with virtue. Roger Crisp and Michael Slote note that virtue ethics puts the focus on agents and their lives and character. They ask "is it possible for utilitarians . . . to enlarge the focus of their own theories to incorporate agents' lives as a whole, their characters as well as . . . their actions" (Crisp and Slote 1997, 3). As I contend here, in the case of Mill's utilitarianism, the answer is clearly in the affirmative.

In *The Liberal Self* (Donner 1991), I offered a revisionary reading and defense of Mill's theory of value, including centrally his qualitative hedonism. In Chapter 2 I reassess and further defend Mill on this central component of his moral philosophy. The questions I explore in Chapter 2 include quantitative and qualitative hedonism, value pluralism, and virtue ethics. In *Utilitarianism*, Mill lays down the basic principle of his moral theory, the principle of utility, which "holds that actions are right in proportion as they tend to promote happiness, wrong as they tend to produce the reverse of happiness" (CW 10:210).[1] In a consequentialist moral theory such as Mill's, the rightness and wrongness of acts are determined by their consequences, specifically, in the case of utilitarianism, the consequences that promote happiness or utility. Consequentialists look at whether actions produce good or bad results. Mill analyzes and unpacks good or value as happiness, and bad as unhappiness or suffering. Much of the exploration of Mill's concept of utility centers on examining his views on the nature of good, or what he means by happiness. Of central import also is his method for measuring good or happiness. His method relies upon the judgments of competent agents and one central focus of my examination is the analysis and exploration of what Mill means by a competent agent. Mill's notion of a competent agent is one who has undergone an education best understood as a process of development and self-development. Mill's characterization of competent agency features his indebtedness to virtue ethics.

I examine and defend Mill's value theory in part by comparing it with the quantitative hedonism of Jeremy Bentham, Mill's utilitarian predecessor. Hedonism maintains that the only things that are good intrinsically are pleasurable or happy states of experience. This statement leaves open the question of what properties of valuable states of experience contribute to their value. Bentham contends that only the quantity of happiness produces its value, while Mill counters that the quality or kind of happiness also counts in assessing its value. Mill maintains that the forms of happiness that are the most valuable are those that develop and exercise the higher human capacities and excellences. This claim explicitly ties Mill's theory in with the lineage of virtue ethics, which makes the exercise of the human excellences or virtues a focal point of ethics and politics. The chapter also takes up objections to hedonism. Some objections claim that it is inconsistent with hedonism to include the quality of pleasures in the assessment of value. Other objections come from external challenges. Value pluralists, for example, reject the notion that only happiness is intrinsically good and argue that other things like virtue, knowledge, and love can be considered as valuable in themselves, apart from any essential relation to happiness.

In Chapter 3 I consider core issues about Mill's views on right or obligation and the status of moral rules. I consider whether Mill's theory is best classified as act- or rule-utilitarianism and explore the difficulties confronting any attempt to firmly locate him in either category. The dispute over act- versus rule-utilitarianism concerns whether the principle of utility should be understood as assessing particular actions on a case-by-case basis or as assessing which moral rules are the most generally beneficial in producing good consequences. I explore the objection that the principle of utility is in conflict with the demands of justice. In responding to this objection I examine the relation between utility and justice in the architecture of Mill's theory, as well as the central place of rights grounded in utility in his system. I argue that awareness of the structure of Mill's theory is an indispensable tool for discerning his intentions. The foundation of Mill's theoretical structure is the Art of Life, which delineates the proper domain of Morality in its relations with companion spheres of Prudence or Policy and Virtue or Aesthetics. We need to understand the *scope* of Morality, as well as the place of rules of obligation and rights within the *structure* of his moral and practical philosophy before we can reasonably approach the question of the status of rules of obligation and principles of justice.

Chapter 4 is on liberty. Mill's famous liberty principle in *On Liberty* claims that "the sole end for which mankind are warranted, individually or collectively, in interfering with the liberty of action of any of their number, is self-protection" (CW 8:223). Liberty can be interfered with only to prevent harm to others. This classic statement raises an array of questions. What is the extent of the legitimate power which state and society may exercise over members of society? How is harm to others to be construed so as to set clear boundaries to the limits of social coercion to effectively protect vital interests and rights to liberty of speech, action, individuality, and self-development? Things fall into place, I argue, if we draw upon the structure of Mill's theory as set down in Chapter 3 and recognize that the liberty principle is a principle of justice, with the mandate of protecting the most vital human interests from the harms of incursions of compulsion and control. Mill invokes a basic distinction between liberty, which is a bedrock liberal value, and power, which is a harmful fuel for oppression and despotism. Mill's liberalism endorses liberty while rejecting despotic tendencies to gain control and power over others. This distinction runs as a bright line throughout his philosophy. I highlight the centrality of the right to liberty of self-development. I explore the importance of liberty in some of its most important manifestations such as freedom of thought and expression, autonomy, and individuality. His models of public deliberation and freedom of speech and action are particularly well suited to diverse and pluralistic societies and present an ideal of human moral and social progress. I scrutinize Mill's own example of polygamous marriage within Mormon communities of his time, in order to test the limits of application of the liberty principle. The case serves as an entry to look at some of the tensions raised by the need to balance individuality and community.

Chapter 5 brings together the commitments of utilitarianism and virtue ethics and of liberal egalitarianism in Mill's philosophy of education. Historical liberals like Mill place a great deal of importance on the education of members of society. In Mill's system, education is one of the primary moral arts, paired with the moral science of ethology (the science of character formation). In his liberal political philosophy, education is construed very broadly, as the art of character formation, and its ideals and goals then become the proper socialization of the members of society, both children and adults. Mill devotes many writings to an examination of appropriate education seen as processes of development and self-development of distinctive human capacities and excellences. Humans are deprived of the opportunity to lead the happiest lives unless they are afforded the opportunity to develop and use these capacities. To be a "competent agent" is Mill's shorthand for being an agent who has had the opportunity to undergo a process of development in childhood and self-development in adulthood. To be self-developed is both an essential element of and a precondition for appreciating the most valuable kinds of happiness. Thus we are entitled and have a right, founded on a vital interest, to be so educated in childhood (if we are born into a society with the means), and to reach at least a threshold level of self-development in adulthood. These capacities that make up self-development combine appropriate balances of autonomy and individuality and compassion, caring and social cooperation. This conception is fully in harmony with and resonant with conceptions of character in virtue ethics. The same abilities are needed to engage as responsible citizens in the public realm to cooperate and to promote the common good.

Chapter 6 is devoted to some core issues of Mill's political philosophy, namely, his liberalism and egalitarianism and applications to his vision of representative government and political and economic democracy. The discussion of education paves the way for an examination of the potentials and dilemmas of egalitarian liberalism. Contemporary liberal theorists such as Amy Gutmann engage with liberal conceptions of democracy that harmonize with the goals of education for democracy. Gutmann says "like democratic education, democracy is a political *ideal* – of a society whose adult members are, and continue to be, equipped by their education and authorized by political structures to share in ruling" (Gutmann 1987, xi). Mill's liberalism provides a framework for approaching issues such as appropriate democratic education and it is particularly well suited to contemporary multicultural and pluralistic societies. His commitment to active participatory democracy is another example of pursuing avenues for the practice of the virtues in the public domain that is linked to virtue theories. Mill's theory propounds a vision of deliberative, participatory democratic politics that is as radical today as it was in his time.

Mill's bold hopes for the prospects of liberal education for democratic practice and progress have faced objections about the limitations of his liberalism's capacity to address problems of inequality and elitism. I explore tensions between the elitist and the egalitarian strands of Mill's philosophy, and offer arguments that the egalitarian commitments are more fundamental and prevalent. The right to liberty of self-development is the right to have one's capacities and faculties developed in childhood so that one is able to carry on the process of self-development once adulthood is reached. This is a basic right since the development of these capacities is a precondition for engaging in and appreciating the moral and intellectual virtues, or the kinds of pleasures that are deemed most valuable, in adulthood. This central notion is the seed for some of the response to these objections. Mill's extensive writings examining the democratic and educative potential of social, political, and economic institutions are guided by these commitments. Mill argues for participatory and democratic workplace partnerships and associations, and hoped that this would bring about "the conversion of each human being's daily occupation into a school of the social sympathies and the practical intelligence" (CW 3:792).

In Chapter 7 this spirit is carried through in Mill's classic liberal feminism and arguments for sexual equality. In *The Subjection of Women* Mill promotes a liberal feminist argument for equality and claims that the family should be "a school of sympathy in equality, of living together in love, without power on one side or obedience on the other" (CW 21:295). His theory is defended by some for its groundbreaking insights on the path to equality between men and women and his clear understanding of the brutal effects of oppressive power and domestic violence. Mill is a classic proponent of liberal feminism, both in theory and in activist practice. I examine some details of his analysis, including his dissection of the brutality of domestic violence, his insights into the corrosive effects of patriarchal oppression upon women's happiness and liberty, and his analysis of how the subtler forms of this induce compliance without resort to violence. This stance has drawn its share of criticism from some contemporary feminist philosophers who see in Mill's work what they contend are the flaws of a liberal feminist framework writ large. I examine the objection that Mill's defense of gendered division of labor indicates that his goal is to mitigate rather than eliminate patriarchy.

In Chapter 8 I explore Mill's contribution to environmental philosophy. Mill is often cited in discussions of environmental ethics as an historical friend of sustainable development in his advocacy of the stationary state in economics and his opposition to the desirability of permanent economic growth. This progressive stance must be considered in balance with his expressed views in the essay "Nature" where he calls for moderate human interventions in nature to improve human prospects. His perspective on the environment is not as widely discussed in treatments of his own moral and political theory. I explore his value theory and how it fits in with the commitments of contemporary radical environmentalists who defend non-anthropocentric theories. I examine how his value theory serves as a foundation for a stance on appropriate appreciation of nature which goes part of the way with radical environmentalism. Finally, I see how his connections with Romanticism underscore this appreciation of wilderness and nature.

Introduction to Part II, Mill's Logic, Metaphysics, and Epistemology

Richard Fumerton

In his lifetime, Mill's philosophical influence in logic, philosophy of language, metaphysics, and epistemology was perhaps almost as significant as his influence in ethics and political philosophy. It cannot, however, be plausibly claimed that his work in the former fields had the same lasting importance. His colossal *A System of Logic* was a work not only in logic but also in philosophy of science, philosophy of language, metaphysics, and epistemology. It contains, however, at least some views that are simply outdated. Formal logic is one of the (perhaps relatively few) areas of philosophy in which it seems uncontroversial that huge advances have been made since the time Mill wrote. Similarly, in the philosophy of language, distinctions have been made that render more perspicuous the terms of various debates, even as the debates rage on. In *An Examination of Sir William Hamilton's Philosophy*, Mill's heroic efforts at reducing meaningful discourse to claims that are experientially verifiable through straightforward enumerative induction have largely been rejected, both in detail and in theory (though there are a few of us still sympathetic to the theory). Nor can one even say that Mill was always the most original of thinkers in these fields. Many of his ideas had their seeds in earlier British empiricists such as Berkeley and Hume.

Even if the above claims are true, however, we should not underestimate Mill's importance in the development of philosophy. As I argue later, Mill's work was very much the *culmination* of British empiricism. If Mill was undeniably heavily influenced by the views of earlier empiricists, he developed those views in the kind of detail that allows subsequent generations of philosophers to see more clearly their implications. As a result the philosophical community was much better positioned to evaluate those views. Mill's conception of matter, for example, as the permanent possibility of sensation was one of the inspirations for positivist reductions of the early twentieth century. However short-lived it was, positivism in its heyday owed a great debt to John Stuart Mill. And even after the more extreme versions of positivism were largely rejected, Mill's suspicions concerning an intuitionist metaphysics and his emphasis on grounding justified belief in empirical evidence have an influence that is still profound.

In my discussion of Mill's logic, metaphysics, and epistemology, I could not do justice to the intricacies of Mill's many views and arguments. I tried instead to give the reader a feel for what I take to be the *heart* of Mill's philosophy. I tried to work almost exclusively with primary texts, and to carve out of those texts the conclusions that I think Mill was most interested in defending. The interpretation of Mill is nowhere near as straightforward as my prose might sometimes imply. Reasonable philosophers might disagree on how to understand any number of theses I attribute to him.

As I suggested above, I don't think that it is possible to understand and appreciate Mill without seeing his work against the backdrop of earlier empiricism. With that in mind, in Chapter 9, I try to describe the metaphysical and epistemological tenets of British empiricism that so dominated Mill's conception of the problems that needed to be addressed. In particular, I set out in some detail the threat of skepticism that so concerned philosophers like Berkeley and Hume.

In Chapter 10, I try to make explicit the epistemological presuppositions of Mill's own brand of empiricism, beginning with some perhaps surprising and potentially significant observations about Mill's willingness to allow into the foundation of empirical knowledge either truths about past experience or truths about probabilistic connections between present apparent memories and past experiences. Mill's liberal attitude towards incorporating non-inductively based knowledge of the past certainly didn't expand to knowledge of the external world. Mill was squarely in the empiricist camp that limited direct empirical knowledge to the phenomenally given character of subjective and fleeting sensation. Unlike Berkeley, who tried to combine that view with an idealism that reduced objects to bundles of actual ideas (either in the minds of humans or in the mind of God), or Hume, who seemed resigned to a radical skepticism concerning belief in an external world, Mill argued that we can find a way of understanding physical objects that will avoid skepticism. He argued that our thought about external reality is just thought about the "permanent possibilities of sensations." Mill's view was a rough forerunner of the phenomenalism defended by some positivists of the twentieth century. As a solution to the epistemological problem of justifying belief in external reality, it is no more plausible than the reduction of physical objects to permanent possibilities of sensation, a view I discuss in more detail in Chapter 11.

In Chapter 10, I group together the examination of Mill's views on logic and his views on epistemology because I think that for Mill himself the two fields are intimately connected. Mill makes some truly startling claims about the subordination of deductive to inductive reasoning. One of these claims concerns the status of mathematical knowledge. Mill is one of very few philosophers who seem willing to claim that even simple arithmetical truths like $2 + 2 = 4$ are only inductively supported, an idiosyncratic claim that I critically evaluate.

Mill is so taken with the fundamental place of inductive reasoning that, on one natural reading, he even seems to claim that all *genuine* reasoning is properly viewed as inductive. While in one sense the claim is patently false, it becomes more understandable when interpreted as an *epistemological* claim. His idea, I argue, is that deductively valid syllogistic reasoning often masks the underlying inferences involved in justifying a belief. Because inductive reasoning is so pivotal to Mill's understanding of epistemic justification, I devote one section of Chapter 10 to his discussion of the justifying ground of our employment of induction.

No discussion of Mill is complete without a discussion of his famous methods for discovering causal connections, and I follow an examination of Mill's more abstract views on induction with an examination of these more applied epistemological principles.

In Chapter 11, I turn to Mill's views in metaphysics, construing the field broadly so that it includes his views about the way in which language represents the world. Again, I argue that it is not really possible to understand Mill's metaphysics without understanding his radical empiricism, a radical empiricism driven by the firm conviction that we must rely on empirical foundations consisting of direct apprehension of the "phenomenally given." The problem is how to avoid skepticism within such a framework. As I indicated above, Mill's solution to the problem of perception critically involves a claim about how to understand the content of claims about the physical world. To successfully reduce talk of physical objects to talk about the permanent possibility of sensations, we must not allow the language of physical objects to creep into our characterization of permanent possibilities of sensations. It is an understatement to suggest that succeeding in this task is an uphill battle.

Just as Mill's views on the metaphysics and epistemology of perception are intimately connected, so also his views on the metaphysics and epistemology of causation are intertwined. In Chapter 11, I give a brief critical evaluation of Mill's metaphysical account of causation.

As was briefly indicated above, there has been something of a resurgence of interest in Mill's views in the philosophy of language, largely due to passages in *A System of Logic* in which he appears to endorse the now somewhat fashionable direct reference theory for names. While I don't even try to do justice to the intricacies of the many distinctions Mill makes concerning meaning and reference, I do suggest that one ought to move slowly before embracing Mill as a forerunner of contemporary direct reference theorists.

I conclude my discussion of Mill's metaphysics by returning to the topic of ethical judgments. Mill was obviously fundamentally interested in ethical theorizing. But for a philosopher who was clearly concerned with careful analysis of the concept of other sorts of claims (such as claims about the physical world), Mill's ethical writing is surprisingly free of straightforward meta-ethical discussion of the *content* of moral claims. There are, I argue, hints of a view about the meaning of ethical statements in utilitarianism, but there are also some surprising passages, usually overlooked, in *A System of Logic* that bear on the interpretation of Mill's implicit commitments in this area. In what might well seem like fairly wild speculation, I suggest a reason why Mill might want to have kept in the background his considered view on this matter.

note

1 With a few clearly indicated exceptions, page references to Mill's writings are to *The Collected Works of John Stuart Mill*, ed. John M. Robson, 33 vols. (Toronto: University of Toronto Press, 1963–91). Hereafter *Collected Works*, cited as CW.

mill's moral and political philosophy

Wendy Donner

utilitarianism: theory of value

Introduction

Utilitarianism is an intriguingly intricate moral philosophy with many facets, and it is open to a plurality of readings and interpretations. In this multifarious landscape, John Stuart Mill's version of utilitarianism still stands out as one of the more complex varieties. It is an exemplar of intricacy and its complex structure invites reflection and dialogue on an assortment of theoretical puzzles and questions about its plausibility and most accurate interpretation. Mill's theory is rich and substantial. It is constructed for the purpose, if not the mission, of ready application to a wide range of social and political questions. It is undoubtedly an activist and reformist theory, well suited to Mill's own lifelong commitments to social and political campaigns and issues of his day.

Despite its intricacy, which does perplex and challenge, its core is pristinely simple and strikingly compelling. The starting point and the anchor are the reality of suffering in the world and the awareness this brings for the ethical life. The foundational claim is that the starting point of ethics is this suffering and the aspirations and obligations to alleviate suffering and promote happiness that flow from this in ethical life. Mill's statement of the foundational principle of utilitarianism as a moral theory is unequivocal. "The creed which accepts as the foundation of morals, Utility, or the Greatest Happiness Principle, holds that actions are right in proportion as they tend to promote happiness, wrong as they tend to produce the reverse of happiness" (CW 10:210). Mill's classic utilitarian theory thus contends that actions are judged to be right or wrong according to their consequences. Utilitarianism is a form of consequentialism, because it is by referring to the consequences of actions that we morally assess them. In a consequentialist moral theory such as Mill's, the rightness and wrongness of acts are determined by their consequences, specifically, in the case of utilitarianism, the consequences that promote happiness or utility. Mill analyzes and unpacks good or value as happiness, and bad as unhappiness or suffering.

The principle of utility functions as the ultimate standard and foundational principle of morality. However, in Mill's utilitarianism, the principle of utility serves a much broader purpose than that of simply grounding morality. It is a general principle of the good, and does full duty as the ultimate standard for all practical reasoning, for all of the "practice of life" (CW 8:951). This generality of function has significant implications, which are sometimes overlooked, for the rest of Mill's utilitarianism. Here is Mill's statement of the principle clarifying its status as a principle of good. "The utilitarian doctrine is, that happiness is desirable, and the only thing desirable, as an end; all other things being only desirable as means to that end" (CW 10:234). He adds that "by happiness is intended pleasure, and the absence of pain; by unhappiness, pain, and the privation of pleasure" (CW 10:210). He expands this meaning in claiming that "pleasure, and freedom from pain, are the only things desirable as ends; and . . . all desirable things (which are as numerous in the utilitarian as in any other scheme) are desirable either for the pleasure inherent in themselves, or as means to the promotion of pleasure and the prevention of pain" (CW 10:210).

The full distinctiveness of Mill's theory emerges in the examination of the details of the nature of good. The wide reach of this principle of good in a utilitarian consequentialist theory is unsurprising. Much depends upon the conception of this good, and I now turn to an investigation of the nature of good.

Qualitative Hedonism

Jeremy Bentham, James Mill, and John Stuart Mill are all classical utilitarian philosophers, sharing core concepts, frameworks, and principles. While the singularity of Mill's theory of value is indisputable, in acknowledging this distinctiveness it is crucial not to overlook this core common ground. Mill adhered to the basic principles that Bentham advocated and thought that Bentham was right about the essentials. The shared core is that the good for human beings consists in experiences or states of consciousness of pleasure or happiness. Hedonism maintains that the only things that are intrinsically good are pleasurable or happy states of experience. I argue that this statement of the basic claim of hedonism leaves open further questions that need exploring.

The differences appear in the detailed analysis of the nature of states of pleasure or happiness. All these philosophers hold to mental-state accounts of utility, locating value in states of mind and experiences such as pleasure, happiness, satisfaction, enjoyment, or well-being. It is convenient in some respects to label Mill's value theory as qualitative hedonism, in part to allow a ready comparison with Bentham's avowedly quantitative hedonism. But as the use of this label can be misleading, it is important that I signal early and clearly that what counts for the philosophical discussion depends upon an accurate understanding of the substance of his views, and not the label we apply to those views. It is also important, in explicating and exploring Mill's views in *Utilitarianism*, that I make full and free use of his voluminous body of work on this subject in other writings for filling in the background and context and for completeness of understanding.

Mill was the designated heir of the Benthamite utilitarian philosophical family lineage. His father James Mill designed his childhood education to train him for this responsibility. Yet Mill's own philosophical theory of value is singular in large measure because of Mill's own acute awareness of the limitations and weaknesses of his philosophical forebears' formulation of utilitarianism, and of the effects of the limitations on his own education and development (CW 1:137–92). Many of those weaknesses Mill located in Bentham's theory of value and especially in his conception of the good. Since in this philosophical tradition the concepts of human nature and of character are intimately linked and connected to the concept of good for agents with this nature, the younger Mill traced the flaws in the view of intrinsic value back to flaws in the Benthamite depiction of character and human nature (CW 10:5–18, 94–100). These two are interwoven and cannot be disentangled. He also departed from Bentham's method of measuring utility, the notorious felicific calculus, which he regarded as being too crude as a measurement instrument.

One promising point of embarkation for a consideration of Mill's differences with Bentham is Mill's comment in *Utilitarianism* that critics of hedonism dislike hedonism and characterize it as "a doctrine worthy only of swine" (CW 10:210). He answers,

> The accusation supposes human beings to be capable of no pleasures except those of which swine are capable . . . a beast's pleasures do not satisfy a human being's conceptions of happiness. Human beings have faculties more elevated than the animal appetites, and when once made conscious of them, do not regard anything as happiness which does not include their gratification. (CW 10:210)

In unraveling the meaning of this we come to the heart of his disputes with his mentor. For he was affected by this objection, and sensitive that it might apply to Bentham's theory of value. In distancing himself, he broke new ground in his presentation of the good for humans. Bentham's brand of hedonism is vulnerable, Mill feared, because Bentham's hedonism explicitly allows only one sort of good-making characteristic or feature – namely quantity – to be taken into account in assessing how much value a particular state of mind is judged to have. In focusing only on quantity, Bentham's theory also tends to focus on the simple pleasurable sensations and components of experience. Mill distances himself from Bentham's quantitative theory in several pivotal respects.

The things that are valuable are satisfying or pleasurable states of experience or consciousness. But Mill's expansive conception of good, reconstructed to overcome Benthamite limitations, goes much further than Bentham in the first of these pivotal differences. While Bentham contends that simple sensations of pleasure are the paradigm mental states that are valuable, Mill demurs. Mill proposes that value is contained in complex, heterogeneous states of consciousness which are the products of the workings of psychological laws of association on these simple mental states. Sensations and ideas are linked through association and in the process of psychological development these originally simple mental states evolve into more complex states of experience. Mill thinks that association often operates as a quasi-chemical process to create chemical unions of elements in which the original parts or elements merge into a new and complex whole. He says,

> When many impressions or ideas are operating in the mind together, there sometimes takes place a process of a similar kind to chemical combination. When impressions have been so often experienced in conjunction, that each of them calls up readily and instantaneously the ideas of the whole group, those ideas sometimes melt and coalesce into one another, and appear not several ideas, but one. (CW 8:853)

The complexes that result occupy an important place in Mill's moral psychology and his value theory. They are the paradigm bearers of value, rather than the simple ideas that generate them.

Secondly, Mill contends that limiting the good-making characteristics of valuable states of consciousness to their quantity is misguided. Mill argues that the quality (or kind) as well as the quantity are both correctly seen as the good-making properties which determine the value of these satisfying states of consciousness. Thirdly, the measurement of utility is of central concern for utilitarianism. The procedures for measuring the value of the states of consciousness that are under consideration widen the distance between Bentham and Mill. Mill's method for measuring value relies upon the judgments of "competent agents." One key question thus is the exploration of what Mill means by a competent agent. I argue that Mill's notion of a competent agent is an agent who has undergone an education best understood as a process of development and self-development. This conception of a competent agent is at the very core of Mill's ethical theory. I explore this central question in Chapter 5, Philosophy of Education (see also Donner 1991; 1998).

To facilitate understanding, it is helpful to keep in mind that, although the bearers of value are pleasurable mental states, what we are seeking to promote and measure is utility or value. In Mill's system, complex mental states are the paradigm entities that are valuable. As these are complex, they have a multitude of features that can be observed through mindful introspection. People can be trained and educated to become adept and skillful at noting their various properties and components. In this introspective scrutiny, many of the properties that come to attention have nothing to do with the value of the experience. And others do come to attention as those that are good-making and contribute to the value of the experience. Bentham maintains that only the quantity (primarily intensity and duration) counts in the reckoning of value of satisfying experiences. Mill contends that, in addition to quantity, the quality or kind of the experience also counts in this reckoning. Their shared common ground is that they both contend that these named features have a dual nature and function. They are both empirical features, that is, features of the consciousness that can be empirically and phenomenally picked out by a discerning, trained awareness. But at the same time, they are also normative, or good-making, or productive of value. This discernment can be done better or worse, well or badly, depending upon the cultivation and education in this ability. This training to discern and appreciate certain properties of experience is one of the basic building blocks of the education and training of competent agents in Mill's system. This means that they are appropriately or correctly picked out or discerned by a trained introspective mind as the basis of value. While value is grounded in these empirical and phenomenal features, and these provide an empirical base for value, the features are not identical with value and they do not constitute value.

Since few would dispute that in many typical cases a greater quantity of happiness or satisfaction is better than a lesser, the trained, discriminative judgments involved in coming to an assessment about what the quantity "amounts to" in Bentham's system may seem too obvious to merit dwelling upon. But pausing here is helpful in understanding what Mill is proposing. When we explore further Bentham's good-making and empirical feature of quantity, we find that there is no simple characteristic of quantity. Instead, Bentham's felicific calculus, his method of measuring value, breaks down quantity into several components. Although he names seven "circumstances to be taken into the account in estimating the value of a pleasure or pain" (Bentham 1970, 38) most commentators collapse these and focus on the first two, namely, the intensity and the duration. Here I pass over many of the problems with measurement long associated with the felicific calculus. I zero in on the point that trained discrimination is called on and necessary even to judge in a rough and ready manner the amount of, at least, the intensity.

But even supposing that adequate judgments of intensity with the definite units required by Bentham's system are available, a further explicitly normative judgment is required in order to arrive at the overall value of the pleasure.

This is because there is no quantity *simpliciter*; ineluctably, there are only properties such as intensity and duration. There is no simple empirical or phenomenal property of quantity, composed of one element that can be measured. Quantity is unavoidably a compound feature of experience, comprised of at least the features of intensity and duration. Bentham assumes too readily that these two features of intensity and duration should be given equal weight. What hides in the background, but must be brought to the foreground for analysis and made conspicuous, is Bentham's assumed normative judgment that the intensity and the duration of a pleasure count equally in estimating and calculating its value. But this cannot simply be assumed, as it is a disputable claim. We may well ask why intensity and duration should count equally. It is possible and indeed plausible to construct scenarios in which a few brief periods of extraordinary happiness or ecstatic bliss are taken to be the central defining moments of a life. In such scenarios some people would be willing to make enormous sacrifices of other periods of happiness in order to attain and achieve these brief moments of intense satisfaction. Lives of adventurers are plausibly interpreted in this light. It is also possible and plausible to construct scenarios in which the feature of duration is given overriding weight. In such scenarios the agents choose to eschew or abstain from intense pleasures in order to pursue and protect the peaceful and calm enjoyments that are constant and enduring. It is not required that such cases be typical or common in order to make the point that Bentham's measurement procedure is not merely one of straightforward calculation. From these scenarios we can draw out the point that different agents, similarly trained and educated, can be expected to differ in their judgments, assessments, and weightings of intensity and duration. What I claim must be noted is that a normative judgment about how to weigh these two separate components of quantity (for there is no simple property quantity) is unavoidable. No straightforward empirical calculation of quantity absent this normative weighting judgment can be obtained. Moreover, agents of different character and outlook will inevitably differ about the best way to weigh these features, according to whether they are bold and exuberant thrill-seekers, to take one extreme, or peaceful contemplatives, to take the other. Pluralism and diversity of judgment are unavoidable.

This clarification of the requirements of Bentham's calculus is helpful in approaching Mill's proposals. Mill claims that quality, as well as quantity, is a good-making feature of pleasurable experience. He says that by quality of experience he means kind. In *Utilitarianism* he says,

It is quite compatible with the principle of utility to recognize the fact, that some *kinds* of pleasure are more desirable and more valuable than others. It would be absurd that while, in estimating all other things, quality is considered as well as quantity, the estimation of pleasures should be supposed to depend on quantity alone. (CW 10:211)

What is there to decide whether a particular pleasure is worth purchasing at the cost of a particular pain, except the feelings and judgment of the experienced? When, therefore, those feelings and judgment declare the pleasures derived from the higher faculties to be preferable *in kind*, apart from the question of intensity, to those of which the animal nature, disjoined from the higher faculties, is susceptible, they are entitled on this subject to the same regard. (CW 10:213)

According to the Greatest Happiness Principle . . . the ultimate end . . . is an existence exempt as far as possible from pain, and as rich as possible in enjoyments, both in point of quantity and quality. (CW 10:214)

Mill mirrors Bentham in maintaining that the relevant properties of experiences are both empirical and normative. Much confusion about Mill's meaning has its source in a failure of critics and commentators to note that in Mill's philosophy quality and value are not synonymous. Value, Mill holds, is what we are trying to promote or produce and what we measure when we follow the principle of utility. The quality of pleasurable experience is best understood as its kind, and indeed Mill says, as explicitly as possible, that by quality he means kind of pleasure: "it is quite compatible with the principle of utility to recognize the fact, that some *kinds* of pleasure are . . . more valuable than others." In Mill's system, value or good is produced by the two basic good-making properties, quantity (intensity and duration) and quality (kind). Experiences are ranked on the scale of value; in other words what is being measured is the value of experiences. The scales are not cardinal, as in Bentham's system, for Mill maintains that these sorts of value judgment do not lend themselves to cardinal measurement. Mill allows for different categories of kind to be brought into the measurement procedure. In his most basic statements of the theory, the qualities or kinds of happiness that are the most valuable are those that develop and exercise the higher human capacities and faculties (see Donner 1991; Brink 1992; Crisp 1997). Put alternatively, the exercise of the intellectual and moral virtues or excellences exemplify the most valuable kinds of happiness. This claim explicitly ties in Mill's theory with the lineage of virtue ethics, which makes the exercise of the human excellences or virtues a focal point of ethics and politics (see Berkowitz 1999; Semmel 1984). Mill's standard example is that "the pleasures derived from the higher faculties [are] preferable *in kind*" (CW 10:213). Thus kinds can be classified as those resulting from the exercise of the higher human faculties. But kinds of pleasure are also classified by cause or source and by phenomenal differences in the experience. Causal and intentional properties form their own categories of kinds. Mill's theory is characterized by its flexibility in part because he identifies quality and kind, and yet also has a pliant view of the categories of kinds.

Bentham's measurement procedure combines empirical, factual judgments and discriminations about the amount of intensity and duration with incontrovertible normative judgments about how they are to be weighted and then integrated onto the primary scale of value, which is what we are measuring. Mill's measurement procedure follows Bentham to an extent and then takes a radically new direction. Mill's procedure must deal with combining the dimensions of intensity and duration, but his procedure must also have a process for integrating judgments of quality (kind) onto the primary scale of value. Agents must make normative judgments, not just about how to weigh intensity and duration, but also about how to weigh quality against quantity in combining them on the primary scale. There is a more extensive normative component in Mill's measurement procedure. The further normative judgment that Mill's procedure calls for is that some kinds (qualities) of satisfactions are more valuable, and thus should be ranked more highly on the central scale of value. Mill's frequent references to "higher" pleasures are thus best understood as meaning pleasures of a kind (quality) that is more valuable. The measurement procedure leads Mill in the new direction of eliciting the judgments of competent agents to resolve, determine, and arrive at overall judgments of the value of pleasurable experiences. These judgments are best understood as being evidential, and thus they may be mistaken – indeed, Mill's expectation of progress over time has built into it the expectation that judgments are regularly discovered to be mistaken. The method allows for a vote among judges in cases of disagreement, in the public realm. As the diversity and pluralism of contemporary societies increase, a philosophy that explicitly allows for and expects diversity among educated and trained agents is plausible and helpful; one that expects conformity is not. Roger Crisp says:

> Because the views of the judges are only evidential, it is of course conceivable that they may be mistaken, and Mill implicitly accepts this in allowing for disagreement among them . . . Mill is claiming not that the majority *must* be right, but that it is only reasonable to respect the decision of the majority. (Crisp 1997, 36–7)

The caveat to this claim is, of course, that in the area of life defended in *On Liberty*, where actions do not affect the vital interests or rights of others, the judgments of individuals must be respected.

These roads lead to the central role of a philosophy of education to explain the proper education of developed and self-developed agents. It is indicative of the deep links with virtue ethics. And this distinctive and new direction of the theory leads directly to some persistent objections to Mill's qualitative hedonism.

Objections to Mill's Qualitative Hedonism: Internal Inconsistency and Value Pluralism

Mill's revision of Bentham's hedonism and his attempts to distance himself from the problems he perceived in the Benthamite theory of value have not always been well received in the discussions of his theory. Indeed, his bold revisionism and his inclusion of quality as a good-making property have faced strong criticism. Mill's shift away from quantitative hedonism produces a theory notable or notorious for its complexity and its openness to a variety of readings and interpretations. His procedure for measuring value is similarly intricate and complex, and open to a range of interpretations and attendant objections. However, I contend that many of the most persistent and often-repeated criticisms of Mill are misguided and based upon confusion. One result of this focus upon confused objections, I contend, has been to misdirect attention away from the objections to Mill's value theory which are more intractable and more deeply challenging and puzzling. These more substantial objections are put by value pluralists, who argue that things other than happiness are valuable in themselves.

One of the most persistent objections is that Mill's qualitative hedonism is internally inconsistent, or alternatively that Mill's theory abandons hedonism by including quality in the measurement of the value of pleasurable experience. According to this perspective, if you are a hedonist, then the only property that can count in measuring the value is quantity, or how much of the pleasurable experience there is. This objection is bluntly stated by F. H. Bradley:

> If you are to prefer a higher pleasure to a lower without reference to quantity – then there is an end altogether of the principle which puts the measure in the surplus of pleasure to the whole sentient creation. (Bradley 1962, 119)

Although this objection put by Bradley is persistently raised, its persistence does not reflect its strength. It is based upon a misconstrual of the basic claim of hedonism, which is that pleasurable experience is the only thing that is good in itself. I argue that it is a separate question what dimensions or properties of these experiences produce their value and should be taken into account in the measurement of their value. This objection to Mill's value theory falls prey to the error of conflating two separate questions: (a) what things are intrinsically valuable (pleasurable mental states) and (b) what properties of these mental states are productive of their value. A position on the first question leaves yet undetermined an answer to the second.

In assuming the very claim that needs to be argued, namely, that only quantity matters in assessing the overall value of pleasure, Bradley simply begs the question against Mill. Mill has a classic response in anticipation of this objection that has occupied such a prominent place in the literature. His response is succinct but compelling. Mill says:

> It would be absurd that while, in estimating all other things, quality is considered as well as quantity, the estimation of pleasures should be supposed to depend on quantity alone. (CW 10:211)

It is indeed absurd to assume as the baseline position that if you value satisfying experiences, then the only thing about them that matters is how much or what quantity you have. Few, if any, actual rational moral agents care only about the amount of happiness they have. Mill's theory of value is constructed as a guide for actual agents in living worthwhile lives. He apprehends clearly that quantity does not capture the whole picture, and he constructs an account that more accurately reflects and guides judgments of practical wisdom. Roger Crisp sees the similarities of Mill's perspective and Aristotelian virtue accounts:

> Those who can judge the value of experiences correctly are those who are not only sensitive to the salient features of those experiences, particularly their intensity and nature, but able to attach to those features the evaluative weight they deserve. (Crisp 1997, 39)

It simply does not follow from the basic claim of hedonism, namely, that the only intrinsically valuable things are experiences of happiness, that we are committed to the further claim that only the amount of happiness matters. This is clearly mistaken. Moreover, it is deeply at odds with how reflective people make comparative choices about good things, beautiful things, noble things, and other similar value choices. In such choices, the kind as well as the amount is standardly taken into account in making value judgments. The anomalous perspective in these practical and rational judgments in daily life is the approach that only quantity matters.[1]

There are substantive and persistent challenges and objections to Mill's value theory which are not as easily laid to rest. Thoughtful readers will find themselves puzzling over these. Value pluralism presents one such challenge to all forms of hedonism. Value pluralism maintains that all forms of hedonism are too limited in the list of things allowed onto the list of intrinsically valuable things. Surely, the value pluralist contends, other things like virtue, knowledge or wisdom, and enlightenment are, at least on some occasions, valuable in themselves, apart from any connection to or presence of happiness or satisfaction.

Mill's reply draws upon his psychological theory of associationism. He uses virtue as an example.

> To illustrate this further, we may remember that virtue is not the only thing, originally a means, and which if it were not a means to anything else, would be and remain indifferent, but which by association with what it is a means to, comes to be desired for itself. (CW 10:235)

Mill's point is that through psychological association virtue becomes part of our happiness. Originally we desire virtue as a means to happiness, but through psychological association virtue becomes pleasurable and so a component of happiness. Virtue is pleasurable especially when a person has developed and exercises the moral and intellectual capacities. I claim that the development and exercise of the virtues is so interwoven with happiness in Mill's system that this response is plausible. A bigger test to his system is the example of knowledge. Although the development and exercise of the intellectual virtues is also interwoven with happiness, we can construct examples of human knowledge which seem to lack this connection to human well-being, and which even seem strongly connected with deep and massive harm and suffering. One immediate example is the knowledge that led to the construction of the atomic bomb. The horror inflicted upon Hiroshima seems to be a clear example of knowledge separated and severed from human well-being. The proliferation of nuclear weapons and other horrifying weapons of mass destruction are further examples. We can add in knowledge severed from well-being in some examples like the expertise that destroys the natural environment. Viewed in this light, examples of knowledge severed from well-being and satisfaction are plentiful. But is this what value pluralists intend to propound? This is not the sort of counterexample to hedonism to which they appeal. The objection from pluralists is rather looking for knowledge that is valuable in itself, and knowledge leading to mass destruction does not seem to fit the bill. At this point the question arises as to where the burden of proof lies, as well as the question what impact these examples should have. The opponent of hedonism replies that the sorts of examples she has in mind are decidedly not those that cause deep suffering (which also have a connection to well-being, albeit a negative one). The sorts of examples rather are those valuable in themselves, apart from happiness, and not as a means to something further, as would be the case in knowledge as instrumentally, rather than intrinsically, valuable.

Is Mill correct in asserting this essential link to experienced happiness of these other purported good things? In his favor, a very strong case can be made that in cases of other good things, if a link to happiness is not present we are inclined to question the intrinsic nature of the value. Whether this applies to all such proposed examples is a good question to ponder. This is the sort of question to which a definitive answer seems elusive, for both supporters and opponents of qualitative hedonism.

But, while counterexamples to Mill's theory can be constructed in which the link to happiness may seem neutral, are we not entitled to more from the value pluralist? Do examples in the absence of a more complete alternative theory constitute a compelling objection to Mill? For the claims of value pluralism to be convincing, we need the apparatus of a theory, not simply examples in isolation from a theoretical structure. A contrary case needs also to be constructed showing how virtue and knowledge are valuable apart from this connection to happiness. Generally what occurs in these discussions is that value pluralists point to proposed examples without making the extensive positive case for the claim that they are good in themselves. This would need to include an analysis of how knowledge can be good in itself in cases in which massive suffering results. For if knowledge is indeed valuable in itself, then must it not be valuable even in the cases in which it has no link to happiness, as well as in cases in which it results in great suffering? Perhaps this is too stringent a requirement. But, at minimum, there must be an analysis similar to that proffered by Mill, setting out the good-making features of knowledge, or an alternative apparatus. So Mill's argument that there must be connections to happiness in order to claim that knowledge is valuable is bolstered by some counterexamples to value pluralism.

Perhaps the value pluralist will respond that we don't know what good consequences this knowledge will provide in the future. But this line of reply supports hedonism, since it appeals in the end to enhancement of human happiness and undercuts the objection. Does value pluralism claim that knowledge is a good even if it leads to horrific suffering? Or merely that there are some examples of knowledge that are neutral with regard to well-being, yet good nonetheless? We may be led to the conclusion that Mill's case is far stronger than that of the opponents.

The Judgment of Competent Agents: Self-Development and Value Measurement

A thorough understanding of Mill's value theory needs an examination, not just of his views on the nature of value, but also of his approach to measuring the value at the heart of his system. Mill sets out an expansive conception of good and he develops a method for measuring the value of satisfying experiences that is consonant with this enlarged view. Mill's method for measuring value relies on the judgments of competent agents who have undergone an education best understood as a process of development and self-development. Mill signals his method of value measurement in *Utilitarianism*. He says,

> If I am asked, what I mean by difference of quality in pleasures, or what makes one pleasure more valuable than another, merely as a pleasure, except its being greater in amount, there is but one possible answer. Of two pleasures, if there be one to which all or almost all who have experience of both give a decided preference, irrespective of any feeling of moral obligation to prefer it, that is the more desirable pleasure. If one of the two is, by those who are competently acquainted with both, placed so far above the other that they prefer it, even though knowing it to be attended with a greater amount of discontent, and would not resign it for any quantity of the other pleasure which their nature is capable of, we are justified in ascribing to the preferred enjoyment a superiority in quality, so far outweighing quantity as to render it, in comparison, of small account. (CW 10:211)

> From this verdict of the only competent judges, I apprehend there can be no appeal. On a question which is the best worth having of two pleasures, or which of two modes of existence is the most grateful to the feelings, apart from its moral attributes and from its consequences, the judgment of those who are qualified by knowledge of both, or, if they differ, that of the majority among them, must be admitted as final. (CW 10:213)

Mill is not primarily concerned with judgments about particular pleasures and satisfactions. The focus of his theory is as much on good character and good lives as it is on particular satisfactions. Because of the broad scope of concern, and the education needed to be a competent agent, he devotes much of his attention in his writings to his philosophy of education. I examine this in Chapter 5.

Mill believes that agents who have been properly socialized and educated are better equipped to lead satisfying and worthwhile lives in the private sphere, as well as to engage as responsible and active citizens in the public domain. We are all entitled to social resources and access to cooperative endeavors to allow us to lead lives of self-development as adults. Self-development is both an essential element of and an essential precondition for appreciating the most valuable kinds of happiness. Members of society who have been denied the basic education needed to become self-developed agents, or competent agents with the training and ability to make astute judgments of value, are wronged by their society. Thus a lot of theoretical weight is put on the philosophy of education in Mill's theory. The form of political liberalism consonant with Mill's value theory is egalitarian (Donner 1991, 160–87). People have a right to liberty of self-development and are wronged and harmed if they are shut out from an appropriate education.

His perspective on self-development also has significant implications for Mill's form of liberalism, as I explore in Chapter 6, on liberalism and democracy. If, as Mill holds, a threshold level of self-development is needed in order to lead a good life, then to deny someone the opportunity of self-development violates some of their most vital interests – and thus their basic rights. Since almost all members of society have the potential to attain the status of self-development, the social context and institutions have a large influence in determining whether these potentials develop. According to Mill's moral and political philosophy, people have the right to liberty of self-development, and their rights are violated if their society actively bars them or does not take action to provide the means to develop and exercise their human capacities.

Assessments of value based upon the judgments of self-developed agents have some measure of legitimacy or authority. But the authority of the judgments is not, in the long term, final or definitive, as these judgments can be mistaken and overturned by later evaluations. Indeed, Mill's faith in moral and social progress is a fixture of his theory. The judgments can be challenged and they are progressive; there is the expectation of change, improvement, and progress over time. There is also the expectation of disagreement, dispute, dissent, plurality, and diversity of views and judgments. This process, and the agents and their judgments, even highly educated ones, are all fallible, as the arguments of *On Liberty* take great pains to establish (CW 18:216–310). However, educated agents are the best situated and have the greatest chance to make correct discriminations and judgments.

I interpret Mill's method of assessing the value of satisfactions as laying out a comprehensive approach that allows in principle for the inclusion and comparability of the full range of the good-making features of enjoyments. This full range includes all of the areas of daily life that fall under what Mill calls the Art of Life – morality, prudence, and nobility, or "the Right, the Expedient, and the Beautiful or Noble, in human conduct and works" (CW 8:949). It also includes a vast array of what Mill calls the moral arts – all of the practical arts of daily living. My interpretation is consistent with Mill's own understanding of the broad reach of the principle of utility as the general principle of the good that guides and justifies all practical judgments about the ends of life. The principle of utility is a general principle of the good with a wide jurisdiction over all of the areas of private and public life and all of the arts of life. The implications of this are far reaching, for if the principle is to fulfill its function, the conceptions of the good at its basis must be general enough to carry into all of these areas of public and private life. The evaluative judgments and assessments of satisfactions and pursuits must be appropriate for all these different areas of life, and judgments of value must be sensitively attuned to the different contexts under perusal. The education required to make such judgments of the good becomes of central importance as a fulcrum of the theory.

This approach could not, then, without missing the spirit of the principle of utility and the range of areas under its jurisdiction, restrict the domain of the kinds of satisfactions that can be scrutinized and compared for value or disvalue. Mill himself undoubtedly regards the enjoyments of intellectual activity and pursuit of justice as primary examples of the highly valuable pleasures that develop and exercise the higher human capacities. However, it is important, I contend, to interpret his comments on the high value of these enjoyments as simply providing enduring examples of the application of the principles of his theory. Since his value theory is a general one, it is a mistake to restrict or try to determine in advance the good-making properties that are to be assessed and compared.[2]

Self-Development and Virtue Ethics

Mill's commitments to a progressive conception of human nature and a concept of the good fundamentally oriented to self-development connect his theory to the tradition of virtue ethics. The focus on the development and exercise of the human excellences as an ongoing lifelong pursuit is reminiscent of the priorities of ethics of virtue. This is not surprising considering the priority given in Mill's own childhood education to exposure to classical Greek philosophy. The spirit of Aristotelian virtue ethics pervades and permeates Mill's ethics, and Mill emphasizes its powerful influence on his outlook in the *Autobiography* (CW 1:9–53). Mill's extensive explanation of the educational processes of development and self-development can be read as setting out a program for the cultivation, inculcation, and development of essential mental and moral virtues. Although Mill gives these Aristotelian ideas a liberal egalitarian face, he follows Aristotle in propounding the claims that a good human life must be one that allows for the development and exercise of the human mental and moral excellences (see Berkowitz 1999; Crisp and Slote 1997; Urbinati 2002). He writes extensively about activities developing these traits in both public and private realms. I develop these themes further in Chapter 4 (Liberty), Chapter 6 (Political Philosophy: Liberalism and Democracy), and Chapter 7 (Sexual Equality and the Subjection of Women).

The foundations of Mill's theory are utilitarian, because habituation and exercise in the virtues provide the best means for promoting happiness for all. But the characterization of human happiness is essentially inter-woven with virtue. Roger Crisp and Michael Slote ask whether it is "possible for utilitarians . . . to enlarge the focus of their own theories to incorporate agents' lives as a whole, their characters as well as . . . their actions" (Crisp and Slote 1997, 3). Mill's utilitarianism offers a clear affirmative response. It would be incomprehensible to Mill to attempt to understand the good for humans without according a prime place to virtuous character traits and capacities. Virtues are admirable character traits that are generally productive of good and that have become habitual, through association with pleasure. The development of admirable character traits that become habitual through practice and participation is one key mark of an ethics of virtue.

A second mark of virtue ethics is the employment of exemplars or models for students to emulate in these practices. These models embody and teach ideals that others can choose to use as examples to follow. Mill himself gives many examples to illustrate his intentions regarding appropriate models or exemplars of the intellectual and moral virtues. In the essay "Theism," Mill proposes Christ as an ideal of virtue for others to emulate. He draws attention to those who have used Christ "as the ideal representative and guide of humanity" (CW 10:488). He adds "nor, even now, would it be easy, even for an unbeliever, to find a better trans-lation of the rule of virtue from the abstract into the concrete, than to endeavour so to live that Christ would approve our life"(CW 10:488). Such models and examples can be more personal, as Mill demonstrates in his dedication to and depiction of his wife Harriet Taylor Mill as his inspiration. She is "the friend and wife whose exalted sense of truth and right was my strongest incitement" (CW 18:216). *On Liberty* uses a range of examples of this sort, including both specific examples like Christ and Socrates and general examples like people with highly devel-oped individuality as models. He explains that

> Many have let themselves be guided . . . by the counsels and influence of a more highly gifted and instructed One or Few . . . The honour and glory of the average man is that he is capable of following that initiative; that he can respond internally to wise and noble things, and be led to them with his eyes open. (CW 18:269)

Mill is quick to add that he is advocating emulation of models, and he is not proposing "hero-worship" or forceful imposition of values. "All he can claim is, freedom to point out the way. The power of compelling others into it, is not only inconsistent with the freedom and development of all the rest, but corrupting to the strong man himself" (CW 18:269).

The richness of Mill's approach to education understood as self-development explains why Mill had confidence in the measurement procedure he proposed in his theory and in the judgments of competent agents to evaluate and measure value. His liberal philosophy of education is substantial. But doubts remain. Mill's method of assessing value and the philosophy of education it mandates raise a slew of questions to ponder and objections to consider.

One significant challenge is the objection that Mill's system is elitist. If the development and exercise of the higher human capacities and the education that is needed are prerequisites for appreciating the most valuable satisfactions, then the elitist argument could be propounded that those who have had this education are better able to judge and appreciate value, and even to impose their judgments on others. This is a challenging question for Mill's theory, and I take up this complex issue in Chapter 6. But the preliminary response to this comes from Mill's deepest commitments and the fundamental egalitarianism of his theory. It follows from the basic tenets of his theory that people are wronged if they are denied this education, and doubly wronged then if their self-development is further impaired by having the judgment of others imposed, rather than simply offered as a model. The argument of *On Liberty* adds power to the reply to the elitist, for the benefits of individuality and autonomy cannot be obtained on the elitist model.

Another substantial objection is that, although the education process is designed to produce autonomous and reliable judges of value, yet the very process of education will have favored certain sorts of enjoyments (most notably the intellectual ones) and thus there will be a built-in bias or predetermination for self-developed agents to favor some enjoyments over others. This brings us face to face with the bedrock question of how to educate citizens to lead autonomous lives. It is a problem faced by all liberal democracies, and the only answer and counter is to encourage the sort of education for freedom that Mill proposes, and back up the commitment with effective development of autonomy. Mill's theory cannot escape this common puzzle faced by all democratic educational philosophies, and yet his bottom line commitment to educate all citizens for autonomy provides the most promising avenues to meet these challenges.

Mill's value theory continues to challenge and intrigue contemporary students of moral and political philosophy. His theory defies attempts at easy categorization, and its intricacy is designed to provide a framework for practical wisdom and for living well. It is an activist theory, constructed to be used and tested in the light of its application to daily life. If ethical life is as complex as it seems to be in contemporary pluralistic and diverse communities, then we need a theory as sophisticated as Mill's to guide our reflections and judgments. My discussion in later chapters will illustrate Mill's value theory in its connections and applications.

notes

An earlier version of this chapter appeared as "Mill's Theory of Value," in Henry West, ed., *The Blackwell Guide to Mill's Utilitarianism* (Oxford: Blackwell, 2006), 117–38.

1 For other noteworthy discussions of these questions see Scarre 1997; Brink 1992; Crisp 1997; Riley 1988; West 2004; Skorupski 1989; Long 1992; Hoag 1992; Berger 1984.

2 Jonathan Riley's reading of Mill on the values of different kinds of enjoyments is an example of an interpretation that is prone to be too restrictive. Riley's reading permits only four kinds of enjoyments: "'utilities of justice' . . . 'private utilities' (including 'aesthetic utilities') . . . 'utilities of charity,' and . . . 'merely expedient utilities'" (Riley 1988, 87). These fixed categories of kind are too rigid to accurately convey the complexity of Mill's actual position on the myriad kinds of satisfactions which may be enjoyed and evaluated. Riley's interpretation is also restrictive in arguing for the lexical dominance of some kinds of utilities or enjoyments, and is especially problematic in its claim that different kinds of utilities cannot be compared. Riley contends that "each kind of utility is non-comparable with other kinds in terms of quantity or intensity" (166). However, this is difficult to uphold as a general approach to value measurement and lacks plausibility. In the course of daily life agents are constantly called upon to make such comparisons, and they do so successfully, albeit in a rough and ready way. Mill's intention is to argue for a general and comprehensive method that can be used to construct actual agents' plans of life and to guide actual value assessments.

further reading

Brink, David O., "Mill's Deliberative Utilitarianism," *Philosophy and Public Affairs* 21, no. 1 (1992), 67–103.

Crisp, Roger, *Mill on Utilitarianism* (London: Routledge, 1997).

Donner, Wendy, *The Liberal Self: John Stuart Mill's Moral and Political Philosophy* (Ithaca: Cornell University Press, 1991).

Griffin, James, *Well-Being: Its Meaning, Measurement, and Moral Importance* (Oxford: Clarendon Press, 1986).

Hoag, Robert W., "Happiness and Freedom: Recent Work on John Stuart Mill," *Philosophy and Public Affairs* 15, no. 2 (1986), 188–99.

Long, Roderick T., "Mill's Higher Pleasures and the Choice of Character," *Utilitas* 4, no. 2 (1992), 279–97.

Riley, Jonathan, "On Quantities and Qualities of Pleasure," *Utilitas* 5, no. 2 (1993), 291–300.

Skorupski, John, *John Stuart Mill* (London: Routledge, 1989).

Sumner, L. W., "Welfare, Happiness, and Pleasure," *Utilitas* 4, no. 2 (1992), 199–206.

West, Henry, *An Introduction to Mill's Utilitarian Ethics* (Cambridge: Cambridge University Press, 2004).

West, Henry, ed., *The Blackwell Guide to Mill's Utilitarianism* (Oxford: Blackwell, 2006).

utilitarianism: morality, justice, and the art of life

Introduction

I n this chapter I engage with the core questions raised by Mill's views on right and wrong, obligation, rights and justice, as well as issues regarding the status of moral rules. I consider whether or to what extent Mill's theory is best classified as act-utilitarian or as rule-utilitarian. One common objection posed to Mill's moral philosophy is that the principle of utility is in conflict with the demands of justice. In responding to this objection I examine the relationship between utility and justice in the architecture of Mill's theory, as well as the central place of rights grounded in utility within his system.

In *Utilitarianism*, Mill lays down the fundamental principle of his moral theory, the principle of utility, which "holds that actions are right in proportion as they tend to promote happiness, wrong as they tend to produce the reverse of happiness" (CW 10:210). The principle of utility is the ultimate principle of utilitarianism. This principle is a principle of the good or value and as such it governs the ends of all of the practical and moral arts of living. The principle of utility serves to justify and ground moral principles of right and obligation, including those justice principles concerned with rights owed to particular individuals. This is the territory of Morality within Mill's Art of Life. It is now time to turn attention to different positions that have been adopted on the question of the role played by the principle of utility in morality. What is the relation between the good and the right or the obligatory? Just as utilitarians can advocate different positions regarding the nature of the good, so they also differ over the question of the relation of the principle of utility to the moral rules setting out obligations. Discussions of the last few decades have tended to frame these debates by categorizing the proffered positions as act-utilitarian or rule-utilitarian. These are not terms that Mill himself used and it is open to question whether he would have welcomed being aligned with either of these perspectives, and whether these categories successfully capture his intentions. There is now a vast literature on these questions, and this literature does not show any signs of abating, even though there is increasing awareness among Mill scholars that the question of Mill's placement in the schema may never be satisfactorily resolved. This is not simply because of the nature of philosophical inquiry. It may also be that Mill is not a cooperative player in this game.

Mill's theory does not sit perfectly comfortably in either the act- or the rule-utilitarian camp, and some straining and tugging is needed to place him in either mold. It is a question worth pondering whether the upshot is to reveal weakness in Mill's theory, or limitations in the way that these theories have been classified, conceived, or configured in recent dialogues. My goal in this discussion is, therefore, to reflect upon which category offers the best fit with Mill's theory.

The categories of and discussions of act- and rule-utilitarianism have been featured prominently in twentieth-century debates. Mill himself did not use these words and probably was unaware of this particular method of classifying consequentialist and utilitarian theories. Therefore, scrutiny of the textual evidence and care in interpreting it are essential for the task of reflecting about whether Mill's theory is best classed as act- or as rule-utilitarian.[1] The debate is lively, as recent commentators continue to argue that Mill is an act-utilitarian, that he is a rule-utilitarian, or that his theory does not fit comfortably into either category. Care is needed in proceeding and the textual evidence for these competing readings must be approached in the context of awareness of the structure of Mill's moral philosophy. Indeed, I will argue that the *structure* of Mill's theory, often neglected in discussions, radically undermines the prospects for several of these interpretations as candidates for furnishing accurate readings of his theory. Central in this theoretical structure is Mill's Art of Life, which delineates the proper domain of Morality in its relations with companion spheres of the Art of Life. So an understanding of the *scope* of Morality, as well as the place of rules of obligation and rights within the *structure* of his moral philosophy, is an essential tool for scrutiny of the status of rules of obligation and principles of justice.

There is an underlying substantive issue at stake – the question of the *strength* of the moral rules in Mill's moral philosophy. The relevant concern is that moral rules must be strong enough to avoid being overturned easily, yet not so strong that they are rigidly adhered to in extreme circumstances where catastrophe will ensue if the rule is followed. In such cases, rare though they may be in real life, reflection is called for to examine whether the rules should, morally speaking, be followed. A more common practical concern arises because moral life inevitably features cases where rules come into conflict, and we must reflect on which rule it is our duty to follow in these circumstances. Mill argues that all moral rules have exceptions and notes that to expect moral rules (or any rules for the practice of living) to be without exceptions is fanciful.

The substantive question is important, because it could provide fodder for an objection to Mill's utilitarianism if it is not addressed. There is a general objection to (generic) utilitarianism that claims that this theory permits or sanctions cases of injustice which are at odds with the moral intuitions of reflective moral agents. A classic example, adapted from H. J. McCloskey by Roger Crisp, is the following:

> A town in the Wild West has been plagued by a series of violent crimes. The sheriff is confronted by a deputation led by the mayor. The deputation tells him that, unless he hangs the vagrant he has in his jail, whom the whole town believes to be the criminal, there will without doubt be a terrible riot, in which many people will almost certainly be killed or maimed. This vagrant has no friends or family. The sheriff knows he is innocent.[2]

Crisp goes on to raise the question whether by "breaking the normal rules of justice that people should be given fair trial, and that those known to be innocent should not be punished, he could produce the best outcome" (Crisp 1997, 118). Crisp says that Mill would reject this line of reasoning and hold fast to the rule because of the bad consequences of breaking the rule. In this case, the sheriff's agenda may well be found out, but his more general point is that it "is just not clear in practice whether, in any particular case, one might maximize by breaking the rule" (118). Therefore, ignorance and uncertainty about future outcomes should lead us to follow the rules of conventional morality. There are other substantial considerations that can also be brought in to argue for rule adherence. For example, pandering to the mob instincts at work could have disturbing consequences. This line of thought backs up the general utilitarian case for following rules and thus it helps answer the objection. But Mill's particular brand of utilitarianism has a further response. Mill's theory, unlike Bentham's, accords a central place to rights, which protect vital interests – and this furnishes a far more robust rebuff to critics who claim that utilitarianism sanctions injustice in such scenarios.

The exploration of the status of moral rules within Mill's theory, that is, the important question of whether Mill's theory is best classified as act-utilitarian or rule-utilitarian, is complicated by the fact that Mill's utilitarianism is a complex variant of this family of theories. Often objections that are directed at more simple forms of utilitarianism miss the mark when applied to Mill's theory. On the other hand, the complex form that Mill defends faces other objections and raises other puzzles to which more simple forms are not subject. Before we can fruitfully examine act- and rule-utilitarianism, we must have in place an understanding of the intricate structure of Mill's moral philosophy, and the scope of Morality within its design.

The Art of Life and Morality

Mill's moral philosophy is intricate. It is a form of indirect utilitarianism in which utility is promoted indirectly, through adherence to the rules that will produce the greatest welfare if practiced generally. The structure of Mill's variety is explained in some detail in Chapter 5 of *Utilitarianism*, "On the Connexion between Justice and Utility." Essential background for this is found in Book VI of *A System of Logic* where Mill explains the function of the principle of utility as the ultimate principle of teleology, grounding all of the moral or practical arts. The principle of utility, as I have noted, is a general principle of the good, underlying all of the practical arts. There are numerous moral and practical arts of human nature and society, and the principle of utility is the foundational principle governing all of them. There is room for confusion here, in part due to Mill's terminology. He regularly uses the words "moral arts and sciences" to refer to the whole expanse of the practical arts of life, and the term "morality" to point to a specific department of this, namely, the domain of right, duty, and obligation. In the first instance, this category of Morality is one of three components of what Mill presents as the Art of Life.

As the first stage of explaining the architecture of his theory, Mill lays out the three departments of the fundamental Art of Life. As Mill explains, Morality occupies only a portion of this Art of Life. The three departments are: "Morality, Prudence or Policy, and Aesthetics; the Right, the Expedient, and the Beautiful or Noble, in human conduct and works" (CW 8:949). The other practical arts, and they are numerous, are subordinate to the Art of Life. For example, in Book VI of *A System of Logic*, Mill examines in depth a number of other significant moral arts and sciences, including psychology, ethology (the science of the formation of character), education, politics, government, economics, sociology, political economy, and history. The list is extensive. The practical arts of living all rely upon the arbitration and justificatory powers of the general principle of teleology, to decide questions of precedence when disputes arise and to determine rankings among the ends of all of these spheres of conduct. Practical reasoning, he maintains, requires a first principle of teleology. "There must be some standard by which to determine the goodness or badness, absolute and comparative, of ends, or objects of desire" (CW 8:951). Arguing against his nineteenth-century opponents, the moral sense theorists, he says that the principles of their theories, even if true, would provide only for that portion of the field of conduct which is properly called moral. For the remainder of the practice of life some general principle, or standard, must still be sought; and if that principle be rightly chosen, it will be found, I apprehend, to serve quite as well for the ultimate principle of Morality, as for that of Prudence, Policy, or Taste. (CW 8:951)

He argues that this general principle and standard is that of "conduciveness to the happiness of mankind . . . the promotion of happiness is the ultimate principle of Teleology" (CW 8:951). When Mill claims that we ought to promote happiness, in many cases he is speaking about a general value ought, and not a moral ought. It is only within the specified domain of Morality that the ought he refers to is moral. In the early pages of *Utilitarianism*, Mill says that utilitarianism is accurately understood as a "theory of life on which this theory of morality is grounded" (CW 10:210). Utilitarianism is a theory about how to live *the good life*. Living *the moral life*, that is, following justified moral rules, doing one's duty, respecting the principles of justice and the rights of others, and so on, is an essential part of living the good life. However, if we inflate the importance of this component of the good life, we fail to give the other compartments of the good life their due, and we risk becoming the "moral police" or the "moralists by profession" that Mill regularly excoriates as agents whose actions and misconceptions undermine some of the most essential elements of human well-being (CW 18:284).

In *Utilitarianism*, Mill's first move is to mark off the sphere of rules of morality or obligation from the broader class of general promotion of good. He explains that in this first move he is also demarcating Morality from its two companion spheres in the Art of Life. Morality is cordoned off from "the remaining provinces of Expediency and Worthiness" (CW 10:247). This latter is the domain of Nobility or Virtue. This clarifying comment is often ignored, leaving confusion in its wake. Mill's moral theory separates out the territory of rules of obligation from rules of general promotion of good *in all of the numerous areas of practical life*, as follows:

We do not call anything wrong, unless we mean to imply that a person ought to be punished in some way or other for doing it; if not by law, by the opinion of his fellow creatures; if not by opinion, by the reproaches of his own conscience. This seems the real turning point of the distinction between morality and simple expediency. It is part of the notion of Duty in every one of its forms, that a person may rightfully be compelled to fulfill it . . . I think there is no doubt that this distinction lies at the bottom of the notions of right and wrong; that we call any conduct wrong, or employ, instead, some other term of dislike or disparagement, according as we think that the person ought, or ought not, to be punished for it; and we say that it would be right to do so and so, or merely that it would be desirable or laudable, according as we would wish to see the person whom it concerns, compelled, or only persuaded and exhorted, to act in that manner. (CW 10:246)

David Lyons' argument clarifies that Mill here conceptually links moral obligation and punishment and so his theory of morality has "a model based on coercive social rules" (Lyons 1994, 54). Lyons continues,

> These considerations suggest that Mill had the following view. To call an act wrong is to imply that guilt feelings, and perhaps other sanctions, would be warranted against it. But sanctions assume coercive rules. *To show an act wrong, therefore, is to show that a coercive rule against it would be justified.* The justification of a coercive social rule establishes a moral obligation, breach of which is wrong. (Lyons 1994, 55)

Justified moral rules are those that would lead to the greatest balance of happiness over suffering if moral agents generally complied with them. Compliance has its costs. And so Mill's justification of utilitarian rules of obligation takes into account the costs of setting up and enforcing a coercive moral rule; such costs include the sanctions tied to breaking the rule as well as the restrictions on freedom of following it.

Mill's first move is to delineate the province of moral rules setting out obligations. His next move is to distinguish a special sub-group of rules within the territory of obligation. These are the moral rules of justice, which defend rights. He says that rules of justice "involve the idea of a personal right – a claim on the part of one or more individuals" (CW 10:247). He defines a right as follows:

> When we call anything a person's right, we mean that he has a valid claim on society to protect him in the possession of it, either by the force of law, or by that of education and opinion. If he has what we consider a sufficient claim, on whatever account, to have something guaranteed to him by society, we say that he has a right to it.
> ... To have a right, then, is, I conceive, to have something which society ought to defend me in the possession of. (CW 10:250)

This is Mill's analysis of the *concept* of a right. His utilitarian *justification* for rights follows. He claims that "if the objector goes on to ask why it ought, I can give him no other reason than general utility." The justification is based on "the extraordinarily important and impressive kind of utility which is concerned" (CW 10: 250–51). He emphasizes that justice and utility are not in conflict, for rules of justice must be grounded on utility: "While I dispute the pretensions of any theory which sets up an imaginary standard of justice not grounded on utility, I account the justice which is grounded on utility to be the chief part, and incomparably the most sacred and binding part, of all morality" (CW 10:255).

The interests protected by rights are, as I have noted, special or impressive in Mill's books. They merit the weightiest protection, and they are in the designated inner sanctuary within the structure of Mill's theory. They are not to be overturned or pushed aside except when they conflict with competing sets of interests that are equally weighty: in almost all cases, competing rights. Mill explains what happens in cases of exception, which are rare:

> justice is a name for certain moral requirements, which, regarded collectively, stand higher in the scale of social utility, and are therefore of more paramount obligation, than any others; though particular cases may occur in which some other social duty is so important, as to overrule any one of the general maxims of justice . . . In such cases . . . we usually say . . . that what is just in ordinary cases is, by reason of that other principle, not just in the particular case. (CW 10:259)

Mill notably does *not* permit rules of justice to be overruled except by another "social duty." The example Mill uses as illustration is of the duty to take or steal food or medicine needed to save someone's life. A point of special importance is that such rules of justice cannot be overruled to obtain small or moderate utility gains even for large numbers of others, as in Crisp's example. (And this is in addition to the key point that feeding unjustified feelings of revenge is a disutility, not a utility, and habituates the vices, not the virtues.) Cases in which small benefits to large numbers of people are gained by violating the rights of a minority, even a minority of one, are ruled out by the very *structure* of Mill's theory. Mill's complex form of utilitarianism is not the generic utilitarianism that is so often the target of objections that posit fanciful scenarios having little to do with real-life dilemmas. In Mill's carefully constructed theory, rights claims conceptually ward off the casual trade-offs permitting some people's vital interests to be overturned to promote other people's trivial or even moderate interests. So the general sorts of example that Crisp presents evoke a strong reply from Mill, and his theory is well equipped to handle them. Mill says that rules of justice, protecting rights, are "incomparably the most sacred and binding part, of all morality. Justice is a name for certain classes of moral rules, which concern the essentials of human well-being more nearly, and are therefore of more absolute obligation, than any other rules for the guidance of life" (CW 10:255). Mill says that the two most basic rights are the right to security and the right to liberty (including liberty of self-development). He reiterates that rights are placed in the inner sanctuary of his theory in order to protect these most vital human interests, the ones most essential to well-being. In Mill's indirect utilitarianism, such rights are enshrined and socially guaranteed. Social and political institutions are collectively set up and maintained to ensure them (CW 10:251). The costs associated with and built into the coercive social rules of morality more than pay off in the radically increased level of human happiness that follows from securing and respecting the most vital human interests. Since the very analysis of the concept of a right involves possession of a valid claim for its social protection, it would be inconsistent to maintain, on the one hand, that rights should be socially guaranteed, and, on the other hand, that it would be morally permissible to trade them away for small gains in happiness to others, even many others. This decision-making strategy is self-defeating, since it would virtually guarantee that massive misery rather than maximum happiness would follow in its wake. The slightest reflection on the suffering that would result from the prospect of cavalier treatment of and threats to people's most important rights, in real-life settings, leads inescapably to the conclusion that rights cannot be traded away. Mill's carefully constructed indirect utilitarianism prohibits such trade-offs and robustly protects the rights. His philosophy of education underwrites this with prescriptions for the inculcation of appropriate moral sentiments. Rules of justice therefore are "guarded by a sentiment not only different in degree, but also in kind; distinguished from the milder feeling which attaches to the mere idea of promoting human pleasure or convenience, at once by the more definite nature of its commands, and by the sterner character of its sanctions" (CW 10:259). Educated Millian agents, acting in character and according to properly cultivated moral capacities, could not bring themselves to act in the way that the examples of sacrifice of the innocents presume. It is not merely rules of the moral code that are internalized. The character traits that underwrite the code and ensure its respect also are cultivated by the educational processes of development and self-development. Reason and rational foresight conclude that moral codes will not survive if they are treated with cavalier disregard in most everyday scenarios. Compassion, kindness, and empathy all disallow temptations to sacrifice important interests of others.

The structure delineated in the last chapter of *Utilitarianism* is an important part of the picture. But it is only a part, for it focuses on the domain of Morality. Recall that Morality is only a portion of the Art of Life. Mill is also engaged in marking off the legitimate sphere of Morality in order to prevent it from trespassing on its neighbors' territory. To see how this works, we must turn to other writings and to Mill's critique of other thinkers whom he castigates for making too much of Morality. For example, Mill heaps scorn upon Auguste Comte for being a "morality-intoxicated" man who does not know how to draw reasonable boundaries around Morality and who erroneously expands Morality's legitimate authority. Every question of practical life, or of the good life, is transformed into a moral question by the misguided Comte, who shares the Calvinist error of believing that

> whatever is not a duty is a sin. It does not perceive that between the region of duty and that of sin there is an intermediate space, the region of positive worthiness. It is not good that persons should be bound, by other people's opinion, to do everything that they would deserve praise for doing. There is a standard of altruism to which all should be required to come up, and a degree beyond it which is not obligatory, but meritorious. It is incumbent on every one to restrain the pursuit of his personal objects within the limits consistent with the essential interests of others. What those limits are, it is the province of ethical science to determine; and to keep all individuals and aggregations of individuals within them, is the proper office of punishment and of moral blame. If in addition to fulfilling this obligation, persons make the good of others a direct object of disinterested exertions, postponing or sacrificing to it even innocent personal indulgences, they deserve gratitude and honour, and are fit objects of moral praise. So long as they are in no way compelled to this conduct by any external pressure, there cannot be too much of it; but a necessary condition is its spontaneity . . . Such spontaneity by no means excludes sympathetic encouragement . . . The object should be to stimulate services to humanity by their natural rewards; not to render the pursuit of our own good in any other manner impossible, by visiting it with the reproaches of other and of our own conscience. The proper office of those sanctions is to enforce upon every one, the conduct necessary to give all other persons their fair chance: conduct which chiefly consists in not doing them harm, and not impeding them in anything which without harming others does good to themselves. To this must of course be added, that when we either expressly or tacitly undertake to do more, we are bound to keep our promise. And inasmuch as every one, who avails himself of the advantages of society, leads others to expect from him all such positive good offices and disinterested services as the moral improvement attained by mankind has rendered customary, he deserves moral blame if, without just cause, he disappoints that expectation. Through this principle the domain of moral duty, in an improving society, is always widening. When what once was uncommon virtue becomes common virtue, it comes to be numbered among obligations, while a degree exceeding what has grown common, remains simply meritorious. (CW 10:337–8)

He continues,

> Demanding no more than this, society, in any tolerable circumstances, obtains much more; for the natural activity of human nature, shut out from all noxious directions, will expand itself in useful ones . . . But above this standard there is an unlimited range of moral worth, up to the most exalted heroism, which should be fostered by every positive encouragement, though not converted into an obligation . . . Nor can any pains taken be too

great, to form the habit, and develop the desire, of being useful to others and to the world, by the practice, independently of reward and of every personal consideration, of positive virtue beyond the bounds of prescribed duty. (CW 10:339)

Mill argues that Comte is not the only philosopher who overextends the moral domain at the expense of the other categories of the Art of Life. His fellow utilitarian Jeremy Bentham also makes this error. Bentham's

one-sidedness, belongs to him not as a utilitarian, but as a moralist by profession, and in common with almost all professed moralists, whether religious or philosophical: it is that of treating the *moral* view of actions and characters, which is unquestionably the first and most important mode of looking at them, as if it were the sole one . . . Every human action has three aspects: its *moral* aspect, or that of its *right* and *wrong*; its *aesthetic* aspect, or that of its *beauty*; its *sympathetic* aspect, or that of its *loveable-ness*. The first addresses itself to our reason and conscience; the second to our imagination; the third to our human fellow-feeling. According to the first, we approve or disapprove; according to the second, we admire or despise; according to the third, we love, pity, or dislike. The morality of an action depends on its foreseeable consequences; its beauty, and its love-ableness, or the reverse, depend on the qualities which it is evidence of . . . It is not possible for any sophistry to confound these three modes of view-ing an action; but it is very possible to adhere to one of them exclusively, and lose sight of the rest. Sentimentality consists in setting the last two of the three above the first; the error of moralists in general, and of Bentham, is to sink the two latter entirely. This is pre-eminently the case with Bentham: he both wrote and felt as if the moral standard ought not only to be paramount (which it ought), but to be alone; as if it ought to be the sole master of all our actions, and even of all our sentiments. (CW 10:112–13)

Morality's domain is crucial to the good life, but it is restricted to the territory of protecting vital interests. Mill's theory conceptually links moral duty, punishment, and coercive sanctions. The costs of setting up a coercive social rule include these sanctions. By definition morally wrong actions are liable to punishment. It follows from this analysis that *not all actions that fail to maximize the good are morally wrong.* Many erroneous objections to Mill's utilitarianism assume mistakenly that there is a standing moral obligation to maximize utility in all of our conduct. The objection that utilitarianism requires us to be moral saints on all occasions is misdirected and flounders on failure to understand Mill's view that this stance exhibits intoxication with morality. The objection springs from the mistaken view that morality has authority over large swaths of practical life. This fails to appreciate the signific-ance of the distinction between Morality and the other two companion spheres of the Art of Life. By restricting morality's authority to the

Wendy Donner

protection of the most vital interests, Mill propounds the theory of life that sanctions are out of place in these other companion spheres. He says that by "demanding no more than this, society . . . obtains much more." This allows room to expand the domain of what Mill refers to on various occasions as that of Virtue, Nobility, Beauty, or positive Worthiness. It allows room for liberty, individuality, and autonomy to unfold unfettered. Mill has a doctrine of Virtue to complement his theory of Morality. In "Thornton on Labour and Its Claims," Mill is quite explicit about the survey of the territory. He says

> utilitarian morality fully recognises the distinction between the province of positive duty and that of virtue, but maintains that the standard and rule of both is the general interest. From the utilitarian point of view, the distinction between them is the following: – There are many acts, and a still greater number of forbearances, the perpetual practice of which by all is so necessary to the general well-being, that people must be held to it compulsorily, either by law, or by social pressure. These acts and forbearances constitute duty. Outside these bounds there is the innumerable variety of modes in which the acts of human beings are either a cause, or a hindrance, of good to their fellow-creatures, but in regard to which it is, on the whole, for the general interest that they should be left free; being merely encouraged, by praise and honour, to the performance of such beneficial actions . . . This larger sphere is that of Merit or Virtue. (CW 5:650–51)

A related error collapses the domains of moral obligation and supererogation. This error claims that Mill's theory ignores supererogation and that there is no space in his theory for the notion of actions that are above and beyond the call of duty. But this is clearly false, as Mill explicitly carves out a healthy space for these actions. The quotes above establish this beyond any doubt. Mill does not ignore supererogation; these actions according to Mill's schema are assigned to the sphere of Worthiness or Virtue in the Art of Life. We are not morally bound to do them, but we deserve praise, honor, and gratitude for their performance. And they are an essential part of our good, for practices of such human excellence, while not required of us, yet enhance the process of our self-development and development of the highest human excellences.

The enlarged perspective on Mill's utilitarianism as engaged with promoting happiness in *all* of the spheres of the Art of Life accurately captures Mill's vision, even as it raises vexing questions about how to balance the demands and entitlements of these different categories of actions, all of which have as their end the promotion of the good life. But what is for sure is that the requirements of Morality, and the sanctions attached to violations of its coercive rules, cannot be exported into the other spheres of life. In these other spheres, the inducements of encouragement, praise, honor, and gratitude replace sanctions and punishments.

Promotion of happiness remains steadfastly the justification, ground, and controller of actions, rules, character, lives, and numerous objects of assessment and evaluation. It is a clear mistake to interpret Mill as maintaining that there is a standing moral obligation to maximize happiness and that therefore we are always "on call" in our moral duty to maximize the good. If we take this stance, then we play the role of the moralist by profession. We go far beyond Mill's actual requirements and we work to the detriment of well-being on many occasions.

In Chapter 4, I examine in more depth the implications of this framework of the Art of Life for liberty. The liberty principle propounded in that essay has the announced purpose of setting the reasonable and legitimate boundaries of social and political coercion over individuals and allowing for it only in cases of harm to others through violation of an other-regarding duty. My argument here is designed to explore the realm of duty and obligation. So it is not out of place to underscore that liberty is the beneficiary of Mill's fundamental claim that it is only in cases of duty that coercion and compulsion have a place. Many rival moral philosophies carve out an assigned place for moral duties to self. This would permit coercion in this private realm. But this path is blocked in Mill's theory, since he emphatically denies any place at his table for the notion of self-regarding duty, or duty to oneself. In *On Liberty* Mill strongly contrasts violations of moral duties with

> the self-regarding faults . . . which are not properly immoralities, and to whatever pitch they may be carried, do not constitute wickedness. They may be proofs of any amount of folly, or want of personal dignity and self-respect; but they are only a subject of moral reprobation when they involve a breach of duty to others . . . What are called duties to ourselves are not socially obligatory, unless circumstances render them at the same time duties to others. The term duty to oneself, when it means anything more than prudence, means self-respect or self-development; and for none of these is any one accountable to his fellow creatures. (CW 18:279)

While Mill repudiates the *self-regarding duties*, he fully accepts and promotes the *self-regarding virtues*. Self-regarding virtues have their assigned place in the domain of Worthiness and Virtue in the Art of Life, and therefore the rules of engagement are of that sphere.

> Human beings owe to each other help to distinguish the better from the worse, and encouragement to choose the former and avoid the latter. They should be forever stimulating each other to increased exercise of their higher faculties . . . But neither one person, nor any number of persons, is warranted in saying to another human creature of ripe years, that he shall not do with his life for his own benefit what he chooses to do with it . . . In this department, therefore, of human affairs, Individuality has its proper

field of action . . . Considerations to aid his judgment, exhortations to strengthen his will, may be offered to him . . . but he himself is the final judge. All errors which he is likely to commit against advice and warning, are far outweighed by the evil of allowing others to constrain him to what they deem his good. (CW 18:277)

The rules of engagement of the sphere of Morality – coercion and sanctions – are out of place in the other sphere of Virtue.

Back in the territory of moral obligation, we have some enhanced understanding of its proper scope (the sphere of Morality) and role (protection of vital human interests). With these tools, we can turn to the issue of act- and rule-utilitarianism afresh.

Morality: Act- and Rule-Utilitarianism

Mill is regularly interpreted as both an act- and a rule-utilitarian. Some recent commentators argue that Mill's theory is not, as strictly defined, either an act- or a rule-utilitarian theory or that there are problems firmly placing him in either of these camps. Often these discussions take place with awareness of the importance of the Art of Life as Mill's framework.[3] The issue of act- and rule-utilitarianism must be examined in the context of the structure of Mill's moral philosophy and the designated scope of Morality within that framework. First, we need working definitions of act- and rule-utilitarianism. Then we can proceed to some textual evidence for the readings.

Both act- and rule-utilitarianism are forms of consequentialism, according to which the rightness and wrongness of acts are determined by their consequences, specifically, in the case of utilitarianism, the consequences that promote happiness or utility. According to utilitarianism, the standard or test of the rightness or wrongness of actions is based upon the promotion of happiness or utility and the minimization of unhappiness or suffering which results from those actions. Both act- and rule-utilitarians turn to the principle of utility to ground their decisions. According to Mill's utilitarianism, we also critically assess or evaluate many things like moral rules, character, the ends of all of the practical moral arts of social and political life, and so on, by this test or standard of utility. In the question of the moral assessment of action, consequentialism is contrasted with deontological theories which maintain that certain classes of actions, like murder, lying, promise-breaking, and so on, are wrong in themselves, and not simply because of any bad consequences that they produce.

Act-utilitarians claim that we decide what is morally right or wrong by examining the consequences of performing a particular act in a particular situation or set of circumstances. This employs a case-by-case methodo-logy to determine right action and moral obligation. Act-utilitarianism is a form of direct consequentialism. Moral decision-making requires agents to scrutinize the available options or possible alternative courses of action and choose the course of action which is most likely to produce the maximum happiness. Act-utilitarian agents are obligated to pursue the particular course of action that is the most likely to promote the greatest good. Rule-utilitarians claim that moral agents perform or fulfill their obligations by following general moral rules, and these rules are themselves justified moral rules. These are the rules that Mill refers to as secondary moral principles, such as the rule prohibiting murder. The rules are justified in turn by consequences, namely, the consequences of their being generally or widely adopted. The rules are justified if they would produce the greatest balance of happiness over suffering if they were generally adhered to by moral agents. As we shall see, there are several variants of this.

The principle of utility furnishes the test or standard for determining morally right action. However, the question of the best strategy about how to proceed in order to produce the greatest happiness is a separate ques-tion. It is still left open. The most common strategy for act-utilitarians to adopt is to follow conventional moral rules such as those prohibiting murder and theft and enjoining promise-keeping and truth-telling. This strategy is deemed preferable to the strategy of attempting to decide on each occasion what will maximize happiness directly. So a "strategy conception" of moral rules is often associated with act-utilitarianism (Berger 1984, 82–120). There is considerable overlap between these two approaches *in practice*. Act-utilitarians can and often do claim both that the maximization of utility in particular cases provides the correct *test* of right action, and also that the best *decision strategy* to adopt is to fol-low justified moral rules rather than to try to calculate the utility of each possible course of action in each case. Indeed most act-utilitarians do in fact adopt the strategy of following justified rules, which they regard as rules of thumb. They will follow the secondary or conventional moral rules. Mill says that these rules can be overturned and direct appeal made to the principle of utility in exceptional cases. We may find ourselves in extraordinary circumstances when we must consider whether to violate a well-entrenched secondary moral rule in order to avert catastrophe. It is rare to encounter any form of moral theory, utilitarian or not, that does not make allowance for non-adherence to a moral rule in order to avoid catastrophe. Also, in circumstances in which the rules conflict, we must determine which rule in the situation should prevail.

There are numerous varieties of rule-utilitarianism. For our purposes, the two most prominent and promising versions are "utilitarian general-ization" and "moral code" varieties of rule-utilitarianism. "Moral code" theories in turn are of two sub-varieties: actual or conventional and ideal moral codes. However, one notable point is that all varieties of rule-utilitarianism maintain that the rules are of such strength that agents are not permitted to violate or break a justified moral rule in a particular case just because they judge that a small increase in happiness would result from this violation. In all varieties of rule-utilitarianism, the justified rules are conceived to be of sufficient strength so as to resist permitting non-adherence simply for modest increases in resulting utility in particular circumstances.

Act-utilitarianism does have a place for moral rules, but these are perceived as general guidelines summarizing the results of the accumulation of past human experience and wisdom. In *Utilitarianism* Mill sharply replies to the objection that utilitarianism is flawed, since it requires us to make moral decisions based upon consequences of action, and "there is not time, previous to action, for calculating and weighing the effects of any line of conduct on the general happiness" (CW 10:224). The objection presumes that utilitarian agents will spend too much time calculating consequences of available courses of action and too little time actually acting. An additional objection claims that they are liable to err because rational capacities are unequal to the task of anticipating all of the consequences that may ensue from any of the available options. Mill's reply features his reliance upon secondary rules or corollaries from the principle of utility. He responds that people have been learning about the tendencies of actions during the whole of human history and know full well that murder and theft are detrimental to happiness. Mill is not impressed by the objection. "It is truly a whimsical supposition that if mankind were agreed in considering utility to be the test of morality, they would remain without any agreement as to what *is* useful, and would take no measures for having their notions on the subject taught to the young, and enforced by law and opinion" (CW 10:224). Humans have acquired considerable expertise about the effects of kinds of actions on happiness. But there is also much room for improvement and progress. Mill signals that he considers moral rules, just as all other precepts of the Art of Life, to be improvable and he expects moral progress. "But to consider the rules of morality as improvable, is one thing; to pass over the intermediate generalizations entirely, and endeavour to test each individual action directly by the first principle, is another. It is a strange notion that the acknowledgement of a first principle is inconsistent with the admission of secondary ones" (CW 10:224). The critics are here talking nonsense, he says. Proper education ensures knowledge of the basics of right and wrong, wise and foolish. "Whatever we adopt as the fundamental principle of morality, we require subordinate principles to apply it by: the impossibility of doing without them, being common to all systems, can afford no argument against any one in particular" (CW 10:225).

Mill acknowledges clearly that moral *rules* are indispensable. The question is, then, what is their status? Are they the rules of act-utilitarianism, or the stronger rules of rule-utilitarianism?

Mill also signals that absolute moral rules that permit no exceptions are an unattainable fantasy in real life. All moral doctrines held by "sane persons," he says, allow that actual moral life presents us regularly with situations of conflicting moral considerations. Human affairs are so complex that

> rules of conduct cannot be so framed as to require no exceptions, and that hardly any kind of action can safely be laid down as either always obligatory or always condemnable. There is no ethical creed which does not temper the rigidity of its laws, by giving a certain latitude, under the moral responsibility of the agent, for accommodation to peculiarities of circumstances . . . There exists no moral system under which there do not arise unequivocal cases of conflicting obligation. (CW 10:225)

Such complex situations of conflict are part and parcel of the moral life; we cannot pretend that any moral philosophy will make them disappear. Faced with real-life scenarios, having recourse to an ultimate standard to arbitrate can therefore only be regarded as helpful by reasonable people. When conflicts confront agents, their cultivated habitual traits of wisdom and virtue are also helpful.

Mill's explanation of moral conflict resolution has implications for the question of the plausible classification of his theory. Mill's explanation runs counter to act-utilitarian resolution. When agents engaged in moral deliberation face conflicting rights and duties, they invoke the principle of utility. Mill argues that utilitarianism has what many other moral systems lack, namely, an umpire to decide which secondary principle has authority and is determined to be obligatory. Mill states firmly that the role and authority of the principle of utility in such cases is to adjudicate conflicts among secondary principles. This position has a strong rule-utilitarian tenor. We have no standing moral obligation to maximize utility *simpliciter*, as act-utilitarianism might in theory suggest. Mill says that "[w]e must remember that only in these cases of conflict between secondary principles is it requisite that first principles should be appealed to. There is no case of moral obligation in which some secondary principle is not involved; and if only one, there can seldom be any real doubt which one it is" (CW 10:226). In other words, we do not have an ongoing duty always to maximize utility, or to break an established moral rule simply because we calculate that doing so will marginally increase utility. The principle of utility's umpire role is restricted to determining which moral rule has authority or precedence in situations of conflict. Its authority does not extend to permitting rule violations to gain a small benefit. This particular scenario of moral conflict painted by opponents does not apply to Mill's version of utilitarian deliberation.

The question of the strength of the rules in utilitarianism is the subject of much discussion. Are rules to be abandoned lightly whenever it appears that even a modest gain in utility in the circumstances can be gained by breaking them? If so, critics of utilitarianism face an easy target. If rules can be easily spurned, then moral rules in such a system are very unstable. The deportment of agents relying upon such a system for moral deliberation would be unreliable and untrustworthy. Trust in the institution of moral rules and respect for such rules must be upheld. Rule-utilitarians argue that agents should follow generally useful rules, because there is the real danger of undermining confidence in the reasonable expectation that moral rules will be respected if agents are encouraged to break rules on particular occasions. Rule-utilitarians maintain that we should adhere to a rule even if on a particular occasion following it would not lead to the best consequences. Now of course act-utilitarians will often do exactly the same thing, as I have noted. Despite this convergence in practice, this factor is often perceived as the dividing line separating rule-utilitarians from act-utilitarians. This is because the case-by-case methodology of act-utilitarians would, at least in theory, sometimes appear to incline act-utilitarians to break the rule on particular occasions and follow the course of conduct that would yield a small utility gain in this setting.

One further question calls for some elaboration. Rule-utilitarianism builds in a method for mediating conflicts among moral rules when they arise. That the theory makes provisions for an umpire in the form of the principle of utility is one of its strong points, Mill argues. But there is room for different readings on the question of how Mill conceives of this mediation process. Does Mill conceive of the process as one in which the principle of utility determines the *weightiest* rule, the rule which has precedence, or does he conceive of it in terms of determining the *scope* of each competing rule, with exceptions and complexities added in? In cases of conflicts among these moral rules, there are two ways of seeing how Mill's theory proceeds in the adjudication. What role does the principle of utility play when it is invoked in the resolution of these conflicts? Does it weigh the utilities expected to result from adhering to one or the other of these rules? Or does the principle play the role of examining the scope of each of the contending rules, and determining which one, in the circumstances, has jurisdiction? This interpretive question is difficult to settle conclusively, since Mill's exposition uses language pertaining both to weight and precedence, on the one hand, and to scope and limitation, on the other. What's more, this language sometimes is present in the same passage.

Even essential moral rules have exceptions, as Mill explains. First, he makes the point that secondary rules of morality are integral to his system and fully compatible with the role of the principle of utility as the ultimate ground. Then he explains that even rules as central to morality as the ones prohibiting lying and requiring truth-telling have exceptions, and certain kinds of exception are agreed upon by moralists. Mill uses the example of that exception to the rule against lying of deliberately acting to withhold information from someone, such as a "malefactor" or a seriously ill person, when such withholding will prevent "great and unmerited evil" (CW 10:223). We withhold information that a loved one has been killed in a car accident from someone clinging to life from injuries sustained in that same accident, until they are out of danger. Or, if we are sheltering a woman fleeing from a husband who has threatened to kill her if she leaves him, we lie if he comes to the door looking for her. Then Mill adds,

> But in order that the exception may not extend itself beyond the need, and may have the least possible effect in weakening reliance on veracity, it ought to be recognised, and, if possible, its limits defined; and if the principle of utility is good for anything, it must be good for weighing these conflicting utilities against one another, and marking out the region within which one or the other preponderates. (CW 10:223)

The interpretive issue raises its head, for Mill uses words pertaining *both* to weighing and to scope in this passage. In "Whewell on Moral Philosophy," he repeats that all moral rules have exceptions, but that the essential point is that the exceptions must be incorporated into a more complex rule that determines the scope of the moral rule and limits its authority outside of that area:

> The essential is, that the exception should be itself a general rule; so that, being of definite extent, and not leaving the expediencies to the partial judgment of the agent in the individual case, it may not shake the stability of the wider rule in the cases to which the reason of the exception does not extend. (CW 10:183)

Thus there remains some uncertainty about the best mode of interpreting Mill's adjudication procedure when we employ the principle of utility in cases of apparent rule conflict. Does the principle weigh the outcomes of following each rule, or does it determine the scope of each rule's legitimate authority in determining which rule to follow?

With these characterizations and preliminary discussions in mind, it is time to look at some textual evidence for interpreting Mill as an act-utilitarian. There are certainly passages in *Utilitarianism* that appear to support this reading. Most prominently, Mill's initial presentation of the principle of utility has an act-utilitarian appearance. Recall that Mill states that the "creed which accepts as the foundation of morals, Utility, or the Greatest Happiness Principle, holds that actions are right in proportion as they tend to promote happiness, wrong as they tend to produce the reverse of happiness" (CW 10:210).

However, although there are passages in Mill's writings that can plausibly be read as bolstering an act-utilitarian interpretation, there is a powerful and even definitive reason against accepting this as the most accurate interpretation of Mill. Act-utilitarianism seems to be eliminated from the competition by the very structure of Mill's moral philosophy, which sets firm limits on the scope of morality and obligation within this edifice. If the scope of morality is contained and limited, then we cannot be *morally* required to maximize utility on each and every occasion or have a standing obligation to do so, as I argued previously. In the companion domains of the Art of Life, we are not *obligated* to maximize happiness. Indeed, we have no obligations whatsoever, although we may have voluntary commitments. Yet it is precisely this standing moral obligation, namely, that agents are morally required on *all* occasions to perform that action which will maximize utility, that is a core requirement of act-utilitarianism. However this requirement of act-utilitarianism is specifically and repeatedly repudiated by Mill. The objection commonly directed against act-utilitarianism that it requires us to be "moral saints," striving to maximize utility with every action we take, has no traction against Mill's utilitarianism. Mill rejects what he disparagingly calls "intoxication with morality." While Mill himself did not use the words act- and rule-utilitarianism, yet his arguments do seem to undermine decisively any attempt to classify him as an act-utilitarian, as this is usually defined.

If the structure of Mill's theory rules out the prospects for an act-utilitarian interpretation, what are the prospects of the two leading branches of rule-utilitarianism? The first version, utilitarian generalization, also looks promising at first sight. Mill makes use of it. For example, in *Utilitarianism* he says that

> In the case of abstinences indeed – of things which people forbear to do, from moral considerations, though the consequences in the particular case might be beneficial – it would be unworthy of an intelligent agent not to be consciously aware that the action is of a class which, if practiced generally, would be generally injurious, and that this is the ground of the obligation to abstain from it. (CW 10:220)

Although Mill employs expressions of the utilitarian generalization form of rule-utilitarianism on occasion, it is also ruled out. In other passages Mill explicitly says that simple rule generalization leaves out some of the elements and factors that need to be addressed by agents in moral deliberation. For example, Mill chides Bentham specifically for limiting consideration to such generalizations in moral reflection. Mill says that he finds fault with Bentham because he "has habitually made up his estimate of the approbation or blame due to a particular kind of action, from a calculation solely of the consequences to which that very action, if practiced generally, would itself lead" (CW 10:8). Mill points to character traits as the features that Bentham leaves out of the picture. For example, the general practice of theft or lying yields bad consequences.

> [B]ut those evil consequences are far from constituting the entire moral bearings of the vices of theft or lying. We shall have a very imperfect view of the relation of those practices to the general happiness, if we suppose them to exist singly, and insulated. All acts suppose certain dispositions, and habits of mind and heart, which may be in themselves states of enjoyment or of wretchedness, and which must be fruitful in *other* consequences, besides those particular acts. No person can be a thief or a liar without being much else: and if our moral judgments and feelings with respect to a person convicted of either vice, were grounded solely upon the pernicious tendency of thieving and of lying, they would be partial and incomplete. (CW 10:7)

Further, he adds, it is an error not to consider whether an act or habit is evidence of a pernicious character, one which is deficient in traits that yield happiness. In sum, Mill criticizes Bentham for ignoring the importance of character. In *Utilitarianism* Mill emphasizes the interconnection between action and the habits and characters which are reliable and trustworthy.

> But inasmuch as the cultivation in ourselves of a sensitive feeling on the subject of veracity, is one of the most useful, and the enfeeblement of that feeling one of the most hurtful, things to which our conduct can be instrumental; and inasmuch as any, even unintentional, deviation from truth, does that much towards weakening the trustworthiness of human assertion . . . we feel that the violation, for a present advantage, of a rule of such transcendent expediency, is not expedient. (CW 10:223)

So Mill's theory probably most harmoniously fits into the second rule-utilitarian variety of "moral code" utilitarianism. The "moral code" version relies upon determining obligations and duties by seeing their place in a complete moral code, a comprehensive set of moral rules. The moral code is the one that lays out the group or set of rules of morality that produces the greatest happiness if most members of society internalize the code and follow the rules prescribed therein. Moral codes in turn fall into two categories: actual or conventional, and ideal. In both of these, Mill's emphasis on education and development as essentially meshed with morality can be seen as providing the necessary conditions, the essential training and inculcation, so that the rules are internalized and generally adopted. Thus it takes into account what Mill complains Bentham leaves out, namely, the character and the education of moral agents. Built into this educative process is the program for the cultivation of the traits that lead to trustworthiness and reliability, compassion and empathy. Moral agents understand the importance of respect for and protection of each and every person's vital interests, the very ones that moral rules are designed to provide for through social guarantees. Mill's philosophy of education is designed to provide this necessary social and institutional support for compliance with the moral code.

What about the prospects for actual moral code versus ideal moral code? In attempting to determine which of these two candidates offers the best reading of Mill, we face a dilemma. The dilemma springs from Mill's basic faith in human progress, which includes moral progress. If moral codes are expected to improve over time, then both ideal and actual moral codes bump up against this anticipated progression. The ideal moral code reading is that the code at the core is the entire set of rules that would produce the most happiness if it were generally accepted and adopted. The problem facing this reading is that the conception of the rules is that they are already ideal, that is, the best they could be in their effects on human happiness. But Mill expects there to be continual *progress* in the rules of morality, just as he expects continual progress within human affairs generally. In *Utilitarianism* he says that "[t]he corollaries from the principle of utility, like the precepts of every practical art, admit of indefinite improvement, and, in a progressive state of the human mind, their improvement is perpetually going on" (CW 10:224). In "Auguste Comte," recall, he claims that "the domain of moral duty, in an improving society, is always widening. When what once was uncommon virtue becomes common virtue, it comes to be numbered among obligations, while a degree exceeding what has grown common, remains simply meritorious" (CW 10:338). But if the theory posits an expectation of improvement, then the rules within it can hardly be conceived of as already *ideal*. So the ideal code reading must take account of this dilemma. One plausible interpretation is that conduct that works for progress is situated in the terrain of Virtue or Nobility, as Mill clearly argues in "Auguste Comte." When improvement leads to better conduct becoming generally accepted, and rules evolve such that they become part of the actual conventional moral code of a society, then and only then are they relocated into the terrain of Morality from that of Virtue or Nobility. Thus the conduct of moral reformers such as Mill in his activist battles can be conceived of as providing models of virtuous activity, habitually above and beyond what Morality requires. Such are the exemplars of individuality that Mill extols in *On Liberty*. Working for progress, the reformers would be guided, as was Mill himself, by the spirit that in time their "uncommon virtue" would become sufficiently common that the conduct would enter the realm of Morality.

Conventional or popular moral rules, generally accepted, internalized, and adhered to, do not face this problem. However, the conventional moral code reading faces the objection that actual moral codes of any society are noticeably imperfect and flawed – that is why Mill expects improvement in them. While it may be a reasonable compromise to conceive of the conduct of moral reformers as praiseworthy virtuous activity, yet it is somewhat unsatisfying to claim that Mill's activist battles, for example to overcome domestic oppression and abuse and violence against women and children, can be conceived of as merely virtuous. One unsettling implication appears to be that domestic violence is not morally wrong until such time as the rule prohibiting such violence becomes a part of the conventional code of a society. However, this particular unsettling implication does not follow from the division between Morality and Virtue. The basic rights protecting security and liberty already prohibited the oppression and violence against women and children that Mill battled. Such rights were already entrenched components of the moral code of Mill's society. The activist battle can plausibly be conceived of as over their application, to bring to awareness that the accepted rights were not being reasonably applied, and perhaps also over their extension. This interpretation of the process of moral reform helps to soften the dilemma that moral progress poses for the conventional and ideal moral code interpretations of Mill's moral theory. So conventional moral rules, generally accepted, internalized, and adhered to, seem to have the best fit with Mill's conception of Morality, as outlined in the previous section. This must be placed in the context of the Art of Life, in which the promotion of Virtue is a companion to Morality.

This sets out the contours of Mill's moral theory and the relationship between the companion spheres of Morality (including justice) and Virtue or Nobility. There are adjudication issues in determining the proper balance among the areas of the Art of Life, when they are in tension or pull in different directions. Within the sphere of Morality, the territory of the basic and vital interests, Morality prevails. But on the edges and in grey areas, questions remain. Mill's moral and political philosophy is constructed to be tested, refined, and improved in application and practice. The discussions on liberty, education, politics and democracy, and gender equality which I pursue in later chapters will offer further clarifications and assessments of his utilitarianism.

notes

1 The literature on this question is voluminous. Some important pieces, in historical order, are the following: Harrod 1936; Harrison 1952–3; Urmson 1953; Stout 1954; Rawls 1955; Smart 1956; Mabbott 1956; McCloskey 1957; Lyons 1965; Brandt 1967; Cupples 1972; Brown 1973, 1974; Copp 1979; Sumner 1979; Berger 1984; Lyons 1994; Crisp 1997; West 2004; Skorupski 2005, 2006; Fuchs 2006; Eggleston and Miller 2007.
2 Crisp 1997, 118. Adapted from H. J. McCloskey 1957.
3 See West 2004; Skorupski 2005, 2006; Fuchs 2006; Eggleston and Miller 2007.

further reading

Berger, Fred, *Happiness, Justice, and Freedom: The Moral and Political Philosophy of John Stuart Mill* (Berkeley: University of California Press, 1984).
Crisp, Roger, *Mill on Utilitarianism* (London: Routledge, 1997).
Eggleston, Ben, and Dale E. Miller, "India House Utilitarianism: A First Look," *Southwest Philosophy Review* 23, no. 1 (2007), 39–47.
Fuchs, Alan E., "Mill's Theory of Morally Correct Action," in Henry West, ed., *The Blackwell Guide to Mill's Utilitarianism* (Oxford: Blackwell, 2006), 139–58.
Hare, R. M., *Moral Thinking: Its Levels, Method, and Point* (Oxford: Clarendon Press, 1981).
Lyons, David, *Forms and Limits of Utilitarianism* (Oxford: Oxford University Press, 1965).
Lyons, David, *Rights, Welfare, and Mill's Moral Theory* (Oxford: Clarendon Press, 1994).
Skorupski, John, *John Stuart Mill* (London: Routledge, 1989).
Sumner, L. W., "The Good and the Right," in Wesley E. Cooper, Kai Nielsen, and Steven C. Patten, eds., *New Essays on John Stuart Mill and Utilitarianism, Canadian Journal of Philosophy, Supplementary Vol. 5* (1979), 99–114.
Sumner, L. W., *The Moral Foundation of Rights* (Oxford: Clarendon Press, 1997).
West, Henry, *An Introduction to Mill's Utilitarian Ethics* (Cambridge: Cambridge University Press, 2004).
West, Henry, ed., *The Blackwell Guide to Mill's Utilitarianism* (Oxford: Blackwell, 2006).

liberty

Introduction

Mill's essay *On Liberty* is frequently the first text that his readers encounter. The core of the essay consists of an impassioned defense of the fundamental liberal freedoms, yet the argument of this work is intricately interwoven with the fabric of Mill's moral and political philosophy. Mill states the liberty principle in the early pages of the essay. He says that the object of the essay is to argue for the principle that should govern the extent to which society can legitimately use coercion and control over its individual members.

> That principle is, that the sole end for which mankind are warranted, individually or collectively, in interfering with the liberty of action of any of their number, is self-protection. That the only purpose for which power can be rightfully exercised over any member of a civilized community, against his will, is to prevent harm to others. (CW 18:223)

Following this initial formulation as a single principle, Mill offers clarifications. The liberty principle is explicated in terms of a familiar demarcation.

> He cannot rightfully be compelled to do or forbear because it will be better for him to do so, because it will make him happier, because, in the opinion of others, to do so would be wise, or even right. These are good reasons for remonstrating with him, or reasoning with him, or persuading him, or entreating him, but not for compelling him. (CW 18:223–4)

This is the well-known formulation of the liberty principle, but it is not Mill's only presentation of the guiding principles of liberty. Several chapters later, he explains that the doctrine of the essay can be summed up by two maxims:

The two maxims are, first, that the individual is not accountable to society for his actions, in so far as these concern the interests of no person but himself. Advice, instruction, persuasion, and avoidance by other people if thought necessary by them for their own good, are the only measures by which society can justifiably express its dislike or disapprobation of his conduct. Secondly, that for such actions as are prejudicial to the interests of others, the individual is accountable, and may be subjected either to social or to legal punishment, if society is of the opinion that the one or the other is requisite for its protection. (CW 18:292)

There is now an extensive literature examining and puzzling over the analysis of the concept of harm at the core of the liberty principle. If the concept of harm cannot be pinned down, then the liberty principle is so amorphous and woolly that its usefulness in protecting a domain of liberty is questionable. But this pessimistic view of the prospects of the core principle is untenable once we realize that it fits neatly into the structure of Mill's moral philosophy. That Mill presents the guiding principle of liberty in one formulation using the concept of harm and in a second formulation using the concept of interests is significant. It signals that Mill regards harm and interests as tightly linked. Mill himself provides the answer to this question in Chapter 5 of *Utilitarianism*. The liberty principle is a principle of justice, protecting the inner sanctum of the most vital human interests from the harms of incursions of compulsion and control. In Chapter 3 on morality I looked at the structure of Mill's moral philosophy, featuring the framework of the Art of Life. I claimed there that the structure of Mill's theory has significant implications for liberty. The liberty principle is a principle of justice, with the express mandate of guaranteeing some of the most vital interests, enshrined as rights occupying the inner sanctum of the theory. The liberty principle marks the legitimate boundary and limit of social and political coercion over people. Such coercion is permitted only in cases of harm to others. Harm to others is analyzed in terms of violations of rights or of significant other-regarding duties (grounded on the vital interests). It cannot be traded off or outweighed merely to provide small gains of happiness to others, even large numbers of others. This sort of trade-off is ruled out by the structure of Mill's theory. Liberty is named as one of the most vital human interests, and rights and principles of justice are their designated protectors. Mill says

The moral rules which forbid mankind to hurt one another (in which we must never forget to include wrongful interference with each other's freedom) are more vital to human well-being . . . Thus the moralities which protect every individual from being harmed by others . . . by being hindered in his freedom of pursuing his own good, are at once those which he himself has most at heart, and those which he has the strongest interest in publishing and enforcing by word and deed. (CW 10:255–6)

Thus the zone of liberty is inviolable except in cases in which another competing right or especially weighty other-regarding obligation is at stake. The liberty principle marks off the territory within which compulsion is not legitimate.

I examined the general arguments for limiting intrusions involving coercion to the territory of Morality in Chapter 3. In *On Liberty*, Mill's general utilitarian justification of the importance of the interests in liberty and autonomy follows in Chapter 2, "Of the Liberty of Thought and Discussion" and Chapter 3, "Of Individuality, as One of the Elements of Well-Being." In these chapters Mill explains and argues at length for his claim that liberty in its many forms is a core component and precondition of human well-being and thus it merits protection as a vital interest of the kind that grounds rights. The right to liberty of self-development, especially the rights to individuality and autonomy, are granted special attention. His commitments to autonomy, individuality, and more generally self-development are surely some of the most familiar features of his moral and political philosophy. Since all members of society have the right to liberty of self-development, and are wronged if they are denied developmental opportunities to lead a life that is their own and not imposed by others, the case for these forms of liberty goes right down to the root of his moral and political philosophy.

Liberty of Thought and Expression

Mill's eloquent tribute to liberty of thought and freedom of expression in Chapter 2 of *On Liberty* is required reading of the liberal canon. Freedom of thought and expression is a cornerstone of liberalism. Liberty is multi-faceted, and this core value plays a multi-dimensional role in Mill's philosophy. The liberty principle plays a structural role in his theory, marking some of the boundaries within Mill's theory of justice. Autonomy and individuality are core human virtues and excellences, and key elements of and preconditions for well-being. Liberty is indispensable for seeking and discovering truth. People who aspire to defend and follow freedom of thought are on the route to intellectual cultivation. Commitment to the spirit of free inquiry and engagement in the questioning spirit, Mill maintains, are the heart and driving force of progress and improvement in human affairs.

Mill's case for freedom of thought and expression considers its value under several scenarios. His argument for liberty of thought has two main prongs. He argues for two fundamental claims that "we can never be sure that the opinion we are endeavouring to stifle is a false opinion; and if we were sure, stifling it would be an evil still" (CW 18:229). Open-mindedness, toleration, and appreciation for the merits of the many sides ("many-sidedness") of cases in disputed questions, as well as patience and empathy for opponents are all stalwart attitudes for cultivating the virtues of reason and intellect. Open-mindedness and the capacity to be reasonable and accepting of diversity of opinion are marks of the liberal stance. This liberal attitude combines passionate engagement and the spirit of inquiry with patience, acceptance, and even welcoming of dispute. Mill himself embodied these liberal attitudes, and his life work can be seen as an unrelenting battle with dogmatism and despotism in its many guises. His attack on the "despotism of custom" as an enemy of freedom and progress is part of a systematic battle against despotism in general (CW 18:272). Dogmatism tries to discredit or silence opponents and is the enemy of liberty of thought. Equally troubling are harms resulting from stifling free inquiry and discussion. This is connected to dogmatism, intolerance, and, in extreme cases, even hatred of opponents. It shuts down or impedes progress and improvement. Individual excellences are not hoarded, in Mill's view, but produce benefits that filter out to the entire society. As Mill puts it, "the peculiar evil of silencing the expression of an opinion is, that it is robbing the human race" (CW 18:229).

The first branch of his argument considers the scenario under which society tries to suppress a view that is in fact true. Mill is a fallibilist. He holds that humans are fallible creatures and prone to err in their judgments. As John Skorupski puts it, Mill "takes the fallibilist attitude that *any* of the things we think we know, however seemingly certain, could turn out to be wrong in the course of our continuing inquiry" (Skorupski 2006, 8). Any judgment or opinion held, however certain we may feel of its truth, yet may be false. We therefore need to guard against our fallibility and take precautions in the light of this awareness of it. We must allow the fullest, freest open discussion of all questions, especially controversial ones, to ensure that if the controversial claim is in fact true, society is not robbed of the fruits of knowing the truth. Some of the most renowned sages and thinkers of their ages turned out to be mistaken in their cherished beliefs. Infallibility no more attaches to ages or cultures than to individuals. In this light, he foresees that many views generally accepted in his time will be rejected in future. The conviction of Mill's age that marriage is for life and divorce is morally wrong, even in cases of extreme marital unhappiness and domestic violence, is now recognized as dubious at the very least.

When action is necessary, the benefits of pursuit of liberty are no less. On the contrary, Mill says, "complete liberty of contradicting and disproving our opinion, is the very condition which justifies us in assuming its truth for purposes of action" (CW 18:231). The mark of a reasonable person is that she has the ability to recognize and correct mistakes. Humans may be fallible, but errors are correctable. Experience, free discussion, and argument tend to pry errors loose, to expose them in the light of day. A wise person's judgment merits confidence and authority only if these conditions are met. "The steady habit of correcting and completing his own opinion by collating it with those of others, so far from causing doubt and hesitation in carrying it into practice, is the only stable foundation for a just reliance on it" (CW 18:232).

Reasonable people issue open invitations to others to dispute and challenge their judgments, to argue with them. Acknowledging their fallibility, they seek reasonable confidence in their opinions by ensuring that their beliefs are open to direct challenge and dispute. By thus removing restraints on challenges to their beliefs, they come to rest in such confidence as is attainable in a complex world of fallible people and diverse perspectives. Socrates and Christ in their times both stood on the wrong side of the divide of popular opinion and were condemned by the legal powers for expressing views deemed to be impious and blasphemous, even though they both had reached the pinnacle of wisdom and virtue. Mill emphasizes that the damage done in suppressing unorthodox views does not fall only on the shoulders of the heretics. Rather, "the greatest harm done is to those who are not heretics, and whose whole mental development is cramped, and their reason cowed, by the fear of heresy" (CW 18:242).

Now Mill moves on to the second division of his argument for liberty, that scenario under which the orthodox or popular opinion is true. The core of his argument is that even in the case of true opinion "if it is not fully, frequently, and fearlessly discussed, it will be held as a dead dogma, not a living truth" (CW 18:243). Students of philosophy know full well that writing a philosophy essay in which only one side of the case is argued earns a poor grade. One feature that separates out those who hold true beliefs reasonably from those who hold them as prejudices or dogmas is whether or not the objections and opposing views are fully understood and answered. Knowing the truth, holding to it rationally, developing the intellect, all require that grounds of and objections to these beliefs are equally familiar friends. This harks back to Mill's stated conditions for being a competent judge of value in *Utilitarianism*. The difference between the wisdom of Socrates and the lack thereof of the fool is that fools "only know their own side of the question" (CW 10:212). In *On Liberty*, he complements this point, proclaiming that "he who knows only his own side of the case, knows little of that" (CW 18:245). On matters of such import, then, society should thank those willing to argue for minority opinions and thank devil's advocates for serving public debate by furnishing the strongest arguments for unpopular views when no actual adherents of that view put themselves forward.

The vitality of convictions depends upon subjecting them to intense scrutiny and questioning. Questioning is required in order for the conviction to "penetrate the feelings, and acquire a real mastery over the conduct" (CW 18:247). In cases where this is absent these dead beliefs are severed from feelings, imagination, and understanding and they no longer have the power of conviction. The phrase "the marketplace of ideas" is sometimes used to convey the Millian model of public debate which is designed to promote the best chance for ascertaining truth. Mill himself extols the benefits of Socratic dialogue for unearthing both error and dogmatic belief. The counterpoise is diversity of opinions held by people willing to argue and uphold them. Truth held as dogma has no power to affect development of virtuous habits and character but is a troubling influence on intellectual vice.

In real-life settings, Mill contends, few beliefs, even true ones, are the whole truth. Mill praises many-sidedness. There are many sides to complex issues, and minority beliefs often contain a portion of truth absent in the popular view. In such cases, it is "only by the collision of adverse opinions that the remainder of the truth has any chance of being supplied" (CW 18:258). Despite the tendency of the human mind to grasp onto one-sidedness, "truth, in the great practical concerns of life, is so much a question of the reconciling and combining of opposites, that very few have minds sufficiently capacious and impartial to make the adjustment with an approach to correctness" (CW 18:254). In this respect, the marketplace of ideas model is misleading, for in the economic marketplace, the strongest wins the competition, but Mill contends that in the public sphere of debate, minority views should be encouraged, to allow fairness for all sides. The many-sided nature of truth relies on open-minded habits which allow it to emerge from reflection and discussion.

In sum, there are two interwoven strands to Mill's case for liberty of thought. The search for truth is an important mission of free open inquiry. But equally important is the impact of the free spirit of inquiry on mental, emotional, and imaginative development. If the search for freedom of expression does not penetrate the emotions and yield conviction, it has done but part of its work. Mill defends liberty as bound up with the "permanent interests of man as a progressive being," especially the human vital interests in mental and moral development (CW 18:224). Mental and moral development rely upon the intense, even passionate, desire to lead a reflective life. The absence of these desires thwarts this developmental process.

Individual self-development is tied to freedom. But Mill thinks that social progress is also distinctly tied to these pursuits. In other writings, including *A System of Logic*, Mill pins his hopes for continued progress in human affairs on mental development of path-breaking individuals and the models they set for society. He argues there that the main determinants of social progress are "speculation, intellectual activity, the pursuit of truth" (CW 8:926). Pursuits of searching for truth and exercising the mental capacities are thoroughly intertwined and mutually reinforcing. When society stifles minority opinion it doubles harm by undercutting individual and social development and by threatening inquiries into truth.

Autonomy and Individuality

Studying the grounds for valuing one branch of liberty – of thought and discussion – is a good entry point for probing the general case for liberty. Mill's case for liberty of action ensues, and in the center are arguments for the value and benefits of autonomy and individuality for happiness.

Autonomy and individuality are core components of Mill's conception of self-development. Autonomy and individuality are interconnected excellences. Individuality involves developing an identity that is authentic to the person, and autonomy is clearly essential for this project. To be autonomous is to be self-determining and free from the dominating will of others. Despotism and oppression are the enemies. To be in the position of having one's life determined by others and to be in servitude to their will means being ruled by others rather than oneself. Mill's positive case for participation rests upon the results of these activities for developing virtues. Conversely, he argues that being excluded from participating in decision making and being subject to commands of others regarding crucial intimate aspects of identity corrode the spirit. This despotism adopts many guises and can be direct or indirect. In *The Subjection of Women* Mill's immediate concern is with the command and obedience model of marital relations under which patriarchal despotic husbands directly command their spouses. In *On Liberty* he expresses his concern about the "despotism of custom" that often acts indirectly to deflect individuality and induce stultifying conformism (CW 18:272). Machine-like conformity to the customary in society is one of the main routes for thwarting these crucial excellences and preconditions of happiness. Of course, autonomy is fully consonant with being *influenced* by others, especially those in one's intimate circle, and with carrying on dialogues and being persuaded by others. This process is essential to the inquiring spirit of liberty and the pursuit of truth, as we have seen. Autonomous agents generally are deeply immersed in communities and intimate relations with others. What distinguishes the autonomous agent from the other-determined agent is that the former makes her own choices at the conclusion of the dialogue – albeit with due concern for the welfare of significant others. While there are several varieties of autonomy, Mill defends liberal autonomy, which is organized around capacities of authenticity, reflection, deliberation, and self-determination. Autonomous agents scrutinize and reflect upon their options, often in dialogue with others. This reflective process leads them to endorse and choose their plan of life, conception of the good, commitments, communities, and most fundamentally their character. Autonomy and individuality are connected skills and combine to enable people to construct principled identities. These lives of their own are not lives of isolation but generally involve interconnection with others – by choice, not by force. And, because Mill expects diversity in life plans, a freely chosen life of solitude is part of the range of good lives.

Mill's argument for the value of autonomy and individuality is motivated in part by his apprehension about menaces from the powerful forces of conformism. People have deep desires to belong to and be in harmony with their family and community. However, there is a shadow side to these needs. These laudable desires for attachment and belonging can be manipulated by despots and oppressors so that autonomy and individuality are frequently put under threat. Healthy autonomy and individuality do not conflict with authentic forms of intimacy, belonging, and group identity. Healthy manifestations of autonomy and individuality and of belonging and connection reinforce each other. But there are shadow forms that mask oppression and tyranny and it is these forms that Mill battles and fears. His arguments for freedom provide a positive case for their immense benefits, but also strongly warn about those forms of belonging and community that are unhealthy. They work to diminish individuality by manipulative appeals to questionable forms of attachment that corrode well-being. The cultural context can enhance and support or threaten autonomy and individuality. Mill's arguments for individuality within community bring to the foreground some compelling questions for liberalism which I consider shortly using the example of polygamy within the Mormon society of his time.

Individuality and freedom of action follow the guide set down by the liberty principle. Individuality must be cherished and unhindered for every member of society as long as any risk is to themselves and their conduct does not harm others. Harm to others is analyzed as violating other-regarding duties, especially rights, as mandated by the theory of justice. No one, says Mill, believes that actions should have the same degree of freedom as opinions. "On the contrary, even opinions lose their immunity, when the circumstances in which they are expressed are such as to constitute their expression a positive instigation to some mischievous act" (CW 18:260). If liberty of expression becomes a positive instigation to or incitement to harm others it loses its protected status. Opinions delivered with the intention of inciting a crowd to violence, rather than the intention of inviting them to express their thoughts and feelings in non-violent, albeit impassioned modes, furnish examples of free expression that cross the line into harmful conduct.

Acts that harm others may legitimately be constrained, and liberty limited, but acts that do not are in the liberty-protection zone. Diversity of belief parallels diversity of lifestyle; both have the same aims of advancing happiness, human progress, and pursuit of truth. Individuality requires more than simple toleration in order to thrive; it deserves and needs positive appreciation. It is advanced by people's willingness to engage in diverse experiments in living. Mill says that "if it were felt that the free development of individuality is one of the leading essentials of well-being; that it is not only a co-ordinate element with all that is designated by the terms civilization, instruction, education, culture, but is itself a necessary part and condition of all those things; there would be no danger that liberty should be undervalued" (CW 18:261). Mill has special regard for the qualities of spontaneity and activity, since they act as conformity's antidote.

But, sadly, it is an ongoing battle to get people to recognize that individuality is indeed a chief component of happiness and of progress. If its value were properly acknowledged, it would not be difficult to discern the legitimate boundaries between individuality and the zone of social control. But widely held attitudes of indifference or hostility to individuality get in the way. Individuality properly understood is not at odds with the accumulated wisdom of human experience. Mill is careful to give due regard to lessons learned from past history and experience. But people should not be constrained by these past experiences if they no longer serve the ends of happiness and especially if they are not in harmony with the person's own character and feelings. Autonomous choice must be exercised to make choices in favor of what is in harmony with the person's own nature, rather than what others wish for us. Customs may be fine for customary characters, but customs do not serve as models for highly individual, creative, and even eccentric people. Even good customs that harmonize well with our individual character can ossify into dead dogmas if they are not subjected to experimentation and interrogation. If individuality is not recognized, we risk creating a culture of robots and mimicking monkeys. Mill frequently invokes the distinction between machines and spontaneous, living organic things. Robotic patterns of conduct that follow fashion for its own sake can have a stultifying impact on the character and degenerate into the very opposite of virtue.

[To] conform to custom, merely *as* custom, does not educate or develope in him any of the qualities which are the distinctive endowment of a human being. The human faculties of perception, judgment, discriminative feeling, mental activity and even moral preference, are exercised only in making a choice. He who does anything because it is the custom, makes no choice. He gains no practice either in discerning or in desiring what is best. The mental and moral, like the muscular powers, are improved only by being used. (CW 18:262)

Habituation in the virtues of autonomy and individuality requires active use, in other words. We should no more do things simply because others do them than we should believe simply because others believe. If we let others set for us our character and life plans, we behave as ape-like mimics rather than self-determining agents. Autonomy and individuality come together to produce a life that is our own, that is authentic to our character and feelings. We could well be said to be the authors of our own life, as long as this is understood as involving a process – a long process – of prior engagement with others including dialogical and reflective elements. It is an individualized, but not an isolated, process of self-authorship. We use and exercise all of our distinctively human faculties if we determine and then self-determine the contours of our life. If we allow ourselves to be unduly guided by others' authority, then even if we end up in the right place, this is accidental. And it is at the cost of sacrifice of our dignity and worth. Mill's stirring words on these few pages of *On Liberty* are some of the best-known passages in his writing.

He who lets the world, or his own portion of it, choose his plan of life for him, has no need of any other faculty than the ape-like one of imitation. He who chooses his plan for himself, employs all his faculties. He must use observation to see, reasoning and judgment to foresee, activity to gather materials for decision, discrimination to decide, and when he has decided, firmness and self-control to hold to his deliberate decision . . . It is possible that he might be guided in some good path, and kept out of harm's way, without any of these things. But what will be his comparative worth as a human being? It really is of importance, not only what men do, but also what manner of men they are that do it. Among the works of man, which human life is rightly employed in perfecting and beautifying, the first in importance surely is man himself. (CW 18:262–3)

Mill is highly critical of those whom he characterizes as human automatons. They may carry out the usual daily functions, yet they are still starved and withered specimens rather than what they could be. Robots and machines are not desirable models. This point applies also to feelings, passions, and desires. Strong passions are indicative of energy, and energetic qualities are preferable to passive indolence. Indeed, in the absence of these virtues, Mill claims people lack a character.

A person whose desires and impulses are his own – are the expression of his own nature, as it has been developed and modified by his own culture

– is said to have a character. One whose desires and impulses are not his own, has no character, no more than a steam-engine has a character. (CW 18:264)

This could rightly be said to be the very essence of individuality. Absent this, there is no authentic character. "Human nature is not a machine to be built after a model, and set to do exactly the work pre-scribed for it, but a tree, which requires to grow and develope itself on all sides, according to the tendency of the inward forces which make it a living thing" (CW 18:263).

The Calvinist ideal is one of his favorite targets and a prime specimen of cramped, stifled human nature. Those who believe in a supreme Being, he says, should have faith that this Being provided people with capa-cities that should be cultivated rather than eliminated. Rejecting the Calvinist ideal of self-denial and abnegation, Mill endorses the alternat-ive Greek ideal of self-development. Contrary to misguided conformist claims, human beauty and nobility are perfected by cultivating individu-ality with due regard to the rights of others.

Self-development mandates that value choices thrust upon people from the outside, not chosen by them for themselves, detract from the value of a good life. Different experiments in living provide different conditions needed to promote development in pluralistic societies. What may be an obstacle or hindrance for one person can prove to be a bonus for the next. For adventurers or entrepreneurs, stimulation and excitement are spurs to action. However, for reflective contemplatives, they are more likely sources of mind-clutter and distraction from medit-ative pursuits. Humans are sufficiently different that "unless there is a corresponding diversity in their modes of life, they neither obtain their fair share of happiness, nor grow up to the mental, moral, and aesthetic stature of which their nature is capable" (CW 18:270).

In sum, Mill claims that individuality is an essential component of self-development and a condition of a happy human life. This is the first part of Mill's argument for individuality. The second prong of his argument for individuality lauds its social benefits. Individuality and diversity are not honed at the expense of sociality, with whom they must keep company and be in balance, but rather self-development incorporates compassion and sociality and strengthens human bonds. The benefits spread out generously to others. "In proportion to the development of his individuality, each person becomes more valuable to himself, and is therefore capable of being more valuable to others" (CW 18:266). Mill is careful to state that he does not advocate selfishness, which in his mind is a surefire route to misery. "As little is there an inherent necessity that any human being should be a selfish egotist, devoid of every feeling or care but those which centre in his own miserable individuality" (CW 10:216). Respecting rights and the rules of justice cultivates social feelings. However, restrictions in areas which do not involve rights of others "dulls and blunts the whole nature" (CW 18:266). It is insidious despotism to crush another's individuality.

The second prong of the argument is that self-developed people are of great value to their fellow beings. Their originality and creativity break open the limited varieties of beliefs, attitudes, and lifestyles prevalent at any time, for they have problems fitting into the relatively small range of options currently favored in their culture. In the absence of these creative and original models, society runs the risk of stagnation and perpetuation of collective mediocrity. Mill hopes that some will freely choose to endorse and try out the models offered by these exemplars of individuality. Many people "can respond internally to wise and noble things, and be led to them with . . . eyes open" (CW 18:269). The "eyes open" proviso is crucial, for without this people would still be mimics rather than self-determining agents. Quickly follows the clarification and proviso that this must not turn into hero worship, for any people who attempt to impose judgments of the good on others would thereby brand themselves as despots. "All he can claim is, freedom to point out the way. The power of compelling others into it, is not only inconsistent with the freedom and development of all the rest, but corrupting" (CW 18:269). In an age of hyped-up conformism then, eccentricity, a type of individuality, is especially welcome to counteract it. Eccentrics and people of unusual originality may come up with more valuable pursuits or ways of living that create ripple effects and in turn become more generally accepted by the culture. For example, vegetarianism used to be considered a proclivity of eccentrics, but now it is almost a mainstream diet. To be called a "granola lover" no longer is an insult, but instead is a compliment to a taste for healthy living. Similarly, the organic food movement has created tastes for these products so they are now found not only in health food stores but also occupy increasing supermarket shelf-space. So the value of individuality does not accrue only to eccentrics and true originals, but the ripple effects are quite widely experienced.

Mill's argument for freedom of expression accentuates that diversity of opinion spurs progress and improvement. Diversity of lifestyle serves precisely the same goal, and conformity to custom, as conformity of opinion, equally obstructs improvement in human affairs. Progress dwindles when individuality ceases to be a driving force in society. The threats are the same as those faced by freedom of expression: intolerance and the desire to compel others to be and live like the rest. This is the tendency to turn us into moralists by profession, to expand the proper place of rules of conduct to encompass what are correctly seen as lifestyle or mode of life choices. Fighting the encroachments of moralists by profession is one of Mill's most cherished projects.

The drive to be a distinct individual is a powerful motivation, even for twins or triplets. For example, Elisabeth Kübler-Ross was born a triplet in Switzerland, but her drive to individuality led her to become a pioneer researcher on death and dying. Her childhood plan and dream was to become a doctor. Her father had other plans for her future and pressured her to work in his office until she found a suitable husband and became a wife and mother (Kübler-Ross 1997, 22). At great cost and effort, she refused her father's plans for her life and fought for a life of her own design. She describes her unusual life plot.

> I could never, not in my wildest dreams – and they were pretty wild – have predicted one day winding up the world-famous author of *On Death and Dying*, a book whose exploration of life's final passage threw me into the center of a medical and theological controversy. Nor could I have imagined that afterward I would spend the rest of my life explaining that death does not exist. (Kübler-Ross 1997, 15)

She is undeniably a true original. Her path-breaking research and clinical work on the process of dying helped to shatter cultural attitudes towards death that were the cause of unnecessary suffering and indignity to terminally ill people. Prevailing attitudes dictated denial of death, and terminally ill people were often prevented from even talking about their impending death, since it was considered better to refrain from telling them the truth about their prognosis. Kübler-Ross conducted research into the process of dying that led to the founding of the hospice movement. Her activism helped bring about a radical transformation in attitudes to and treatment of people with terminal illness, so that now it is considered unethical to deny them the dignity of communicating with others about their condition. Kübler-Ross is an excellent example backing up Mill's argument that encouraging individuality allows for the emergence of "better modes of action, and customs more worthy of general adoption" (CW 18:270). She is the exemplar of one who develops her individuality, resulting in great social benefits, opening up new social paths, and dissipating outdated cultural practices that no longer serve to promote happiness.

Autonomy, Individuality, and Community: The Case of Mormon Polygamy

The virtues of and entitlements to individuality and autonomy, to an authentic identity and a life of one's own, are basic to the good life. The liberty principle is a principle of justice guaranteeing these basic rights within Mill's philosophy. He argues eloquently for the liberal essentials of freedom of thought and discussion and individuality and autonomy. His theory is holistic, and the excellences of individuality and autonomy are balanced with those of compassion, cooperativeness, and community. The framework of his theory sets some clear limits to intrusions into the domain of liberty. But in other cases, on the edges especially, the structure offers rather a framework for deliberation. Things change over time, and these changes, hopefully progressive improvements, bring out new dilemmas and puzzles and new ways of scrutinizing questions. The balancing between individuality and autonomy and values of culture, community, and belonging can bump up against each other and be in tension, and sometimes radical conflict. Mill himself presents some examples of applications of his theory in the later chapters of *On Liberty*, after the early chapters in which he sets out the liberty principle and defends some of its core forms of liberty of thought and of individuality. One of these examples offers a useful entry point for exploring some of the dilemmas and tensions raised by the balancing of individuality and community belonging.

In Chapter 4 of *On Liberty*, Mill looks at the case of polygamous marriage within Mormon communities of his time. He uses this example to test the limits of application of the liberty principle. In Mill's day, the Mormon community had moved to then far-off Utah. Mill claims that this remote Mormon community was suffering persecution. Some even advocated sending a British expedition to Utah to end this marital practice by force.

After Mill's strong defense of individuality and autonomy, his comments on polygamy within the Mormon community come as something of a surprise. Against the backdrop of Mill's previous arguments about the fundamental value of autonomy and individuality to each person, and of the dangers of conformism in response to pressure, the question to be asked is, under what circumstances could the women of this community be characterized as exhibiting individuality and autonomy in their marital choices? The standard option in this community is polygamous marriage in which women are one of several wives. The reverse scenario under which men are one of several husbands does not occur.

Mill says that "no one has a deeper disapprobation than I have of this Mormon institution" (CW 18:290). Yet he claims that the women's conduct in engaging in polygamy is "voluntary." At the same time he admits that the institution does not comply with the liberty principle, for "far from being in any way countenanced by the principle of liberty, it is a direct infraction of that principle, being a mere rivetting of the chains of one-half of the community, and an emancipation of the other from reciprocity of obligation towards them" (CW 18:290). Despite this, he says, this kind of marital union is as voluntary as other forms of marriage. In this community, the only options for women are to be one of several wives or to remain unmarried. Since the group has moved away, Mill argues that outsiders would be behaving tyrannically by attempting to stop them from living according to their divergent system of marriage. The provisos are that they do not attack other communities, and that they permit dissenters the right to exit the community.

Mill departs from his previous arguments in *On Liberty* and defends the communal rights of the group while abandoning the substantive rights of its individual members. He views them through the lens of the outsider, keeping them at a distance. He loses sight of the obvious – that this group is composed of individuals and is not a homogeneous mass. Mill's core point in *On Liberty* is that the mandate of the right to liberty of self-development is to defend each individual's right to autonomy and individuality within their society, to lead their lives according to their own way of being. Some members of any culture will be content to endorse the dominant community values and traditions after due reflection. But the mandate of liberty is to defend the rights of all members, including dissenters and rebels. In any case, in closed religious communities women who dissent face the force of community power, including violence and abuse. Although in *The Subjection of Women* Mill emphasizes that women's compliance in marriage is often the result of coercion, including violent coercion, he does not take this problem seriously in his example of polygamy.

Adopting the vantage point of the insider within his own culture, Mill perceives correctly that diversity, pluralism of life plans, and even eccentricity are the natural results of individuality and autonomy. He concludes that uniform outcomes are suspect and likely result from capitulation to the pressures of conformity. This is a major feature of his arguments defending individuality. Yet he does not sufficiently question the strange and disquieting supposedly "voluntary" acceptance of polygamy by the women and girls of the community. Mill views the group stereotypically, accepting too easily that their choices are all similar. He attacks his own society for using despotism to produce conformity. But the pattern of Mormon marriage, which all the evidence suggests is even more so the result of despotism, strikes him as needing protection from persecution by liberal outsiders. He claims that this marital choice is as voluntary as the individual heterosexual marriage institution of his own society. This claim was clearly false even in Mill's time, but is certainly so in the present time. The tinted lens of stereotype that he looks through leads to the expected result that Mormons all have the same "voluntary" choices in marriage. A vantage point internal to that community, when people are seen clearly as individuals, might yield a different perception. Mill displays a lack of empathy and sympathy for the vulnerable and powerless women and girls who are coerced into polygamous unions. This is a lapse of judgment on his part. But it is an instructive error, and serves a useful purpose in illustrating how his liberal theory has corrective insights to overturn the error.

Liberal rights to self-determination defend the right to evaluate the meaning of our own experiences, and reach our own decisions about what is worth pursuing. Millian persons recognize their fallibility, and acknowledge the need for experiments and investigations to ratify their current views about the good life, or to change them when they are revealed as mistaken. This process of reflection about the good has preconditions. The rights to autonomy and individuality are socially guaranteed. We need the opportunity to be presented with and engage with a range of options concerning the good life for all of the elements of this life, including most saliently educational, occupational, and marital arrangements. We need, in other words, to be in the position such that we are aware of various perspectives on the good life as live options, not as distant fantasies, and we require the social conditions to nurture the intellectual and imaginative capacities required critically and sensitively to look at the available options. While our society and culture generally furnish the backdrop for these deliberations and imaginations, Mill's feared conformism occurs in cases in which the community tries to enforce one particular conception of the good (marriage) and in the process thwarts the vital interests which are at stake. The liberal tenet is that "individuals are considered free to question their participation in existing social practices, and opt out of them, should those practices seem no longer worth pursuing" (Kymlicka 2002, 221). Autonomy in this context means that people are free to question and endorse, or to revise and reject, conceptions of the good, including particular components such as marital, educational, and occupational practices. This questioning is part and parcel of the healthy autonomy that does not undermine belonging and interconnectedness. The result is that persons are in a position to choose relationships and attachments from the perspective of conviction and awareness, and these tend to be enduring.

Mill recognizes the role of culture and community in providing the context of life choices. However, his preferred perspective on the community is that it will nurture and support eccentrics and true originals who reject the prevalent range of choices offered in their society and push back the boundaries and horizons of choice to come up with new ways of life through their experiments in living. His assessment of the traditional practices of the Mormon community is out of step with these expressed commitments. It falls under the scenario he fears and combats of the "hurtful compression" of "the small number of moulds which society provides in order to save its members the trouble of forming their own character" (CW 18:267–8).

Mill's liberalism does not endorse atomism, and Millian individuals are embedded in community. However, for liberals, the delicate balance between individuality and interconnection must be approached with awareness of the hazards when the balance tips against nonconformist members. Autonomy can fall prey to the expectations of family and community about their children's marital and occupational choices. If these go against the grain of entrenched community expectations, they can be viewed as betrayals and the consequences can be painful. Coercion is frequently employed under the rationale of preservation of traditional cultural practices. This definitely clashes with Mill's argument that preserving tradition for its own sake is not a justification for thwarting the individuality of nonconformists. The coercion to marry within the community is often served up as a means of preserving traditional ways or cultural practices that bond. The result is to capitulate and allow others to determine one's destiny and take control of major life decisions. In such cases, there is the risk of volatile clashes between individuality and autonomy on the one hand, and tradition and community on the other. Mill's liberalism sets very definite limits on the power granted to the community over individual life plans.

Mill's reflections on polygamy, despite their disquieting tension with the core of his arguments on individuality and autonomy, do not expose a problem with his theory. Rather, I argue, the case underscores that it is important to separate out his basic principles and the architecture of his theory from the examples he uses to illustrate the philosophy. The examples are often outdated and not readily applicable today. Even when the examples are current – as his cases of violence against women – it is yet a mistake to read too much into examples. For what this particular example exposes, I claim, is weakness in Mill's application of his theory, rather than a weakness in the theory itself. By regarding an entire social and religious group through the lens of stereotype, Mill shows a failure of empathy and sympathetic imagination in not seeing the distinct individuals who make up the group.

The fundamental arguments and principles of *On Liberty* present the response to this example. Mill thus corrects his own mistake. In Chapter 5 of *On Liberty* Mill strongly criticizes excessive parental control over their children. He argues that children's rights should be protected by the state when their parents fail in their obligations to educate them. The form of education called for by his commitments is a liberal education. I delve deeper into Mill's philosophy of education in Chapter 5.

The Subjection of Women features a very clear explanation of the basic distinction between liberty (individuality and autonomy) on the one hand and power over others on the other. Power over others fuels despotism and its corruptions. The distinction between liberty and power runs throughout his philosophical system, furnishing the means to promote the liberal freedoms and condemn oppressive power over others. *On Liberty* uses this distinction between liberty and despotic power to attack marital tyranny of husbands over wives and children. The state must respect the liberty of each individual in the self-regarding sphere. The state must equally "maintain a vigilant control over his exercise of any power which it allows him to possess over others" (CW 18:301). The family ought to be a sphere of friendship and equality between spouses. It is instead a zone of despotism of husbands over wives. The state fails miserably to fulfill its duties to protect the rights of children. Children also suffer from patriarchal control of fathers. Children have a basic right to an education which must include the right to be educated in the capacities of self-development, including prominently the capacities of autonomy and individuality. "Is it not almost a self-evident axiom, that the State should require and compel the education, up to a certain standard, of every human being who is born its citizen?" (CW 18:301). Parents have a clear duty to educate their children, and it is a "moral crime" to fail to provide an education along with other essential conditions of well-being. The state should force compliance when parents fail to fulfill their obligations to their children. The state also has a clear duty to ensure that all its members are properly educated.

Mill's philosophy of education commits him to propounding an education of a liberal kind, one that allows adults the capacities to function as autonomous individuals, embedded in community. These capacities must be nurtured in childhood if they are to be sufficiently developed by the time children reach adulthood. These capacities do not simply emerge on their own. This means that children have a right-in-trust to be autonomous in adulthood (Feinberg 1983). If their childhood education is so arranged that some possible futures are shut off as live prospects when they are adults, then their rights have been violated. Mill's philosophy of education is set up so that parents cannot determine their children's future lives when they reach adulthood. The extent of legitimate parental expectation is limited to the domain of hopes that their children will voluntarily choose to follow the traditions of community in adulthood. Mill's powerful arguments for liberty of thought and expression and individuality in combination with his philosophy of education lead inexorably to this conclusion.

Contemporary liberals also grapple with the delicate balance between individuality and community. As Will Kymlicka puts it, those defending traditional cultural ways have fears about liberal freedoms.

> They fear that if their members are informed about other ways of life, and are given the cognitive and emotional capacities to understand and evaluate them, many will choose to reject their inherited way of life, and

thereby undermine the group. To prevent this, fundamentalist or isolationist groups often wish to raise and educate their children in such a way as to minimize the opportunities for children to develop or exercise the capacity for rational revisability . . . Their goal is to ensure that their members are indeed "embedded" in the group, unable to conceive of leaving it or to succeed outside of it. (Kymlicka 2002, 228)

The Mormon community of Mill's example fits this model. Mill's discussion of the example is anomalous with his core commitments which do not permit parents and communities to close off the rights to open futures of the younger generation or of future generations. Mill's philosophy requires that adults must be able to have some ability to detach from the customary norms of their community in order to be able to choose to endorse or reject them. His philosophy does not have the means to differentiate among societies in this respect. His reflections upon the factors that cause societies to stagnate and become stationary rather than progressive illustrate this. For example, he claims that China is an example of a stationary society even though its customs were designed long ago by "sages and philosophers." But since then, he says, they have not changed and progressed. Mill complains that they "have succeeded . . . in making a people all alike, all governing their thoughts and conduct by the same maxims and rules" (CW 18:273). This complaint applies with equal logic to the marital rules of the Mormon community, yet Mill does not draw the proper conclusion.

Mill's argument allows ample room for recognition of the dialogical elements of identity construction, and for acknowledging the importance of the advice and counsel of others, and allowing for the influences of significant others. The argument pays due regard to the accumulated wisdom, rather than the biases, of cultural tradition. But there is no substitute for the liberal virtue of the ability to prevent these influences from becoming determinants of choices. Mill's mantra is "persuasion, not coercion." When the proper liberal educational and social conditions are secure, it is doubtful that many women would choose polygamy. These proper educational and social conditions include the ability and the liberty to scrutinize the reasonable range of family and marital options available to equal and self-respecting women. Polygamy is not likely to survive as a popular option when children are educated for freedom, because polygamy relies upon sanctions ranging from control and oppression to abuse and violence against young women and girls of the community. Mill's philosophy does not permit supporting traditional cultural practices that cannot survive critical scrutiny of all members of the community, vulnerable ones as well as members of dominant groups of the community. These are the lessons that Mill ought to draw from his own philosophical principles and commitments.

further reading

Appiah, Kwame Anthony, *The Ethics of Identity* (Princeton: Princeton University Press, 2005).

Baum, Bruce, *Rereading Power and Freedom in J. S. Mill* (Toronto: University of Toronto Press, 2000).

Baum, Bruce, "Millian Radical Democracy: Education for Freedom and Dilemmas of Liberal Equality," *Political Studies* 51 (2003), 404–28.

Berger, Fred, *Happiness, Justice, and Freedom: The Moral and Political Philosophy of John Stuart Mill* (Berkeley: University of California Press, 1984).

Gray, John, *Mill on Liberty: A Defence* (London: Routledge, 1983).

Hart, H. L. A., *Law, Liberty, and Morality* (Stanford: Stanford University Press, 1963).

Lyons, David, *Rights, Welfare, and Mill's Moral Theory* (Oxford: Clarendon Press, 1994).

O'Rourke, Kevin C., *John Stuart Mill and Freedom of Expression: The Genesis of a Theory* (Lanham, MD: Routledge, 2001).

Riley, Jonathan, *Mill on Liberty* (London: Routledge, 1998).

Skorupski, John, *Why Read Mill Today?* (London: Routledge, 2006).

Ten, C. L., *Mill on Liberty* (Oxford: Oxford University Press, 1980).

Ten, C. L., ed., *Mill's "On Liberty": A Critical Guide* (Cambridge: Cambridge University Press, 2009, in press).

philosophy of education

Education: Development and Self-Development

The discussion thus far has offered strong indications of the significance of education for Mill's liberalism and utilitarianism. Mill holds a conception of happiness organized around the notion that human flourishing consists in the development and exercise of certain capacities and virtues. The conception of happiness is closely linked with liberal educational processes of development and self-development. It is an education in the virtues which are preconditions of valuable and happy lives. Developed and self-developed agents are pivotal to the theory. Mill's method for measuring value relies upon judgments and preferences of those who have undergone a process of development in the virtues as being positioned to make wise value discriminations. In the private domain, where conduct does not violate moral duties, the pursuit of the mental and moral virtues bolsters opportunities to pursue a life that is our own, that expresses our individuality. The education of the competent agents of whom Mill speaks in *Utilitarianism* as those best positioned to make judgments of value is precisely this liberal education of development and self-development. These self-developed agents are called upon to make reasonable and wise judgments concerning a range of questions. For example, the moral progress and improvement which Mill promotes rely upon the judgments of moral reformers who work to bring about change in certain arenas of morality. Mill's activism on issues such as extending the suffrage to women and reform of marriage laws can be examined in this light. Their activities also naturally expand into the domain of Virtue in numerous ways that go well beyond the moral requirements and that constitute meritorious conduct.

John Stuart Mill's philosophy of education is a model for his liberalism that is rooted in his utilitarian philosophy and Art of Life. We have seen how the utilitarian theory of morality is grounded on the "theory of life . . . that pleasure, and freedom from pain, are the only things desirable as ends" (CW 10:210). The utilitarian theory of life is fundamentally a theory of the good life, which includes the moral life as one compartment. In Chapter 2, on theory of value, I argued that Mill propounds a sophisticated form of qualitative hedonism in which the things which are desirable as ends are certain kinds of complex satisfying mental states. The principle of utility is concerned with promoting utility "in the largest sense, grounded on the permanent interests of man as a progressive being" (CW 18:224). As a principle of the good it governs morality, but it also grounds the entire array of the moral arts and sciences.

Mill's philosophy of education can be approached fruitfully by exploring his claim in *A System of Logic* that education is one of the primary moral arts. In Book VI of the *Logic*, Mill explores the moral arts and their companion moral sciences. Mill's philosophy of education fits neatly into this structure of the moral arts and sciences. The purpose of a moral art is to define or set down the ends that are desirable or that promote utility, and thus ought to be aimed at. Each moral art is conjoined or linked with a moral science that investigates the "course of nature" in order to formulate effective means to promote the ends of the art. Mill explains as follows:

> The art proposes to itself an end to be attained, defines the end, and hands it over to the science. The science receives it, considers it as a phenomenon or effect to be studied, and having investigated its causes and conditions, sends it back to art with a theorem of the combinations of circumstances by which it could be produced. (CW 8:944)

Mill's philosophy of education is best understood in this context. Education is one of the more important particular moral arts and it is paired with its companion moral science, ethology, or the science of character formation. Mill devotes an entire chapter of *A System of Logic* to an exploration of the place of the science of ethology within this schema (CW 8:861–78). Seen in this light, it is apparent that Mill construes education very broadly as the art of character formation guided by its corresponding science, ethology. As he says in the *Logic*,

> There exist universal laws of the Formation of Character. And since it is by these laws, combined with the facts of each particular case, that the whole of the phenomena of human action and feeling are produced, it is on these that every rational attempt to construct the science of human nature in the concrete, and for practical purposes, must proceed. (CW 8: 864–5)

If the goal of education is interpreted broadly, as the appropriate socialization or character formation to encourage the development of certain character traits and the nurturing of certain human excellences, then the goals and principles of liberalism and utilitarianism are advanced. With tools of social science provided by ethological research, these laws can be aptly applied to bring about the desired ends. He adds, "[w]hen the circumstances of an individual or of a nation are in any considerable degree under our control, we may, by our knowledge of tendencies, be enabled to shape those circumstances in a manner much more favourable to the ends we desire, than the shape which they would of themselves assume" (CW 8:869–70). These goals are to educate and socialize autonomous persons of individuality and responsible democratic citizens. The goal is decidedly not to encourage the development of more specific forms of personality, since this would undermine autonomy and individuality. The point of education for freedom or autonomy is that developing these excellences will lead to unexpected results, to a diversity of outcomes. His conception of education is radically democratic and egalitarian, as is fitting for his liberalism. He advocates processes of education that are concerned not just with a narrow form of freedom, but with social, economic, and political liberty. His conception of education for freedom is designed to prepare people for emancipation from economic, political, and marital oppression.

Mill's utilitarianism and liberalism are ultimately grounded in the principle of utility. But if the principle of utility, which governs all of the practical arts including education, calls for the promotion of utility, much will depend upon the conception of utility at its core. In Mill's view, utility is analyzed in terms of a conception of the good that is appropriate for human beings with a certain nature. The most valuable kinds of happiness for humans consist in the self-development and exercise of our higher human capacities. C. B. Macpherson discusses Mill's philosophy as an example of developmental democracy, a major model of liberal democracy. Macpherson says that according to Mill's model, "man is a being capable of developing his powers or capacities. The human essence is to exert and develop them . . . The good society is one which permits and encourages everyone to act as exerter, developer, and enjoyer of the exertion and development, of his or her own capacities" (Macpherson 1977, 48). Mill's philosophy of education sets down a program in which people are educated in childhood to develop their human cognitive, emotional, and moral capacities. In adulthood, this process continues as self-development, in which the person herself develops the higher-order capacities of autonomy, individuality, compassion, and sociality. For this process to continue, the support of and participation in various social and political institutions are prerequisites. For these capacities to become stable and habitual, ongoing practice is necessary. Such practice naturally occurs through active participation in various social, political, economic, and domestic sites. I have already discussed *On Liberty*'s arguments for the educational purposes of public debate.

I further elaborate Mill's arguments for the educational potential of the political, social, and family domains in subsequent chapters.

For many liberals, the cultivation of the rational capacities is the pinnacle of education. Many stop there. Mill gives its due to training the intellect in childhood, and returns often to his conviction that cognitive training requires active exercise of the mind, to develop habits of critical awareness (CW 1:33–7). He expresses admiration for Socratic methods of mental training.

> The Socratic method, of which the Platonic dialogues are the chief example, is unsurpassed as a discipline for correcting the errors, and clearing up the confusions . . . The close, searching *elenchus* by which the man of vague generalities is constrained either to express his meaning to himself in definite terms, or to confess that he does not know what he is talking about . . . as an education for precise thinking, is inestimable. (CW 1:25)

A key principle of his philosophy is that education does its work by encouraging active use of our capacities rather than passive receptivity and conformity to other people's ideas. The use of any method of rote learning, such as memorizing facts without understanding, does not promote the development of critical cognitive ability. Mill regularly criticizes the passive sort of education which relies upon cramming. He describes his own education in the *Autobiography* and he notes the beneficial effects of pedagogical methods of cultivation rather than cram. Those educated by cram "grow up mere parroters" and are thus predisposed to lead lives of stunted conformity rather than active individuality as adults (CW 1:35).

> Most boys or youths who have had much knowledge drilled into them, have their mental capacities not strengthened, but overlaid by it. They are crammed with mere facts, and with the opinions or phrases of other people, and these are accepted as a substitute for the power to form opinions of their own . . . Mine, however, was not an education of cram. My father never permitted anything which I learnt, to degenerate into a mere exercise of memory . . . Anything which could be found out by thinking, I was never told, until I had exhausted my efforts to find it out for myself. (CW 1:33, 35)

Unlike some other liberal theorists, Mill places equal value upon emotional development. In the *Autobiography* he recollects and reflects upon his own education, describing in detail its content, scrutinizing the principles that guided it, exploring those aspects which he endorses from the perspective of adulthood as well as those elements which he rejects and revises (CW 1:3–191). The element he most strongly rejects is its excessive rationalism, which, he later comments, had threatened to turn him into "a mere reasoning machine" (CW 1:111). The imbalance is addressed by giving a central place to emotional and moral cultivation. Mill's philosophy of education has a notable place within it for the cultivation of the emotions and the imagination, as well as for the emotional virtues of compassion, empathy, and sensitivity to the suffering of others. While he appreciates the importance of reason, as his comments on Socratic dialogue demonstrate, he maintains that this faculty must be kept in balance. He praises his father's use of active learning techniques, but he does not appreciate his father's undervaluing of emotion, which had negative consequences on the son. He reacts against the rationalistic excesses of his own education which produced an emotional crisis in early adulthood. After this crisis, he recognized acutely the need for the "internal culture" of the feelings, and subsequently argued that the educative process is incomplete without due attention to cultivation of feelings and imagination (CW 1:147–57). He recommends appreciation of poetry and encounters with natural beauty as two reliable methods for promoting emotional sensitivity. The significance of the link Mill draws between emotional and imaginative cultivation and the human–nature connection will be further explored in Chapter 8 on environmental ethics.

Discussions of the liberal virtues typically point to the steadfast qualities of reason, reflection, autonomy, self-authorship, and individuality as capacities that Mill endorses. While it is certainly correct to characterize Mill as a champion of these excellences, it often happens that half of the portrait is omitted. Mill himself typically uses the phrase "mental and moral excellences" to convey that he is not simply encouraging intellect, and he never leaves out of the picture that half of the human excellences are composed of emotional, compassionate, and social capacities. In this respect, his theory is an ally of contemporary virtue ethics and feminist care ethics in their common advocacy of feeling and sentiment. All these theories emphasize that affective abilities are crucial moral and psychological capacities that are essential for personal and moral agency. Mill champions educative processes of development and self-development which are designed to produce habits and attitude structures that go far beyond simple dispositions to act in certain characteristic ways. They have become part of confirmed character. Utilitarianism is often depicted as focused on the promotion of happiness, and indeed it is. But we should not overlook the obvious condition of the world that means that often the efforts of moral agents are focused as much on minimizing suffering as on promoting happiness. Self-development includes emotional awareness of and the capacity to respond to the suffering of the world. Development of compassionate responsiveness cannot proceed in the absence of feelings. Mill's utilitarianism is anchored to awareness of the reality of suffering in the world and what this suffering means for the ethical life. The spheres of Virtue and Morality link aspirations and duties to alleviate suffering and promote happiness in ethical action.

Sympathetic imagination and social sentiments dispose people to be attuned to the happiness and suffering of others. Self-development produces attitudinal structures and habitual responsiveness to others. Mill contrasts this utilitarian sensibility with the insensitive lack of feeling or shallowness of response of those whose self-development is off key, whose reason and autonomy are predominant and out of balance with emotional engagement and receptivity. Millian self-development with virtues and abilities cultivated in balance, by contrast, habituates and conditions people to be attentive, to recognize, acknowledge, reflect on, and respond to the world in certain ways and not in others, and this includes sympathetic and compassionate responses. Mill argues that the basis of moral development, including compassion, is fellow feeling that is a natural propensity in humans. There is a reliable natural basis for utilitarian sentiment and it is on this foundation that moral training proceeds. Cooperative social practice "leads him to identify his *feelings* more and more with their good . . . He comes, as though instinctively, to be conscious of himself as a being who *of course* pays regard to others. The good of others becomes to him a thing naturally and necessarily to be attended to" (CW 10:231–2).

Mill's personal experiences, described in the *Autobiography*, laid the groundwork for his promotion of emotional cultivation. Mill describes the period of his mental crisis as having the effect of transforming both his opinions and his character. He was depressed and dejected. He confesses that "if I had loved any one sufficiently to make confiding my grief a necessity, I should not have been in the condition I was" (CW 1:139). He experienced his condition as absence of love and absence of feeling. While the tradition of virtue ethics has a great deal to say about love as a central good of human life, other ethical theories often seem to avert their eyes from what common sense places at a fulcrum of flourishing life. Mill recognized poignantly the effects of absence of love on his psyche. He judged that his father's educational plans had failed, erected as they were on an excessively rationalist foundation. His education had emphasized reason and analysis, and so he was left without a sail, "without any real desire for the ends which I had been so carefully fitted out to work for: no delight in virtue or the general good" (CW 1:143). His depression lifted when he was moved to tears while reading a passage in Jean-François Marmontel's *Memoires*. He was relieved to discover that he still had the capacity to feel, "some of the material out of which all worth of character, and all capacity for happiness, are made" (CW 1:145). From this discovery arose his conviction that internal culture is an indispensable condition of well-being. No longer content to grant priority to reason, action, and external circumstances, as his prior education had insisted, he now accepted the need for cultivation of feelings and the receptive susceptibilities. He perceived the advantages of a holistic model of interconnection and balance of the faculties, and rejected a hierarchical model of capacities. Poetry, art, and nature were his reliable sources for engendering emotional sensibility. Mill thereafter remained a steadfast advocate for the perennial power of poetry to encourage affective responsiveness and sensibility in readers.

Mill's transformed perspective sits well with the virtue ethical tradition's distrust of moral theories that denigrate emotion. Millian competent agents cannot rely solely on reason and dispense with emotion. Michael Stocker, for example, argues that modern ethical theories suffer from schizophrenia in permitting a split between emotions or motivation and value, and that values and emotions must come together if theories are to have sound views about human nature and the good life. This is especially the case when it comes to the important goods of love and friendship whose actualization depends upon this union of value and motivation. Recall Mill's words about his depression. Stocker's analysis of the importance of emotional development and sensitive attentiveness is congruent with Mill's perspective on the centrality of emotional development to self-development. His comments also resonate with Mill's preference for models featuring balance between reason and emotion over those with hierarchical ordering or dualistic splits between reason and emotion. This is also a prominent theme of feminist care ethics. Stocker argues that emotions are required for evaluative knowledge and so lack of emotional development can interfere with sound evaluations. While modern theories often lose sight of the importance of the emotions, it is actually a settled part of western ethical thought "that being good at noticing and appreciating value – being a good judge – is of utmost value" (Stocker 2003, 177).

Emotions are also core to certain specific goods, as well as certain forms of exercising the human excellences involving emotional care and engagement. For example, in love and friendship we want to give and receive engaged care. Stocker argues, harmoniously with Mill, that value involves engagement of self with others. The upshot is endorsement of shared emotional, interpersonal, and social life, of the entire gamut of human emotions from sorrow and grief to happiness and joy. As well, we need to be concerned about the specific emotions from which we carry out action. Often what we want is not simply to do something, such as write a great novel, but we also are concerned with the emotional tenor of action. We want engagement "rather than alienated, machine-like, dead activity" (Stocker 2003, 182). In Mill's exploration of individuality in *On Liberty*, he draws on just this metaphor, lambasting machine-like activity performed by "automatons in human form" (CW 18:263).[1]

Mill's shared agenda with virtue ethicists is that emotional development is promoted by engaging emotionally with others. A central claim of the feminist care ethic is that attentiveness and loving care are central goods and that ethical knowledge is not possible without emotional knowledge. These common commitments and goals link Mill's theory to the virtue tradition, with its endorsement of emotional awareness. Mill's endorsement of emotional intelligence is emphatic, but the methods he proposes are sometimes more limited in comparison with the practices honed by some other virtue traditions. Other moral theories with sympathetic treatments of emotional virtue, such as the feminist care ethic and the Buddhist tradition, have more explicit practices and methods for training. For example, feminist care ethics promotes emotional sensibility through everyday practice of care and nurturing of children and "those who cannot take care of themselves" (Okin 2003, 229). In feminist ethics, such care itself often can be a virtue and a form of practice. For thousands of years, the Buddhist ethical tradition has developed numerous techniques and meditative practices to cultivate the awakening and training of the emotions, to transform attitudes and to cultivate *bodhicitta*, the compassionate awakened heart/mind. These practices range from fundamental cultivation of mindfulness and insight, through the practices of the four positive attitudinal qualities – loving-kindness, compassion, sympathetic joy, and equanimity. All of these traditions share the conviction that emotions ought to be developed in tandem with reason, even when they develop different educative strategies to achieve this.

The process of moral development, which develops empathy, sympathy, benevolence, and compassion, also begins in childhood. Moral development focuses on cultivating these positive traits while discouraging harmful attitudes and habits of mind like egoism, selfishness, and self-absorption. The process of moral development educates children to connect sympathetically with others and to enjoy their happiness. He claims that this feeling of sympathy and connection is firmly rooted in human nature. He says,

> This firm foundation is that of the social feelings of mankind; the desire to be in unity with our fellow creatures, which is already a powerful principle in human nature, and happily one of those which tend to become stronger, even without express inculcation, from the influences of advancing civilization. The social state is at once so natural, so necessary, and so habitual to man, that, except in some unusual circumstances or by an effort of voluntary abstraction, he never conceives himself otherwise than as a member of a body. (CW 10:231)

He rejects the conception of moral agents as pursuing rational self-interest only. He is always careful to balance the intellectual/individualist side with the moral/social side and to deplore the creation of a hierarchy among them. Mill claims that moral development must always accompany mental development and this has important implications for his conception of self-development as well as for his liberal political philosophy.

These three components of mental, emotional, and moral development are embedded in childhood education. In adulthood, the educative process of development matures into the process of self-development which continues under the authority of the person. In self-development, the higher-order capacities of individuality, autonomy, sociality, and cooperativeness are built up on the groundwork of the generic human capacities. The higher-order capacities must also be balanced. The core liberal capacity of autonomy is the ability to reflect on, choose, endorse, and revise the character, relationships, projects, and life plans most reflective of our nature. Individuality encourages our ability to explore the range of these goods most in harmony with our abilities and particularities, to pursue a life that is our own. While Mill does not believe that individuals have fixed essences, there is a range of potential characters and plans of life most in harmony with our individuality, and our happiness is augmented by building on this basis.

Mill is well known for his defense of individuality and freedom in *On Liberty*. However, Millian individuals are deeply rooted in their social and cultural contexts and are not anomic and atomistic. Mill's individualism is characterized by its concern that the primary focus of value is the individual and not the social group. In his view value is located in each individual member of a community and the value of a community flows from the value of its individual members. Individual rights cannot easily be overturned in the name of communal values. Autonomous individuals are self-determining creators and controllers of their lives, and their choices and life plans reflect their particularity. Thus the intricate balance of individual and social plays out.

Self-development cultivates capacities which are higher-order and depend upon the traits developed in childhood. That is one reason why Mill maintains that people are wronged and their right to liberty of self-development violated if their childhood education has not inculcated these capacities in them. I argued in Chapter 4, on liberty, that autonomy and individuality are core components of self-development. Equally important are the higher-order social capacities, those that draw us into community and cooperative enterprises to work jointly with others in the public domain for the common good. On the basis of sympathetic connection, adults develop and exercise higher-order capacities such as empathy, compassion, and kindness.

Two Senses of Education

Mill's *Inaugural Address Delivered to the University of St Andrews* provided an occasion for him to lay out his views about university education. This lecture was delivered to mark his appointment to the position of Rector of the University of St Andrews. The address casts further light on the content as well as the principles that Mill sees as guiding this significant moral art. In the address Mill distinguishes two senses of education, the first much broader than the second. The larger sense refers to the broad meaning of education as socialization elucidated in *A System of Logic*. In his *Inaugural Address*, Mill says of education that

> Not only does it include whatever we do for ourselves, and whatever is done for us by others, for the express purpose of bringing us somewhat nearer to the perfection of our nature; it does more: in its largest acceptation, it comprehends even the indirect effects produced on character and on the human faculties, by things of which the direct purposes are quite different; by laws, by forms of government, by the industrial arts, by modes of social life. (CW 21:217)

This characterization of education seems well equipped to apply to the broadest scope of the Art of Life. This broader sense of education is the predominant one in Mill's writings and the major focus of his concerns. In his *Inaugural Address*, however, he separates out this broadly characterized form from the narrower sense of schooling, the sense most often used in connection with education in our culture. It is the broader sense, however, which distinctively marks Mill out as a representative of liberalism, the sense that education is applicable to every domain of life and is not restricted to schooling.

The broader view is that "whatever helps to shape the human being; to make the individual what he is, or hinder him from being what he is not – is part of his education" (CW 21:217). But even Mill's characterization of what he calls the narrower sense of education – that provided primarily by educational systems of schools and universities – is in keeping with the tradition of liberalism and is clearly weighted in favor of a liberal education in the arts and sciences. He defines the narrower sense as "the culture which each generation purposely gives to those who are to be its successors, in order to qualify them for at least keeping up, and if possible for raising, the level of improvement which has been attained" (CW 21:218). Mill specifically has in mind a liberal education including arts and sciences, and he specifically repudiates and sets aside the view that universities should include professional schools and faculties. A university "is not a place of professional education. Universities are not intended to teach the knowledge required to fit men for some special mode of gaining their livelihood. Their object is not to make skilful lawyers, or physicians, or engineers, but capable and cultivated human beings" (CW 21:218). Other public institutions should take on this task of training and educating for work or the professions. "But these things are no part of what every generation owes to the next, as that on which its civilization and worth will principally depend" (CW 21:218). Specialized education is needed by a small number only. If professionals do also acquire a university education, it should be to "bring the light of general culture to illuminate the technicalities of a special pursuit" (CW 21:218). University public education, although narrower in its scope than the general sense of education, is still distinct from professional or work and business training, and it still has as its goals to promote both intellectual education and, to a lesser extent, moral education.

Returning to an examination of Mill's perspective on the first, broader characterization of education, I revisit his claim that many forms of social institutions can shape and be affected by the qualities that this form of education is intended to promote as part of its utilitarian commitments. The goal of the art of education, as of all the practical arts, is to promote utility, conceived of as the development of desirable human characteristics, specifically as the development and nurturing of certain human capacities and excellences. But because Mill conceives of humans as both social beings and autonomous agents whose good consists in exploring and developing their individuality, the educative process must promote these interrelated goals of bringing to fruition the progressive view of human nature and promoting a conception of the good for humans that is at its core concerned with self-development.

John Rawls claims that Mill's utilitarianism is a comprehensive doctrine, meaning that "the principle of utility . . . is usually said to hold for all kinds of subjects ranging from the conduct of individuals and personal relations to the organization of society as a whole" (Rawls 2002, 13). As a representative of the lineage and tradition of liberalism, Mill holds the view that the heart of the educative and developmental process is the creation and sustenance of autonomous individuals who are prepared to participate in the public democratic forum. There are two senses of education, broad and narrow, yet there is underlying unity. The unified nature of the educative process comes into play because the same educative process, in formal institutional school settings and in other public venues, works comprehensively to produce participatory democratic citizens and also to prepare people to lead meaningful and autonomous lives. A precondition of this latter is, according to a tenet of contemporary liberalism with which Mill would agree, that we "should be free to form, revise, and act on our plans of life" (Kymlicka 2002, 222). So Mill argues for a unified view of the educative developmental process which serves to promote both of the above goals and ends by developing capacities and character traits that allow agents autonomously to form conceptions of and choose meaningful and fulfilling lives while also cooperating with other citizens to promote the common good in the public domain.

While Mill is concerned to promote lifelong education and development in the first, broad sense, he does not neglect the second, narrower sense of education for children. He was a political and social activist and distinguished himself by fighting, not just for universal suffrage, but also for the universal right to schooling in the era before universal rights to education were widely recognized. In *On Liberty*, as well as in other writings, Mill argues that children have a right to an education. He says,

> Is it not almost a self-evident axiom, that the State should require and compel the education, up to a certain standard, of every human being who is born its citizen . . . It still remains unrecognised, that to bring a child into existence without a fair prospect of being able, not only to provide food for its body, but instruction and training for its mind, is a moral crime, both against the unfortunate offspring and against society. (CW 18:301–2)

Mill argues that the state ought to enforce this right, and so there is a "duty of enforcing universal education" (CW 18:302). However, he goes on to argue that, while the state has a duty to enforce the universal right to education, up to certain standards, it should not itself provide universal public education. Parents should have the right to determine the means of education for their children, and the state should subsidize the fees of poor children to ensure they receive an education. "All that has been said of the importance of individuality of character, and diversity in opinions and modes of conduct, involves, as of the same unspeakable importance, diversity of education" (CW 18:302). According to Mill, universal state education would run the risk of undermining diversity and individuality and of "moulding people to be exactly like one another" (CW 18:302). In exploring the case of the Mormon community and its educational and marital practices in Chapter 4, I took Mill to task for granting too much parental power to parents on this matter of the education of their children, arguing that this grants parents the right to educate their daughters for submissiveness rather than autonomy. However, according to Mill, state-controlled education would result in the sort of conformity that he abhors as leading to "despotism over the mind" (CW 18:302). State education should be one alternative among several, he claims. Public examinations would ensure that the diverse educational experiences live up to certain standards, although Mill does not tackle the obvious question of how to balance diversity of experiences with uniformity of standards as tested by public examinations. The aim is to make "the universal acquisition, and what is more, retention of a certain minimum of general knowledge, virtually compulsory" (CW 18:303). Complicating his claims further, he says that to prevent inappropriate influence by the state over opinions, these exams should be "confined to facts and positive science exclusively" (CW 18:303). He advocates the establishment of teachers' colleges to train and examine teachers, an advocacy also ahead of his time. While Mill's perspective on the universal right to education is in advance of his time, his views were undoubtedly affected by his own remarkable education by his father, received outside of any school system, and by the fact that he never attended or taught at any university, although his books were widely used in university instruction.

But it is not just formal and informal schooling that are sites of education. Mill's views on education are expansive. According to Stefan Collini,

> Mill's conception of society is an exceptionally and pervasively educative one . . . he makes their effect on the shaping of character the ultimate test of all institutions and policies, and one could without strain regard his whole notion of political activity itself as an extended and strenuous adult-education course. (Collini 1984, xlviii)

The educative effect of social institutions cannot be underestimated. All institutions can be used to promote the radically progressive, egalitarian, and democratic ends of Mill's utilitarianism and liberalism. Mill's philosophy of education, then, cannot be understood simply by examining those writings whose announced purpose is to discuss this theme. Mill's exploration of social, political, and economic institutions is guided by his conviction that one of their major purposes is educative. I explore these dimensions of his educational philosophy further in Chapter 6 (Political Philosophy: Liberalism and Democracy) and Chapter 7 (Sexual Equality and The Subjection of Women). Thus democratic political institutions are deemed to be agents of "national education" (CW 19:390). In some later writings on economics, Mill argues for a form of economic democracy and workplace partnerships, and expresses the hope that this would bring about "the conversion of each human being's daily occupation into a school of the social sympathies and the practical intelligence" (CW 3:792). In The Subjection of Women, he advances a classic feminist argument for the emancipation of women and argues that the moral principle regarding gender relations, especially within the family, should be "a principle of perfect equality, admitting no power or privilege on the one side" (CW 21:261). The family should be "a school of sympathy in equality, of living together in love, without power on one side or obedience on the other" (CW 21:295). The family is the early major sphere of moral education.

John Stuart Mill's extensive writings on education, rooted in his utilitarianism and emancipatory egalitarian liberalism, furnish a panoramic argument that formal educational systems as well as a wide range of social, political, and economic institutions all offer opportunities for lifelong education and self-development. This is the core statement of the pride-of-place of educational concerns to his liberalism and utilitarianism, which I elaborate in the chapters on liberty, political philosophy, and sexual equality.

note

1   Martha Nussbaum also argues for the centrality of the emotions. See, for example, Nussbaum 2001.

further reading

Baum, Bruce, *Rereading Power and Freedom in J. S. Mill* (Toronto: University of Toronto Press, 2000).

Garforth, F. W., *John Stuart Mill's Theory of Education* (Oxford: Martin Robertson, 1979).

Gutmann, Amy, *Democratic Education* (Princeton: Princeton University Press, 1987).

Heydt, Colin, *Rethinking Mill's Ethics: Character and Aesthetic Education* (London: Continuum, 2006).

Robson, John M., *The Improvement of Mankind* (Toronto: University of Toronto Press, 1968).

political philosophy: liberalism and democracy

Introduction

Exploring the history of liberalism, C. B. Macpherson notices an important shift in perspective that distances John Stuart Mill from his mentors Bentham and James Mill. James Mill is primarily interested in that function of democracy which protects the interests of citizens, but John Stuart Mill propounds more expansive conceptions of human nature and the good, and thus has greater hopes for the prospects of democracy. Macpherson says of John Stuart Mill:

> But he saw something even more important to be protected, namely, the chances of the improvement of mankind. So his emphasis was not on the mere holding operation, but on what democracy could contribute to human development. Mill's model of democracy is a moral model . . . it has a moral vision of the possibility of the improvement of mankind, and of a free and equal society not yet achieved. A democratic system is valued as a means to that improvement – a necessary though not a sufficient means; and a democratic society is seen as both a result of that improvement and a means to further improvement. The improvement that is expected is an increase in the amount of personal self-development of all the members of a society. (Macpherson 1980, 47)

This gets to the heart of Mill's vision. The principle of utility governs and lays out the ends of all practical moral arts, including political philosophy. Mill's conception of human nature and his view of the good appropriate for this nature, with its central place for development and exercise of the human excellences, lead quite naturally to the normative view of the art of politics and government in which democratic life is intimately connected to the promotion of happiness. Mill sets out a central criterion of good government as "the degree in which it tends to increase the sum of good qualities in the governed, collectively and individually" (CW 19:390). A major role of government is to act as an "agency of national education" (CW 19:393). The emphasis upon the political and civic virtues in Mill's theory is striking, as is his commitment to active participatory democracy as a powerful technique for the practice of virtue in the public domain.

Mill's method for measuring value uses the judgments of those who are competently acquainted with the relevant forms of happiness. Mill's conception of the good and his method for measuring it are fully consonant with his liberalism. The "competent agents" who have undergone a process of development and self-development are not an elitist sub-group of society. Rather, they comprise all adult members of society who have been socialized and nurtured by their society to develop and exercise their human excellences and virtues. My argument is focused on Mill's writings on these questions in western liberal democracies. The term "liberal" is intended to encompass a broad spectrum of social and political formations including social democratic societies.

Like many other liberals, both classical and contemporary, Mill holds firmly to the belief that education and socialization are at the heart of the projects of creating and sustaining members of society who are prepared for their role as democratic citizens. Modern liberal democrat Amy Gutmann reflects similar sentiments:

> Education, in a great measure, forms the moral character of citizens, and moral character along with laws and institutions forms the basis of democratic government. Democratic government, in turn, shapes the education of future citizens, which, in a great measure, forms their moral character. Because democracies must rely on the moral character of parents, teachers, public officials and ordinary citizens to educate future citizens, democratic education begins not only with children who are to be taught but also with citizens who are to be their teachers. (Gutmann 1987, 49)

The very same educational and socialization processes that prepare people for citizenship also position and support them in pursuing the Art of Life, in leading a good life which is their own. Modern liberals agree with Mill that a precondition of leading a good life is that we are "free to form, revise, and act on our plans of life" (Kymlicka 2002, 222). Mill's moral doctrine is comprehensive, and he holds a unified view of the educative processes that produce the abilities which are preconditions for the character traits needed for flourishing lives.

In Chapter 5, on philosophy of education, I explored how Mill's more familiar writings such as *Utilitarianism* and *On Liberty* rely upon the extensive backdrop of his views on the educative processes of development and self-development. Mill's procedure for measuring the value of enjoyments, projects, characters, and life plans is also comprehensive, and he claims that if self-developed agents judge certain enjoyments or projects to be more valuable, then these judgments have the best chance of being correct in the long term. While personal autonomy in value choices is strongly protected in the private realm (a realm characterized primarily in terms of conduct that does not violate other-regarding duties or rights), in the public realm democratic procedures govern social choices.

In Mill's theory, then, a lot rests upon these educative and socialization procedures. People need a supportive social context to provide the circumstances in which human excellences develop. Compassion, empathy, autonomy, individuality, and the rest of the array of capacities do not emerge on their own. In the absence of the institutional support base on which liberal democracies depend, development of the mental and moral virtues will be impeded. The institutional base provides the social guarantees for the rights which are the entitlement of every member of society. Absent such institutional arrangements to guarantee and underwrite these vital interests, the rights to liberty of self-development are violated. These principles have significant implications for Mill's form of liberalism. Since most people have the potential to attain the status of self-development, the social and cultural context greatly influence whether this potential is actualized. So Mill's liberalism has egalitarian inclinations. This egalitarianism emerges in his democratic theory.

Political and Economic Democracy

The exploration of Mill's philosophy of education paves the way for an examination of the potential and dilemmas of his egalitarian liberalism. Mill's liberal vision is both clarified and tested by his writings on representative government and political and economic democracy. Mill's liberalism provides a framework for approaching issues such as the forms of education appropriate for democratic society and the role of deliberation and disagreement within a healthy democracy. His liberalism is particularly well suited to contemporary multicultural and pluralistic societies, since he expects disagreements and divergence. As we saw in the exploration of *On Liberty*, disagreement is not simply to be tolerated. It is to be welcomed and sought out whenever it is not readily in sight. Intense public debates foster the mental and moral virtues but also serve as insurance that collectively we are making progressively better choices. We have a better chance of getting it right if we follow these principles. Mill is a fallibilist: he maintains that we are prone to error, but also that we are prone to engaging in inquiries that tend to reveal errors and allow mistakes to be corrected. The activities of debate and interrogation not only enhance the intellectual virtues, but also enhance the probability that truth will prevail in the long run.

The processes of development and self-development are lifelong pursuits. Mill promotes active participation in political and community life as principal avenues for these activities. *On Liberty* provides the general arguments for liberty in those domains in which actions do not harm others. The essay is an appeal for increase in public debates and discussions which Mill sees as crucial means for exercise of the mental and moral capacities. He notes:

> Not that it is solely, or chiefly, to form great thinkers, that freedom of thinking is required. On the contrary, it is as much and even more indispensable, to enable average human beings to attain the mental stature which they are capable of. There have been, and may again be, great individual thinkers, in a general atmosphere of mental slavery. But there never has been, nor ever will be, in that atmosphere, an intellectually active people. (CW 18:243)

Representative Government narrows the focus to the developmental impact of political participation and activity. Mill highlights the benefits of such commitments and claims that people can all participate in governing and benefit from the "mental exercise derivable from it" (CW 19:436). His warning about dangers resulting from the lack of such participatory activity follows:

> Where this school of public spirit does not exist, scarcely any sense is entertained that private persons, in no eminent social situation, owe any duties to society, except to obey the laws and submit to the government. There is no unselfish sentiment of identification with the public. Every thought or feeling, either of interest or of duty, is absorbed in the individual and in the family. The man never thinks of any collective interest, of any objects to be pursued jointly with others, but only in competition with them . . . Thus even private morality suffers, while public is actually extinct. (CW 19:412)

There are numerous pathways into Mill's democratic theory. In this work I focus on his democratic liberal vision as an integral component of the moral arts and sciences and the Art of Life. My discussion is thus framed by Mill's own approach in *A System of Logic*, where he treats politics and government as moral arts and sciences under the authority of the principle of utility. These arts and sciences of government and economics have the same purpose as all the others, namely, to promote human happiness and welfare. Their success is measured and weighed by their achievements in the enterprise of improving human well-being, and this in turn is analyzed in terms of their efficacy in promoting the virtues and excellences. Recall Stefan Collini's perspicacious comment that "he makes their effect on the shaping of character the ultimate test of all institutions and policies, and one could without strain regard his whole notion of political activity itself as an extended and strenuous adult-education course" (Collini 1984, xlviii). This is shrewd insight into the core vision of Mill's liberalism. Mill's philosophy of education is applied to all social, political, and economic institutions. They have as one of their main purposes their usefulness as educational sites for cultivation of the virtues. Mill foregrounds this function of government early in the argument of *Representative Government*:

> The first element of good government, therefore, being the virtue and intelligence of the human beings composing the community, the most important point of excellence which any form of government can possess is to promote the virtue and intelligence of the people themselves. The first question in respect to any political institutions is, how far they tend to foster in the members of the community the various desirable qualities, moral and intellectual . . . it is on these qualities, so far as they exist in the people, that all possibility of goodness in the practical operations of the government depends. (CW 19:390)

He adds immediately,

> We may consider, then, as one criterion of the goodness of a government, the degree in which it tends to increase the sum of good qualities in the governed, collectively and individually; since, besides that their well-being is the sole object of government, their good qualities supply the moving force which works the machinery. (CW 19:390)

There is also a second element to consider. This element is ratified by common sense as a necessary part of any good government. But it also leads to a prime source of contention about the character of Mill's democratic theory. The contentious issue is the question of whether he is most properly characterized as an egalitarian or as an elitist theorist. His political philosophy and democratic theory feature balance between the principle of participation and the principle of competence. The first element, participation, has to do most directly with utilitarian ends; the second element, competence, has to do with the means to those ends. This second element of the merit of a set of political institutions concerns the quality of the governmental machinery. It is balanced with the principle of participation which governs the promotion of activities to nurture self-development. This second aspect of the merit of governments is "the degree of perfection with which they organize the moral, intellectual and active worth already existing, so as to operate with the greatest effect on public affairs . . . Government is at once a great influence acting on the human mind, and a set of organized arrangements for public business" (CW 19:392). Within the framework of *A System of Logic*, the first relates to the moral art of the end and the second relates to the moral science concerned with formulating the best policies to promote the end of human happiness.[1]

Mill's views on the development of the virtues in the economic domain complement his views on politics and government. His commitments to furthering civic virtue in the political domain are also reflected in his later views on economic democracy. Evident in these writings on economics are some familiar tensions and ambivalences. Mill's perspective on the centrality of the virtues of autonomy, independence, and cooperativeness and his battles against the vices of despotism and dependency lead very naturally to his endorsement of the economic arena as a potent site for education in the excellences. In these later writings, influenced by the utopian socialist movement, Mill argues for participatory and democratic workplace partnerships and associations. He greatly admires the cooperative movement in both its producer and consumer manifestations. Producer and consumer cooperatives do not undermine individual responsibility, he says, but they do reduce harmful dependency of workers on capitalist owners. Worker cooperatives boost the development of the communal sentiments, the desires to join with others in shared enterprises. While Mill thought that this transformation in economic relations would take some time, several generations in fact, he had great hopes that the moral regeneration and progress of workers would lead in the long term to certain progressive forms of economic association. This progressive formation is "not that which can exist between a capitalist as chief, and workpeople without a voice in the management, but the association of the labourers themselves on terms of equality, collectively owning the capital with which they carry on their operations, and working under managers elected and removable by themselves" (CW 3:775).

In Mill's eyes, these forms of economic association are more suitable to the task of increasing human dignity than the capitalist forms which cause unhealthy dependency. He hoped that this economic reform, or even revolution, would bring about "the conversion of each human being's daily occupation into a school of the social sympathies and the practical intelligence" (CW 3:792). Strengthening the hand of the principle of participation in the economic domain is the awareness that contrived, manipulative "participation" – in which owners and managers retain effective control of decisions yet foster the illusion that workers have participatory input – does not result in the real thing of development of civic virtues. The contrivance will be revealed and the result will be frustration and alienation rather than self-development. The lesson is that the participation must be authentic to have the intended effects. Genuine control over work and workplace decisions has the desired effects. Without this, participation is ersatz (Pateman 1970, 28–66). The moral development of workers is one key factor, and Mill thinks that those unable to overcome selfishness and develop their cooperative abilities will remain workers for hire. Here is how Mill describes his projection of the progressive changes.

> Associations . . . by the very process of their success, are a course of education in those moral and active qualities by which alone success can be either deserved or attained. As associations multiplied, they would tend more and more to absorb all work-people, except those who have too little understanding, or too little virtue, to be capable of learning to act on any other system than that of narrow selfishness. (CW 3:793)

In this process, capitalism will gradually and almost spontaneously evolve into the superior system of associations and cooperatives.

In the arena of economics, also, balancing principles of participation and competence is still required, at least in the short term. Mill's theory as expressed in his later writings on economics is a form of democratic socialism. He endorses the goal of fostering worker collectives for the simple reason that he expects them to provide valuable training in the social virtues. But his commitment to participation is, of necessity, balanced with other salient factors such as respect for existing property rights and the legitimate claims of economic efficiency and good management. He condemns the poverty and dependence of the working class as deplorable and morally insupportable, and he fully expects that increasing economic democracy will reduce or remove these conditions. The benefits of workplace associations are to be attained over time, thus reducing conflicts with property rights of the owners of capital, and there will be a natural evolution to the new economic system, or so he believes.

Objections: Elitism and Egalitarianism

Mill's hopes for the prospects of liberal education for democratic practice and progress have faced objections primarily about the limitations of his liberalism to address properly problems of inequality and elitism. There certainly are tensions between the elitist and the egalitarian strands of Mill's philosophy. However, I argue that Mill's egalitarian commitments are more fundamental and so prevail. The right to liberty of self-development includes the right to have one's capacities and faculties developed in childhood so that one is able to carry on the process of self-development once adulthood is reached. This furnishes the seed for some of the response to these objections.

My argument thus far has focused on what I take to be the main and fundamental lines of thought in Mill's liberalism. At first glance, participation seems to hold sway very thoroughly. That is, until we remember the cautionary brakes built into Mill's theory. *Representative Government*, *On Liberty*, and his writings on economics display Mill's ambivalence towards the members of his society whom he believes are still developing their mental and moral virtues. His strategy is to promote a plan for improvement which involves a delicate balancing act between the principles of participation and competence. The depth of his commitment to radical participatory democracy is demonstrated in the many passages filled with enthusiastic endorsement of the benefits to be gained from active, sustained, and extensive participation in political activity. But this is balanced by and put side-by-side with his cautionary appeals to the principle of competence, which proposes allowing those with more expertise to put their knowledge to use in order to have an effect upon the public good. The collective affairs of the community should be well organized and competently administered and carried out, and those with specialized training and expertise in administration are in a better position to do so, he thinks. These professional bureaucrats carry out the policies of the government of the day. Their role mirrors that of present-day public servants and bureaucrats. The role of citizens includes their active participation in public debates about the collective goods, the ends to be promoted, as well as choice of their political representatives in parliament. Recall how *On Liberty* contains a sustained argument for the epistemic advantages of free and open debates for increasing the probability that public policy will promote the general good. In this regard, people's freedom of expression and freedom of association and participation should be as extensive as possible and untrammeled.

But yet, Mill hopes that the arguments of the wise will be listened to with respect, given great weight, and perhaps freely granted authority. He wants them to have influence, not control. The demeanor and conduct of those acting as exemplars of wisdom are governed by the principles of the domain of Virtue and must make use of persuasion, never coercion. The arguments of *On Liberty* express Mill's sense of frustration with the "collective mediocrity" (CW 18:268) that seems to be so powerful, paired with his argument that the way forward in progress must involve an educative program of development of the mental and moral virtues of all. This progressive educative process is essentially active and participatory, and involves at its core the internalization of and habituation in the civic virtues, which cannot happen if people are excluded from participation and their input is sidelined. Mill hopes therefore that the exemplars of virtue will be listened to, that they will be influential, and their arguments given great weight. But he decries the scenario under which they would exercise authority at the expense of the development of all. As he puts it in *On Liberty*, his hope is that a person who is less educated will listen to

> [t]he counsels and influence of a more gifted and instructed One or Few . . . The honour and glory of the average man is that he is capable of following that initiative; that he can respond internally to wise or noble things, and be led to them with his eyes open. I am not countenancing the sort of "hero worship" which applauds the strong man of genius for forcibly seizing on the government of the world and making it do his bidding in spite of itself. All he can claim is, freedom to point out the way. The power of compelling others into it, is not only inconsistent with the freedom and development of all the rest, but corrupting to the strong man himself. (CW 18:269)

In other words, the despotism so demonstrated would immediately reveal corruption and disregard for the interests of others; it would undercut claims to virtue and wisdom of ones who attempt to force their judgments on the rest. In *The Subjection of Women* Mill emphasizes how central to well-being is autonomy, and notes the contrast "between a life of subjection to the will of others, and a life of rational freedom" (CW 21:336). His point transfers into this context. In the public arena of collective debate and discussion, due respect means that others must be persuaded, argued with, but not forced or coerced to set aside their rational freedom to be subjected to the will of the supposedly wise, whose very behavior in attempting to impose judgments on others raises questions about the authenticity of their wisdom. Wise judgments and choices must be internally adopted and endorsed in order for self-development to be affected. Mill's underlying point is that wisdom is not a possession of the One or the Few, but all have the right to pursue it. The interiority of the process is essential for its authentication as part of self-development. Mill interweaves his concern to have in place a public process that will increase the prospects for better social choices, those that in fact promote general happiness, and his concern to preserve the integrity of the process so that it positively impacts self-development and cultivation of the mental and moral excellences. Despotic, heavy-handed tactics that undermine or destroy the autonomy of one's fellow members exact a heavy price for "correct" value choices. For in the very process, the vices are enhanced and raise doubts about whether those revealed as attracted to despotism can be relied upon to express wise judgments about the public good. After all, their lack of concern for the autonomy and dignity of others marks them out as unwise self-absorbed egotists in Mill's books, and thus undercuts their claim to wisdom.

Short-circuiting the self-development of the majority will also in the long run hamper the well-being of that majority. Mill's vivid descriptions of the great harms caused by despotism of husbands over wives in *The Subjection of Women* map well onto his arguments about the detrimental effects of those despots masquerading as wise even though they wield their power to impede others' self-development.

Mill soundly rejects the "theory of dependency" which claims that the poor must be deferential to the rich and the rich should make judgments on their behalf. He has only scorn for the view that "the lot of the poor, in all things which affect them collectively, should be regulated *for* them, not *by* them . . . The rich should be *in loco parentis* to the poor" (CW 3:759). Mill's resounding repudiation of that argument should undercut any claim that he countenances elitist coercion in the name of the good of others. The wise members of society may serve as models for others, but their role can never legitimately be transformed into that of acting as *in loco parentis*. Their judgments cannot legitimately be substituted for the independent judgments of their admirers. Wise and compassionate people are willing only to seek a hearing for their arguments, to have the opportunity to persuade and encourage their fellows. They would agree with Mill's mantra of persuasion, not coercion and control. That is how the authentically wise (as distinguished from affluent privileged people with a grandiose sense of themselves and their entitlements) actually behave. The virtues in Mill's system include centrally compassion and sensitivity to the suffering and happiness of others. The virtues exclude self-absorption, self-aggrandizement, and the like – in other words, the vices of elitism.

But this is not the end of the delicate balancing act of participation and competence. Concerns about despotism of elites are real. But Mill is equally concerned that the sinister interests (i.e., those interests that conflict with the community's general good) of the uneducated will lead them to ignore the arguments of the authentically wise. There is much benefit to be gained from increasing the influence, but not the despotic power, of the wiser members of the community. The delicate balancing act is required because, while active and effective participation is in itself educative and conducive to virtue, danger from the operation of the sinister interests and the purported ignorance of those who are still developing their virtues must realistically be held in balance by giving great weight in the public domain to the influence, as opposed to the coercion, of the wiser members of the community. One side of the scale appears in Mill's famous warning in *On Liberty* of the danger that the wise will be overwhelmed by the "tyranny of the majority"; it is one obvious example of this concern (CW 18:219). But on the other side of the scale is the argument that since the self-development that follows from active participation brings increasing competence with it, over time the value of participation will take on greater weight in this balance. The harms arising from exclusion from active participation on the progress of self-development, as well as the loss of the infusion of energy of those constrained in their participation, must also be taken into account in weighing the proper balance. Mill's arguments in *The Subjection of Women* about the detrimental effects and loss of potential value resulting from the systemic exclusion of women's active participation and contribution to social and political life are certainly pertinent here, since exactly the same point applies to the classist exclusion of workers from many political and economic arenas.

Additionally, adequate tests of competence are often elusive and unreliable, and there is the very real danger that those deemed more competent or wise are really just those in positions of power and privilege because of their class, gender, or racial membership. Racism, sexism, and classism produce biased judgments about the competence and abilities of members of these oppressed groups; the perceived competence of members of privileged groups is correspondingly inflated. The causal links between income level and access to education are clear enough in our time; in Mill's day, the connections between class and education were even more pronounced. In such cases, oppression and exploitation based on class, race, and gender will be perpetuated. Mill is crystal clear about this problem of corrupt power masquerading as legitimate authority in his depiction of marital despotism. There are similar dangers of exploitation and unequal treatment of workers arising from sinister class interests in the political and economic domains.

Therefore much care is needed in weighing the principles of competence and participation in political and economic arenas. Mill straightforwardly argues that his theoretical framework uses a model of balance of these two principles, and that the balancing act is intricate. How we interpret and read his balancing act strongly influences whether his theory is perceived as fundamentally egalitarian or as elitist. His concerns about the dangerous combination of despotism and elitism are voiced in tandem with expressions of the positive benefits of allowing the activities of everyday life to operate as schools of practical education.

Egalitarian or Elitist?

In scrutinizing Mill's treatment of political institutions, economic and workplace forums, and the family as educative sites, we repeatedly encounter dynamic tensions between egalitarian and elitist themes. The strands of radical egalitarianism and of elitism in Mill's thought are readily detectable, and often appear side-by-side in his writing. In order to determine, therefore, whether his theory is most accurately depicted as fundamentally egalitarian or as elitist, given that both threads are evident and on the surface in his writings, we must scrutinize the architecture of his moral and political theory. The interpretive principles guiding decisions about the most plausible reading of his theory are best explicitly formulated and defended. My arguments and readings foreground and give priority to basic and foundational principles and structures over the examples Mill provides to illustrate those principles. I do not give much weight to policies and agendas that are of the nineteenth century and that are not commonly defended by twenty-first-century liberals. Plural voting schemes which give more votes to some members of society who are supposedly highly educated are a prominent example of this, since no reasonable liberal theorist of the twenty-first century would promote this as a serious policy proposal. Mill himself was extremely uncertain about the wisdom of this strategy, even for his own time. In the *Autobiography*, he notes that he had never discussed his proposal for plural voting, which he tied to educational level rather than property-owner status, with Harriet, his "almost infallible counsellor" (CW 1:261). He says he does not have evidence that she would have given this proposal her assent. This is a strong reason to reject the idea, in his mind. He admits that other supporters of plural voting of his time diverge from his preferred educational test; they want a property test to determine numbers of votes. This obvious classism will not do. The only fair path to instituting a voting scheme linked to proven educational levels, he says, is to have in place a system of National Education. Otherwise, people are doubly wronged, first by being denied an education, and then by being denied a vote or an equal vote based upon their lack of education. A fair and just system of plural voting is only possible "after the establishment of a systematic National Education by which the various grades of politically valuable acquirement may be accurately defined and authenticated. Without this it will always remain liable to strong, possibly conclusive, objections; and with this, it would perhaps not be needed" (CW 1:262). This is not strong conviction. It is uncertainty and wavering in the extreme.

Additionally, I distinguish, when relevant, means from ends, and give priority to intrinsic value and ends over instrumental value and means to those ends. Mill's utilitarian ends of happiness as self-development are firmly fixed; of means he is often far less certain, as his remarks on plural voting illustrate. He follows the theory laid down in *A System of Logic* in treating policy proposals as governed by their empirically demonstrated success in achieving the end of well-being.

Mill's firm repudiation of despotism makes it very difficult to interpret his theory as fundamentally elitist. He explicitly opposes policy proposals to develop the mental and moral virtues of the elite only, and he equally explicitly endorses the value of cultivating habits of cooperation in all people. "A people among whom there is no habit of spontaneous action for a collective interest . . . have their faculties only half developed; their education is defective in one of its most important branches" (CW 3:943). In *Representative Government* he also raises his dispute with elitism. He objects to the claim made by supporters of despotism "that absolute power, in the hands of an eminent individual, would ensure a virtuous and intelligent performance of all the duties of government" (CW 19:399). Not so, he replies. Too much power in the hands of even the eminent does not answer his potent question: "What sort of human beings can be formed under such a regimen? What development can either their thinking or their active faculties attain under it? . . . Their moral capacities are equally stunted" (CW 19:400). Mill here replies to those who claim that he is overly tempted by the notion of elites wielding power, and that he is so repelled by the idea of "the ignorance, the indifference, the intractableness" of people that he would defend elites who are prepared to use power to bring about better government (CW 19:402). For he says that "those who look in any such direction for the realization of their hopes leave out of the idea of good government its principal element, the improvement of the people themselves" (CW 19:403). On the contrary, well-being depends upon two principles, which he explains.

> The first is, that the rights and interests of every or any person are only secure from being disregarded, when the person interested is himself able, and habitually disposed, to stand up for them. The second is, that the general prosperity attains a greater height, and is more widely diffused, in proportion to the amount and variety of the personal energies enlisted in promoting it. (CW 19:404)

Mill follows with an argument that should put to rest any idea that he is fundamentally classist and that he does not stand up for workers. Mill sides with workers and opposes even well-meaning attempts to marginalize them and remove their power. He decries the exclusion of the working class from participation in government. They are marginalized and excluded by this, and as a result their interests, as a class and as individuals, are ignored by those with political power. The perspectives paid attention to are only those of the employers. Working-class perspectives must, he says, be listened to and not ignored. The way to have that perspective accurately presented is to have it presented by workers themselves, in the setting of parliament. Acting in the collective realm, performing public duties and public service, are essential. A major principle for democratic governance is that of protection of interests by the holders of those interests. Self-protection and self-dependence are the indispensable principles. Those in positions of political power will ignore the interests of the disenfranchised and powerless and they will use their power to promote their own class and individual interests. Representative government means that "the whole people . . . exercise through deputies periodically elected by themselves, the ultimate controlling power . . . They must be masters, whenever they please, of all the operations of government" (CW 19:422).

He says,

> There cannot be a combination of circumstances more dangerous to human welfare, than that in which intelligence and talent are maintained at a high standard within a governing corporation, but starved and discouraged outside the pale. Such a system, more completely than any other, embodies the idea of despotism, by arming with intellectual superiority as an additional weapon, those who have already the legal power. (CW 3:943)

If Mill were fundamentally elitist, he would not express such potent concern about building up the talents of the elite. His concern flows directly from his fundamental commitments, which are liberal and egalitarian.

In *A System of Logic* Mill explicitly lays out the structure of his theoretical model and in particular how he sees the relationship between ends and means and between art and science. A moral-art like education has the responsibility to set out the ends that promote utility in that domain. The corresponding moral science is responsible for investigating what means will most effectively promote these ends. The end of the art of education is to promote those human character traits that are most conducive to human flourishing. The right to liberty of self-development is a fundamental right in Mill's system because it is the very one that protects this educative process. Elitist policies cut against this process and short-circuit it for those who are excluded or whose inclusion is limited. Whenever Mill proposes them, they are qualified and clearly marked as interim measures only. Any exclusionary policies, for example proposals for voting procedures, are temporary. No such qualifications apply to Mill's fundamental commitment to the right to equal self-development and its components. The right to liberty of self-development is part of the fundamental Art of Life. Particular political policies and strategies are part of one of the subordinate moral arts. The structure of the theory creates the strong presumption that the fundamental right shall outweigh the policy of the subordinate art, and that in cases of conflict the presumption is also that the means shall give way to the end.

Mill puts fully on display in *A System of Logic* his awareness of the pitfalls of the demanding task of framing just the right means to promote the ends of human happiness, especially in the complex sets of circumstances in which contemporary democracy typically occurs. He warns that the theorem of the moral science is not ready to be turned into a precept or rule of art until the whole of the moral scientific investigation has been thoroughly carried out. He warns further about what will happen if the rule is framed too early.

> If, in this imperfect state of the scientific theory, we attempt to frame a rule of art, we perform that operation prematurely. Whenever any counteracting cause, overlooked by the theorem, takes place, the rule will be at fault: we shall employ the means and the end will not follow. (CW 8:945)

He remarks that in practice it is often the case that rules must be formulated on the basis of less than complete study, since the social circumstances are so complicated that perfect understanding of them may never come to pass. He concludes then that wise practitioners will only consider rules to be provisional, and so subject to revision and improvement in the light of the experience of their application.

Much discussion in the literature examines and offers explanations for those of Mill's practical proposals that are classified as elitist. Ready examples are his proposals for plural voting, public voting, and other policies deemed to be countervailing forces to the perceived "mediocrity" and sinister interests of many potential voters. I contend that drawing upon the methodology of *A System of Logic* illuminates the spirit in which he presented these proposals. They are particular strategies proposed for specific sets of social and historical circumstances. Not only are these circumstances impermanent, and constantly changing, but our knowledge is generally incomplete and imperfect, because of the complexity of the social circumstances. A degree of uncertainty is present. Dogmatism and over-confidence about policies proposed to promote goals are not reasonable stances to adopt. Reason calls for a spirit of experimentation and a willingness to try out different strategies to see how well they work. This explains the reasons for his willingness to propose different strategies for voting to achieve his fundamental goals. While he wavered on particular policies and strategies, his commitment to the fundamental ends of his philosophy, the promotion of human well-being and flourishing of all members of society, never wavers in the slightest.

Mill's emancipatory vision of education for freedom and democracy is still a work in progress. His vision has yet to come to fruition. Democratic theorists are still grappling with the dilemmas of democratic systems which have not lived up to their ideals. Much of the life seems to be drained out of the ideal of democratic participation on which Mill pinned his hopes. The achievement of expanding suffrage for which he fought has been turned into an exercise in which citizen participation often is limited to voting. Mill certainly never intended democratic participation to stop at the exercise of casting a ballot. Moreover, Mill saw the vote as being a trust in which citizens have the responsibility to vote for the common good rather than their own narrow self-interest. Yet the vote is usually seen in just this light as primarily serving self-interest. The welcome diversity of perspectives has also led to new dilemmas as pluralism of contemporary societies leads inevitably to moral disagreement. In his time Mill called for a revitalized view of political life which places moral considerations at the center and which is deliberative in its emphasis on public reasoning and rational debate. Although this revitalization project is still in progress, we can look to Mill's vision of self-development and deliberative and participatory democracy as its exemplary model.

note

1 For a classic treatment of these questions in depth see Thompson 1976, especially 13–90. Also see Ten 1998; Baum 2000, 2003; Riley, 2007.

further reading

Baum, Bruce, *Rereading Power and Freedom in J. S. Mill* (Toronto: University of Toronto Press, 2000).
Eisenach, Eldon J., *Mill and the Moral Character of Liberalism* (University Park, PA: Pennsylvania State University Press, 1998).
Kinzer, Bruce L., Ann P. Robson, and John M. Robson, *A Moralist In and Out of Parliament: John Stuart Mill at Westminster, 1865–1868* (Toronto: University of Toronto Press, 1992).
Skorupski, John, ed., *The Cambridge Companion to Mill* (Cambridge: Cambridge University Press, 1998).
Thompson, Dennis F., *John Stuart Mill and Representative Government* (Princeton: Princeton University Press, 1976).
Urbinati, Nadia, *Mill on Democracy: From the Athenian Polis to Representative Government* (Chicago: University of Chicago Press, 2002).
Urbinati, Nadia, and Alex Zakaris, eds., *J. S. Mill's Political Thought: A Bicentennial Reassessment* (Cambridge: Cambridge University Press, 2007).

sexual equality and the subjection of women

Mill's Liberal Feminism

Mill is a classic liberal feminist. His feminist theory seamlessly meshes with his political philosophy of liberalism and his distinctive form of utilitarianism. The arguments in *The Subjection of Women* palpably rely upon the concepts and principles of liberalism and utilitarianism: intrinsic value analyzed as happiness linked with self-development; justice, equality, autonomy, and liberty, especially liberty of self-development. Nineteenth-century liberal Mill draws upon a robust philosophical heritage. As a political tradition it is both distinguished and radical. Some of the most revolutionary historical breakthroughs and advances in individual, social, and political progress have been motivated by the ends and principles of classical liberalism. Mill's political philosophy and his moral theory directly fuel his feminist commitments and agendas; there is no separation between his general liberalism and its application to the core questions of gender equality and the emancipation of women. The theme of liberty versus despotism and power, which is a constant presence throughout Mill's corpus, makes a vivid appearance in this essay.

Mill's theory, however, is much richer than some currently popular models of liberal feminism. It sits well with many insights that are now frequently associated with radical feminism. We could conclude from this that Mill's theory is a hybrid, incorporating elements that are currently identified as components of liberal feminism, radical feminism, and the feminist care ethic, among others.[1] However, it is more plausible to argue that historical liberalism is a radical, emancipatory creed and that propounding a watered-down version of liberal feminism as representing fairly Mill's vision is inaccurate and does injustice to the robust form. Historical liberalism, promoting the values of liberty and equality and universal dignity, fuelled some of the most progressive and even revolutionary campaigns for emancipation, including movements to abolish slavery, eliminate child labor, reduce the 16- and 18-hour workday to a more reasonable limit, establish basic health and safety workplace regulations, introduce mandatory universal education and universal suffrage, and so on. This raises questions about the adequacy of the current characterizations of varieties of feminism. I argue that Mill is a classical liberal feminist, and that his theory fits this mold with distinction and panache. The fighting creed of historical liberalism is well suited to play its emancipatory role, rather than the feeble role that is often attributed to it, usually by opponents. Mill relied upon the theory as the guiding framework in his activist battles for women's suffrage, reform of laws governing marriage, and campaigns against domestic violence, including rape and murder. That his liberalism incorporates a shrewd and devastatingly insightful analysis of corrupt power, oppression, despotism, and tyranny in gender and family relations is exactly what one would expect from a theory of this lineage. If contemporary liberal feminism is now depicted as an insipid theory focused primarily on securing equal formal legal rights, then that should not lead to a critique of Mill's robust liberal feminist creed. It should rather lead to revivification of liberal feminism to its fighting form. The current straw person versions of liberal feminism should be brought up to the standard of their venerable predecessors. There is no need to accept weak caricatures such as the view of liberal feminism as organized around limited goals of achieving legal reforms. Mill fought vehemently for changes to the legislation governing marriage, which placed women in legal bondage and denied them their basic legal, economic, and political rights, but that was the beginning of his agenda, not its culmination.

Mill's theory also anticipates some core commitments of the feminist ethics of care, including a critique of excessive rationalism, which I explored in Chapter 5, on education. These points also are a perfectly natural component of his theory, as articulated on its own terms. Mill belongs to a line of historical moral philosophers – including David Hume – who are sensitized to the requirement that cultivated emotional capacities are necessary for competent moral judgment and agency. Empathy and emotional sensitivity to the suffering of others are core human virtues and excellences within Mill's philosophy. In his personal and activist life he was drawn to feminist agendas and outlooks in part because of his keen awareness of the pains of oppression. Mill's long-term intimate friendship and marriage to Harriet Taylor Mill was quite an unconventional relationship by nineteenth-century standards. They collaborated closely on many writings and activist campaigns, so much so that it is difficult to determine definitively the full extent of Harriet's impact on his thought and attitudes. His feminist inclinations were already evident in his early twenties and even in his teens, as his participation in campaigns for birth control displays. Their close relationship could not but impress upon him the pains that a loved one felt at the social restrictions on her marital and work options. Harriet Taylor Mill's influence is unmistakably present in Mill's sensitivity to the pain of gender inequality. Mill could plainly see the debilitating effects of domination, inequality, and dependence in relations between the sexes. In his writings on democratic politics and economics, Mill shows keen insight about the debasement of human self-development caused by class exploitation and economic dependency. In his analysis of political and economic inequality, he shows awareness of the corrupting effects of power on despots and the sufferings of poverty on exploited members of the working class. But, perhaps fueled by personal experience, his insights are especially compelling when he looks at women's oppression and the consequences that ensue when men wield their power to repress the autonomy and individuality of their wives and children.

Two strands of Mill's feminist argument – the case (often associated with liberal feminism) based upon the liberal values of freedom, equality, and self-development, and the case (associated with radical feminism) based upon the harms of oppression and tyranny to women's happiness and self-development – can be detected and separated to a degree. But only to a degree, since they are intertwined and the full impact of Mill's argument depends upon appreciating both aspects in synergy. It seems obvious enough that if the foundational principle of utility calls for promoting happiness and reducing suffering, then the massive harms produced by patriarchal domination must be drastically mitigated, then eliminated, and the conditions that support well-being, characterized as essentially involving development and exercise of human excellences, must be advanced. Mill's arguments in this essay, clear and reasonable as they are, at the same time have a distinctly polemical and rhetorical tenor to them. *The Subjection of Women* is a philosophical treatise with an avowedly activist purpose. In Mill's view it is a salvo in the ongoing battle for human emancipation from despotism. A noticeable theme of *Subjection* is his repeated comparison of slavery with women's oppression under patriarchy. Actually, it is not so much a comparison as an instance, since Mill argues forcefully that women's condition in patriarchal marriage is an example of slavery. Mill frequently invokes this link between patriarchy and slavery, and regularly characterizes the treatment of women in marriage as a kind of slavery. He says that "it is the primitive state of slavery lasting on, through successive mitigations and modifications occasioned by the same causes which have softened the general manners, and brought all human relations more under the control of justice and the influence of humanity. It has not lost the taint of its brutal origin" (CW 21:264).

This wording is no accident. It is a deliberate and calculated move on Mill's part, having both philosophical and activist import. Mill rightly believed that he was dealing with long-entrenched, deeply ingrained prejudices that required the most finely balanced combination of reason and rhetoric to bring them into conscious awareness in order to dissipate and dissolve them. From our present-day vantage-point, it may seem overheated for Mill to invoke an analogy with slavery, which now has the appearance of a long-banished evil. But it would not have appeared so to Mill, because as a young adult he took part in the campaign to abolish the institution of slavery in Britain and the British empire. Even after it was legally abolished in Britain, it had not yet been eliminated outside of Britain. In Mill's lifetime, slavery was not a distant monstrosity, but a still-living abomination. The common threads linking its horrors and the abuses and degradations he observed in the patriarchal family would not seem far fetched in his world.

The strands of Mill's argument concerning the case for liberal feminism include positive statements squarely grounded in the liberal goals and principles, namely, rights, liberty, including saliently liberty of self-development, autonomy, individuality, and equality. The most prominent source for this case is *The Subjection of Women*, but other statements of the bedrock themes are found in writings like *On Liberty*. The case is built by applying liberal principles to questions of gender and family relations and the rights of women. Mill states the guiding principle governing gender and familial relationships at the beginning of *The Subjection of Women*. He will argue:

> That the principle which regulates the existing social relations between the two sexes – the legal subordination of one sex to the other – is wrong in itself, and now one of the chief hindrances to human improvement; and that it ought to be replaced by a principle of perfect equality, admitting no power or privilege on the one side, nor disability on the other. (CW 21:261)

Mill's arguments for gender equality in this essay are grounded in a general defense of liberal equality, in which the circle of inclusion will be expanded. He argues that social progress has reached the historical point at which justice will be the primary virtue. Justice will be based on "cultivated sympathy . . . no one being now left out, but an equal measure being extended to all" (CW 21:294).

Mill's argument is impelled by his repugnance at the negative state of the institution of marriage in his time. It was founded on the command and obedience model of patriarchal marriage. This model of marriage is degrading and damaging to all parties, and Mill's goal is to propound the positive ideal of marriage founded on equality and friendship: "[w]hat marriage may be in the case of two persons of cultivated faculties . . . between whom there exists that best kind of equality, similarity of powers and capacities with reciprocal superiority in them" (CW 21:336). It is a union based on equality, respect, and loving treatment. The other forms of marital union are but leftovers from barbarism, when slavery and rule by force were the norm. This argument has rhetorical power, but Mill also intends it to be read as an accurate statement of history. He sets out an overview of the long process of gradual improvement and progress in human affairs, commencing with the earliest conditions of barbarism and then moving through slow stages to a noticeably improved state of society abiding by moral rules of justice rather than brute force. It is only a recent development in historical progress that moral law founded on rules of justice has stepped in to replace the law of brute force as the regulating principle of human affairs. Mill invokes the framework of philosophy of the social sciences, explored at great length in Book VI of *A System of Logic*, where he elaborates his theories about stationary and progressive periods of history and the causes and conditions for historical and social progress that foster equality and well-being (CW 8:911–30). However, these progressive changes have a long way to go, he thinks, and are only in the relatively early stages of what human beings can achieve in the right political and social contexts. The law of the strongest has been abandoned or is in decline in other spheres, but it remains in force in the family, to great detriment. "The moral regeneration of mankind will only really commence, when the most fundamental of the social relations is placed under the rule of equal justice, and when human beings learn to cultivate their strongest sympathy with an equal in rights and in cultivation" (CW 21:336).

A prime focus for a liberal theorist must be the anticipated gains in personal happiness for individual women that would result from their emancipation. The benefits to women of release from oppression would be immense. It would be nothing less than "the difference to them between a life of subjection to the will of others, and a life of rational freedom. After the primary necessities of food and raiment, freedom is the first and strongest want of human nature" (CW 21:336). But the collective benefits in increased happiness would be equally impressive. Mill holds to the conviction that the clearest indicator of the progressiveness or lack thereof of a society is the level of education and development of women in that society. Experience has shown that women's social and political status provides "the surest test and most correct measure of the civilization of a people or an age" (CW 21:276). He extols the virtues of liberty and emancipation, mirroring the arguments of *On Liberty*. Self-development is the core of well-being for both sexes, and so the basic rights protected by liberalism must extend to women, since it is an essential ingredient of all people's happiness.

Mill calls on all of his argumentative talents to pick away at and attempt to overturn the outdated attitudes and attendant bad arguments which were employed to prop up the edifice of systemic institutionalized injustice against women. If freedom is essential to well-being, then women's degrading dependent position of living under the control of others, even loving others, constitutes a denial of their basic rights. Those who underestimate liberalism may miss the significance of Mill's repeated invocations of the fundamental distinction between liberty (a bedrock liberal value) and power (a malign source of corruption and despotism). A liberal theorist, can, indeed must, fully endorse autonomy and liberty while rejecting control and power over others. Liberals are routinely accused of underestimating the harm of oppression and of mis-understanding the relationship of freedom and power. The objection says that the freedoms touted by liberalism are supposedly linked with the desire for control and power over others. That this accusation does not apply to Mill is evident when he gets to his core convictions.

> The love of power and the love of liberty are in eternal antagonism. Where there is least liberty, the passion for power is the most ardent and unscrupulous. The desire of power over others can only cease to be a depraving agency among mankind, when each of them individually is able to do without it: which can only be where respect for liberty in the personal concerns of each is an established principle. (CW 21:338)

Mill's theory quite naturally includes reliance on the positive liberal principles of liberty and equality and also an astute analysis of the harms of patriarchy and oppression. Mill places autonomy at the core of self-development. He holds to it as a core capacity essential to a good life. But Mill is also keenly aware of the fragility of this essential capacity and the many obstacles in the path to its development and exercise. Indeed, he anticipates and eloquently expresses many of the arguments formulated by contemporary feminists about the diminution of women's self-determination under patriarchy as well as some of the strategies for overcoming these impediments and amplifying empowerment. Many of these strategies are liberal basics such as equal access to education and jobs, rights to vote, to associate in collective struggles for liberation, to control of reproduction, to personal security, most saliently protection from assault, and so on. Autonomy can be easily undermined, distorted, and suppressed. The corrupting power of despotic males to corrode the autonomy of women and children under their domination and cow them into submission is a conspicuous focus of Mill's passionate, unrelenting attacks on patriarchy.

When Mill lists the most basic rights in *Utilitarianism* and other writings, he invariably prioritizes the right to liberty and the right to security (CW 10:250–59). Women's physical safety was not adequately protected, and Mill makes it one of his highest priorities to confront social attitudes that make light of violence against women and children. Children's legal status was equally troubling. Children were the legal property of their fathers, and mothers were excluded from legal authority over their children. In Mill's time, the legal status of women and children in marriage and family was appalling. The "rights" of husbands included coerced and involuntary sex with their wives – in other words, legalized marital rape. Even if the husband was, in Mill's words, a brutal tyrant, he could "claim from her and enforce the lowest degradation of a human being, that of being made the instrument of an animal function contrary to her inclinations . . . she is held in this worst description of slavery as to her own person" (CW 21:285).

Mill's dissection of the harms of domestic violence, including the impact of the terrorizing in inflicting tremendous misery and suffering, is remarkably in advance of the time. In his day, even more than today, violence against women and family violence were not taken seriously and people averted their eyes from it. Mill's utilitarian sensibilities made him aware that many women were afflicted with raw suffering of physical and emotional assault from which they could see no escape and so this cause elicited his full activist and philosophical support. His discussions of these painful topics are not restricted to *The Subjection of Women*. His activist work on violence against women and children prompted him and Harriet to report on trials involving women and children subjected to brutality. The language used in these investigations is uncompromising. They look unflinchingly at the reality of the brutality, and their investigations do not spare the passive onlookers of these crimes from their moral outrage and condemnation. The diagnosis they offer of gender oppression and domestic violence is as relevant today as it was in the nineteenth century. For example, Harriet and John Stuart Mill write in the *Morning Chronicle* on the case of Anne Bird (March 13, 1850):

> Persons who are not conversant . . . with the breadth and depth of popular brutality, have very little idea of what is comprehended in the meaning of the words, "domestic tyranny" . . . Every now and then the public are revolted by some disclosure of unspeakable atrocities committed against some of these helpless dependents – while, for every such case which excites notice, hundreds, most of them as bad, pass off in the police reports entirely unobserved . . . If, through the accidental presence of some better-hearted person than these poor creatures are usually surrounded by, complaint is made to a magistrate, the neighbours – persons living in the same house – almost invariably testify, without either repentance or shame, that the same brutalities had gone on for years in their sight or hearing, without their stirring a finger to prevent them. The sufferers themselves are either unable to complain, from youth or ignorance, or they dare not. They know

too surely the consequences of either failing or succeeding in a complaint, when the law, after inflicting just enough punishment to excite the thirst of vengeance, delivers back the victim to the tyrant. (CW 25:1156)

As part of their campaign against violence, the Mills provide graphic, even stomach-churning, descriptions of some horrifically brutal assaults against women and children. Their description of the impact of the trauma on children growing up in families where violence is prevalent is compelling as they paint a clear picture of the ongoing cycles of suffering and violence that can continue for generations.

> Let any one consider the degrading moral effect . . . of scenes of physical violence, repeated day after day – the debased, spirit-broken, down-trodden condition of the unfortunate woman, the most constant sufferer from domestic brutality in the poorer classes, unaffectedly believing herself to be out of the protection of the law – the children born and bred in this moral atmosphere – with the unchecked indulgence of the most odious passions, the tyranny of physical force in its coarsest manifestations, constantly exhibited as the most familiar facts of their daily life – can it be wondered if they grow up without any of the ideas and feelings which it is the purpose of moral education to infuse, without any sense of justice or affection, any conception of self-restraint – incapable in their turn of governing their children by any other means than blows? (CW 25:1157)

Any argument that Mill's liberalism does not have an adequate account of the damage that oppression causes for women and children is completely mistaken.

Autonomy is a fulcrum of human well-being and the good life, but it requires social and cultural support for its full development and it can easily be deflected. One example of how this can happen is the circumstance in which adaptive preferences take the place of genuinely self-determining, autonomous choice. In such cases women adapt their preferences to fit with their restricted range of options, believing that their choices are freely made, even though they have actually been subverted to conform to the narrowed domain of readily available prospects. Mill devotes considerable attention to dissecting how women's preferences and desires are distorted and debased under patriarchy, and his reflections are not outdated in the least. Intimate spousal and sexual relationships are prime sites for oppression to do nefarious work to produce defective desires and so thwart autonomy. In many such cases, it would be extremely difficult, although not impossible, for women to imagine their lives taking some directions routinely open to men, and the idea that certain options were live prospects for perusal rather than just subjects of fantasy would be shielded from their awareness. There have always been examples of "exceptional women" who break out of their assigned roles despite strong social barriers. The example of Elisabeth Kübler-Ross which I discussed in Chapter 4 is one such case. It is sometimes objected that liberal feminism promotes these examples in the spirit of "if they can do it, why can't more women achieve independence?" Whether such examples serve primarily as inspirational models for emulation, or whether they more often serve to rationalize oppression, by downplaying the power of the impediments to women's autonomy and emancipation, is an interesting point for reflection. Key to Mill's analysis is his insight that women's deference to illegitimate male power routinely causes them to deflect their own liberty to appease male demands for compliance. Realistic and reasonable fear of abuse and violence is one obvious motivator and malefactor, but the corrosive effects of tyranny within the family can take many subtler, almost invisible forms. Legitimate fear of poverty is another key factor in women's constricted self-determination. Barred from working for wages outside of the home, many women were denied economic self-sufficiency and forced into economic dependence upon men. Women then, as now, often stayed with brutal abusers rather than face the poverty that would follow any attempt at independent life. Dependency in all its forms – personal, economic, legal, and political – when substituted for independence is a prime suspect in Mill's analysis of the factors operating to undermine well-being.

Liberalism defends and promotes equal rights to pursue educational and occupational opportunities without discrimination on the basis of gender, class, or race. Mill actively promotes women's rights to compete for and pursue all of the same jobs and occupations that men take for granted as their terrain and privilege. The injustice of being barred from occupations and education is a general one, and is very debilitating. However, Mill argues that certain groups of women are particularly aggrieved by being barred from pursuit of all other occupations except managing a household. These groups include women who deliberately choose not to marry and those whose children have grown up or have died. In such cases, Mill argues that the impact on basic enjoyments of life arising from "the want of a worthy outlet for the active faculties" causes great misery for many women barred from outside employment (CW 21:338). Women who are caring for homes and children have these outlets for their energy and talents, he thinks. But what about those whose children have grown up and left home? Or died? These women have chosen and fulfilled their domestic duties, and yet have no active outlets or employments. The costs are extreme. "What, in unenlightened societies, colour, race, religion . . . are to some men, sex is to all women; a peremptory exclusion from almost all honourable occupations . . . few persons are aware of the great amount of unhappiness even now produced by the feeling of a wasted life" (CW 21:340).

In a passage that could have been lifted straight out of the pages of *On Liberty*, Mill sums it up: "every restraint on the freedom of conduct of any of their fellow human creatures, (otherwise than by making them responsible for any evil actually caused by it), dries up *pro tanto* the principal fountain of human happiness, and leaves the species less rich, to an inappreciable degree, in all that makes life valuable to the individual human being" (CW 21:340). The arguments used to defend liberty, individuality, and autonomy in *On Liberty* have the same mandate in *The Subjection of Women*. The restraints on women in marriage who were under the legal control of their husbands, and the restraints on the activities of women who were barred from most occupations outside of the home were great barriers to justice and happiness.

Progress and advances in civilization have reformed most other institutions, but lamentably the patriarchal family remains almost unchanged. It is also one of the last sites for early training of petty despots who are reluctant to give up this bastion in which their aggression and violence can go virtually unchecked. Mill does not claim that male oppression of women is the most basic form of oppression, or the root cause of all oppression, as some forms of feminism maintain. He propounds the more modest view that patriarchy is the most persistent form of oppression. Patriarchal power is stubbornly enduring; its corruption trades on and gains power from the intimate nature of the relationship between oppressor and oppressed. Such intimacy is absent in other varieties of despotism. In domestic tyranny, the desire of oppressors for power is amplified, "for every one who desires power, desires it most over those who are nearest to him . . . in whom any independence of his authority is oftenest likely to interfere with his individual preferences" (CW 21:268). In the domestic sphere, closeness and intimacy prevent individual rebellion and collective resistance and the kinds of uprisings that often put an end to political tyrants. In marital tyranny, women have no obvious means of collective action, and they have powerful incentives to avoid giving offence to men. In the wave of feminism of the 1960s and 1970s, the slogan "the personal is the political" was employed to counter women's perceptions that their oppression was a personal, individual problem. The result was a surge in collective agendas and struggles. In Mill's time, women desiring their liberty were bribed and intimidated into giving up the struggles. "If ever any system of privilege and enforced subjection had its yoke tightly riveted on the necks of those who are kept down by it, this has" (CW 21:268).

In Mill's time, it was also commonly accepted that male domination was "natural." Mill persistently questions the meaning and the justifiability of the idea of the "natural," since in his view this notion is frequently employed to rationalize illegitimate male domination. In his essay "Nature," as I will examine in Chapter 8, on environmental ethics, he questions the soundness of this notion when it is put in the service of hampering improvements to nature. In *The Subjection of Women* the targets of his interrogation are the supposedly "natural" differences between the sexes, particularly differences in their mental and moral abilities. Although it was frequently asserted that men and women have different natures, Mill asks how we could possibly know this. He uses an apt comparison with slavery, reminding readers that questionable claims about the inherent differences among people of diverse races were routinely invoked to prop up slavery for a very long time. The claims of "natural" differences are suspect, since "unnatural generally means only uncustomary, and . . . everything which is usual appears natural. The subjection of women to men being a universal custom, any departure from it quite naturally appears unnatural" (CW 21:270). Mill responds to the frequently posed objection that the customary form of marital relationship was voluntarily accepted by the very women who were putatively the sufferers. He replies that this claim is false and that actually many women fight this form of oppression. There would be many more resistors were it not for the harsh reality that acting to complain of abuse is often "the greatest of all provocatives to a repetition and increase of the ill usage" (CW 21:271). Women often do not seek redress against marital assaults because they fear reprisal.

Mill is aware that women's desires and emotions are distorted and deformed by oppression. This is a central theme and insight shared by all varieties of contemporary feminist philosophies, and Mill once again is in advance of his era in the clarity of his perception. In this most intimate of relations, men with tyrannical tendencies want more than mere obedience and servitude from their wives – "they want their senti-ments" (CW 21:271). Although threatening violence may be the extreme strategy for gaining compliance and obedience, Mill knows that most men do not resort to violence and "desire to have, in the woman most nearly connected with them, not a forced slave but a willing one, not a slave merely, but a favourite" (CW 21:271). In other forms of the master–slave relationship the main instrument of control is fear. A pernicious form of education for vice is practiced to deform women's character, to subvert their autonomy and individuality.

> All women are brought up from the very earliest years in the belief that their ideal of character is the very opposite to that of men; not self-will, and govern-ment by self-control, but submission, and yielding to the control of others . . . that it is their nature, to live for others; to make complete abnegation of themselves, and to have no life but in their affections. (CW 21:271–2)

Women's affections are thus narrowed by their socialization, and they are expected to reduce the range of objects of their love and interest to husbands, children, and a small circle of intimates and friends. Wider social and political questions are supposedly outside of their region of concern.

Mill draws out the theme of the corrupting effects on both sexes of relationships built on dependency. Members of the working classes are dependent upon their political and economic masters and this has acted to block their self-development and their interests. Women are immeasurably more dependent upon their husbands and deformation of character is the predictable outcome. The social and political arrangements that induce women's utter dependence on their husbands, and that make it their primary goal in life to marry a "suitable" man conspire, so that "it would be a miracle if the object of being attractive to men had not become the polar star of feminine education and formation of character" (CW 21:272). Sexual allure appears then as essential, and this influences them to develop the submissive traits supposedly attractive to men. Thus is autonomy sacrificed and deflected.

It is highly detrimental to social welfare to block half of the population from pursuing and developing their talents and excellences. Freedom of choice over vocation is "the only thing which procures the adoption of the best processes, and throws each operation into the hands of those who are best qualified for it" (CW 21:273). It cannot be determined in advance of actual experience that members of certain groups are or are not qualified to perform a task or a job. Even if a measure of the talents and abilities of members of large gender, racial, or national groupings could be determined in advance for the majority of them, which is unlikely, "there will be a minority of exceptional cases in which it does not hold" (CW 21:274). Mill here calls on the conviction, defended in depth in On Liberty, that people are excellent judges of their own interests and vocations, and so should be allowed the opportunity to pursue them. He emphasizes that a significant cause of women's dependency on their husbands is economic. In his analysis of the ills of the working class, their poverty looms large. Women's fear of poverty were they to give up their dependency on male economic support is a very strong inducement to cultivate submissiveness in domestic and social affairs. Mill relies also on his argument of On Liberty that only experiments in living can yield reasonable evidence about the most beneficial social practices and arrangements. In gender relations, the evidence is very sparse because only one model has been followed. "I deny that any one knows, or can know, the nature of the two sexes, as long as they have only been seen in their present relation to one another" (CW 21:276). The result is that social science had not yet in Mill's time furnished reliable evidence on the question of the differences or similarities between men's and women's natures.

What is now called the nature of women is an eminently artificial thing – the result of forced repression in some directions, unnatural stimulation in others . . . no other class of dependents have had their character so entirely distorted from its natural proportions by their relation with their masters . . . a hot-house and stove cultivation has always been carried on of some of the capabilities of their nature, for the benefit and pleasure of their masters . . . men . . . indolently believe that the tree grows of itself in the way they have made it grow, and that it would die if one half of it were not kept in a vapour bath and the other half in the snow. (CW 21:276–7)

Social science was in its formative period, and the lack of reliable evidence about gender differences was part of the more general absence of knowledge about society. For empiricist Mill, such substantive studies are crucial for knowledge acquisition. Absent this, we accumulate only speculation and conjecture, not knowledge. As things stood, Mill claims, there was massive ignorance about the influences and causes of human character traits. Mill carries out an investigation of the philosophy of social science in *A System of Logic*. He discusses the work to be done in his proposed study of the moral science of ethology – the study of the social and environmental influences regarding the formation of human character and personality. This was one project that Mill never saw to completion. On the subject of women's capacities, he says we already know enough "to make it a tyranny to them, and a detriment to society, that they should not be allowed to compete with men for the exercise of these functions" (CW 21:300). He adds that it is inconsistent with the demands of justice to deprive them of their chance to compete fairly for jobs and occupations.

Lest he be accused of overstating the case for the potential of abuse, it should be clarified that Mill does agree that many, if not most, cases are not extreme. There are feelings and interests which moderate in men the tyrannical impulses. There are intense ties and attachments. Additionally, there are the obvious factors that mitigate the corrupting impact of power on men. These include affection and love, shared interests and concerns about their children, and their daily life together. But Mill's central and uncompromising position on the matter is that power is not freedom. His contrast between power (which he consistently associates with tyranny and despotism) and liberty runs as a clear bright line throughout his writing.

The insights and arguments of *The Subjection of Women* and *On Liberty* dovetail nicely here as in other places. The practice of freedom, for example trying out "experiments in living" in domestic arrangements and in vocational experiments, is the way forward according to the prescriptions and arguments of *On Liberty*. Mill rightly can be critiqued for his dearth of imagination on the question of the sexual division of labor. Could he have foreseen what has followed from subsequent loosening of rigid family structures, most significantly undermining the dogmatic notion that the nuclear family, composed of breadwinner husband, stay-at-home mother, and 2.5 children, is the only "normal" family form? His prescription in *On Liberty* for many "experiments in living" tracks a direct line to the explosion in varieties of families and myriad ways that people now choose to define their domestic arrangements. The traditional nuclear family has been left behind in the dust. In this instance, Mill's prescriptions for experiments in living have been eagerly pursued. Mill and Harriet's own personal experiment in living is no longer unconventional.

Mill's application of his philosophy of education to the family deserves some particular attention. The family is a prime site for the moral education of its members. How parents treat each other, whether with respect or with contempt and abuse, has a profound impact on their children. Mill saw this so clearly that a special component of his philosophy of education looks at the role of the family in education. In his *Inaugural Address Delivered to the University of St Andrews*, a lecture he presented on the role of university education, he makes special note of the place of the family in education. Moral education trains the feelings and habitual conduct, and this largely takes place in the domestic arena of the family in early childhood (CW 21:247–8). Since much early socialization and development of human capacities occurs in childhood, the family is a particularly potent zone for education in the widest sense, for cultivation of the virtues or, deplorably, the vices. Children cannot daily witness and endure violence of the kind reported in the Mills' *Morning Chronicle* writings and be unaffected and unscarred.

Families have strong potential to operate as schools specializing in the training of virtues; children should be taught that "the true virtue of human beings is fitness to live together as equals" (CW 21:294). These domestic virtues of freedom and of living together lovingly could and should be the norm. Parents who practice the moral virtues of equality between the sexes and who treat each other with loving respect provide models for their children to emulate. The training in the virtues or in the vices that children are habituated to in their families has the power to influence their orientation towards liberty or towards despotism, and it also functions as an educative site for parents.[2] Although the family is sometimes viewed as the domain of the private and the personal in liberal theory, it has notable social and political roles within Mill's liberalism.

> But the true virtue of human beings is fitness to live together as equals; claiming nothing for themselves but what they as freely concede to every one else . . . The family, justly constituted, would be the real school of the virtues of freedom . . . What is needed is, that it should be a school of sympathy in equality, of living together in love, without power on one side or obedience on the other. This it ought to be between the parents. It would

then be an exercise of those virtues which each requires to fit them for all other association, and a model to the children of the feelings and conduct which their temporary training by means of obedience is designed to render habitual, and therefore natural, to them. The moral training of mankind will never be adapted to the conditions of the life for which all other human progress is a preparation, until they practise in the family the same moral rule which is adapted to the normal constitution of human society. (CW 21: 294–5)

The educative role of the family impacts parents in Mill's agenda. In a marriage of equals men would perhaps lose some of their self-absorption and their temptation to indulge in "self-worship" (CW 21:293). Women are not immune to the corruptions of the present family institutions. Certain powers that are readily available to the vulnerable can also operate to educate women in the vices. They develop powers which they can use to retaliate against bad treatment and cause misery to their husbands, at the very least as a form of self-protection: as Mill describes it, this is "the power of the scold, or the shrewish sanction" (CW 21:289). Mill's liberal principles thus lead him to conclude that both sexes and society collectively would benefit from emancipation.

Objection: Mill's Defense of Gendered Division of Labor

Now follows a point of real contention: Mill's defense of the sexual division of labor within the family, which is the target of persistent, strong, and perhaps legitimate objections. It is by far the most frequently discussed objection to Mill's feminist theory.[3] Some critics go as far as to claim that this misapplication of his theory sinks the boat of his liberal feminism. It is too extreme to make this strong claim based on an unfortunate misapplication of theory to practice. What does not follow from Mill's substantive theory is the conclusion Mill himself draws about women's choices to remain in the home after marriage. The soundness of the basic tenets of liberalism and liberal feminism are not affected by this faulty logic. These are unscathed by the legitimate critique of Mill's *non sequitur* about women's choices to work or not to work for wages after marriage.

When family income depends upon earnings, he says,

the common arrangement, by which the man earns the income and the wife superintends the domestic expenditure, seems to me in general the most suitable division of labour between the two persons. If, in addition to the physical suffering of bearing children, and the whole responsibility of their care and education in early years, the wife undertakes the careful and economical application of the husband's earnings to the general comfort of the family; she takes not only her fair share, but usually the larger share, of the bodily and mental exertion required by their joint existence. If she undertakes any additional portion, it seldom relieves her from this. (CW 21:297)

In other words, those married women who work for wages undertake a double day of work, a full day working outside the home and a second workday of housework and childrearing, without any equitable arrangement for sharing this second workload with married men. The point, widely recognized in theory if not in practice nowadays, that liberal justice requires men to share responsibility for housework and childrearing did not occur to Mill as a perspective calling for consideration – thus fueling critics' suspicions of his less than full commitment to eliminate rather than just moderate patriarchy.

> In an otherwise just state of things, it is not, therefore, I think, a desirable custom, that the wife should contribute by her labour to the income of the family . . . But if marriage were an equal contract . . . it would not be necessary for her protection, that during marriage she should make this particular use of her faculties. Like a man when he chooses a profession, so, when a woman marries, it may in general be understood that she makes choice of the management of a household, and the bringing up of a family, as the first call upon her exertions . . . and that she renounces, not all other objects and occupations, but all which are not consistent with the requirements of this. (CW 21:298)

Practically speaking, then, Mill contends that domestic responsibilities would preclude working outside of the home for the majority of married women. Mill adds some provisos to this, but they are not sufficient to quell the immediate objections.

> But the utmost latitude ought to exist for the adaptation of general rules to individual suitabilities; and there ought to be nothing to prevent faculties exceptionally adapted to any other pursuit, from obeying their vocation notwithstanding marriage: due provision being made for supplying otherwise any falling-short which might become inevitable, in her full performance of the ordinary functions of mistress of a family. (CW 21:298)

Mill's argument stumbles, but does not collapse, when he accepts rather uncritically that women who choose to marry thereby choose to make childrearing and domestic labor their sole vocation and career. As we saw in the case of Mormon women and polygamous marriage in Chapter 4, although he is firmly committed to the liberal virtues of autonomy and individuality, his vision sometimes is blurred in the application of this to cases that seem obvious to present-day attitudes. In the example of women's choices in work, Mill should reasonably expect to find many women and men both interested in and able to seek fulfillment and economic prospects in working outside the home and childrearing. Instead, Mill perceives married women, in this respect, as having homogeneous desires and choices. Married men retain their individuality in matters of work after marriage, while married women lose it. Despite this significant lapse in judgment, Mill's basic points hold up rather better over time. It should not be overlooked that he argues vehemently that a significant number of women will voluntarily forego marriage, preferring to pursue a life of work outside of the home for which many are eminently able and qualified. Even in the nineteenth century, when there were few opportunities to test the extent of women's abilities in many fields of education or vocation, Mill points to numerous individual examples of women's exemplary talents and performance in fields like government. The notable talents of women who govern well when circumstances have permitted (examples of Queen Elizabeth I and Queen Victoria serve well) rebut any general claims about their lack of ability to perform tasks generally reserved for male privilege.

Mill's limited imagination on the question of the sexual division of labor is all the more surprising and puzzling when we compare his diagnosis of the ills and barriers to self-development of working-class men and of women. Many of their ills are traced back to similar deprivations in social and political conditions needed for development and self-development. Both groups are plagued by social injustice, by having their self-development thwarted by systemic social conditions that hamper their well-being and force them into conditions of dependency and servitude to masters. The prescriptions for their liberation also start in the same soil of liberal values and agendas. Yet without good reason, his vision of women's future prospects is more compressed. In his chapter "On the Probable Futurity of the Labouring Classes," Mill starts off with a direct comparison of the condition of working-class men and women according to the theory of dependency which he rejects as a conservative throwback and rationalization for injustice. Mill is quite scornful of the corruption underlying the rationalizations of the class and gender privileges. He says that, according to the theory of dependence,

> the lot of the poor, in all things which affect them collectively, should be regulated *for* them, not *by* them . . . It is supposed to be the duty of the higher classes to think for them, and to take the responsibility of their lot . . . The relation between rich and poor, according to this theory (a theory also applied to the relation between men and women) . . . should be amiable, moral, and sentimental: affectionate tutelage on the one side, respectful and grateful deference on the other. The rich should be *in loco parentis* to the poor. (CW 3:759)

What is actually needed, he says, is protection by *laws*, not reliance upon the good will of supposed protectors who are often anything but compassionate and loving. "The brutality and tyranny with which every police report is filled, are those of husbands to wives, of parents to children" (CW 3:761). In the case of the working class, he believes that the patriarchal system of government has had its death knell with the education of workers. Now the era of their dependence is drawing to a close, as their independence increases. Their future well-being from now on rests upon their prospects for education and mental development, according to Mill. He is hopeful for radical changes in their conditions. The parallels between the diagnosis of and remedy for the harms to workers and women continue, and then they abruptly end. Workers' condition of dependency will become more and more intolerable, until self-government becomes the only acceptable option for them. Along with increased political independence, the increasing economic independence, of choosing a wider range of occupations, will be part of the new era. This applies also to women's economic independence, and Mill repeats his contention that occupations should be equally open to all classes and genders.

> The same reasons which make it no longer necessary that the poor should depend on the rich, make it equally unnecessary that women should depend on men; and the least which justice requires is that law and custom should not enforce dependence . . . by ordaining that a woman . . . shall have scarcely any means open to her of gaining a livelihood, except as a wife and mother. Let women who prefer that occupation, adopt it; but that there should be no option . . . for the great majority of women . . . is a flagrant social injustice. (CW 3:765)

Yet he does not notice his lapse of allowing women only limited options of occupation as wife and mother and occupation (apart from marriage) of working for wages outside the home. It is laudable that he notably classifies domestic work as an occupation, and it is a common feminist objection to patriarchal attitudes that the unpaid work that women do inside the home is invisible, unrecognized, and not factored into the economy. But Mill's unwillingness to follow his own logic, to extend the occupational freedom of various combinations of working within and working without the home to both sexes, remains contentious and deeply puzzling. Whether it springs from failure of logic and vision or from his decision that extending the argument to its obvious conclusion would be too inflammatory and counterproductive, Mill's arguments seem deficient to twenty-first-century eyes. This is all the more the case since he foresees unlimited horizons for the future of the working class, including the possible dismantling of capitalist relations of production in favor of a kind of democratic socialism featuring worker cooperatives.

However, there is no doubt concerning the power and eloquence of the main lines of argument in *The Subjection of Women* as an analysis of the harms of patriarchy and of the benefits of sexual equality and emancipation.

notes

1 See, for example, Keith Burgess-Jackson, "John Stuart Mill, Radical Feminist," in Morales 2005, 71–97; Morales 2007.
2 For recent discussions of Mill's views on the family, gender equality, and marriage see: Morales 1996; Morales 2005, in particular essays by Mary Lyndon Shanley, "Marital Slavery and Friendship: John Stuart Mill's *The Subjection of Women*," 52–70, Susan Mendus, "The Marriage of True Minds: The Ideal of Marriage in the Philosophy of John Stuart Mill," 135–56, and Nadia Urbinati, "John Stuart Mill on Androgyny and Ideal Marriage," 157–82.
3 See, for example, Okin 1979, 197–230; Pateman 1988.

further reading

Di Stefano, Christine, "John Stuart Mill: The Heart of Liberalism," in Christine Di Stefano, ed., *Configurations of Masculinity: A Feminist Perspective on Modern Political Theory* (Ithaca: Cornell University Press, 1991), 144–86.

Eisenstein, Zillah, *The Radical Future of Liberal Feminism* (New York: Longman, 1981).

Makus, Ingrid, *Women, Politics, and Reproduction: The Liberal Legacy* (Toronto: University of Toronto Press, 1996).

Mill, John Stuart, Harriet Taylor Mill, and Helen Taylor, *Sexual Equality*, ed. Ann P. Robson and John M. Robson (Toronto: University of Toronto Press, 1994).

Morales, Maria, *Perfect Equality: John Stuart Mill on Well-Constituted Communities* (Lanham, MD: Rowman and Littlefield, 1996).

Morales, Maria, ed., *Mill's "The Subjection of Women": Critical Essays* (Lanham, MD: Rowman and Littlefield, 2005).

Okin, Susan Moller, *Women in Western Political Thought* (Princeton: Princeton University Press, 1979).

Pateman, Carole, *The Sexual Contract* (Stanford: Stanford University Press, 1988).

Rossi, Alice, "Sentiment and Intellect: The Story of John Stuart Mill and Harriet Taylor Mill," in Alice Rossi, ed., *Essays on Sex Equality* (Chicago: University of Chicago Press, 1970), 3–63.

Shanley, Mary Lyndon, "The Subjection of Women," in John Skorupski, ed., *The Cambridge Companion to Mill* (Cambridge: Cambridge University Press, 1998).

Wendy Donner

environmental ethics

Green Mill?

Mill's attitude towards nature is ambivalent. His well-known essay "Nature" expresses some core commitments that are clearly human-centered, and he does not hesitate to call for human intervention in the environment when he thinks that this will lead to reducing the harms caused by nature or that it will bring clear improvements to the human condition (CW 10:372–402). In this essay Mill rejects the view that nature provides a guide for human moral conduct. Because of the harms wrought by nature, Mill refuses to accept that there is a moral order in nature that humans should follow. However, this essay sets out only one aspect of his environmental ethics and in other writings he expresses a positive and even exalted view of the natural environment and the human–nature connection. The natural environment has an inspiring effect on humans and encounters with nature are powerful sources of experiences that nurture aesthetic, emotional, and moral cultivation. Mill was an avid walker, and much of his home schooling under the tutelage of his father James Mill took place literally on his feet, as student and teacher discussed his readings and studies during their walks in nature. Mill's accounts in the journals of his walking tours show the great pleasure and inspiration he derived from his connection with nature. Natural beauty also played a significant role in aiding his recovery from his period of depression and emotional crisis. Daily walks in nature were a constant feature of his life. He was an amateur botanist and he collected and classified plant specimens.

His connections with Romantic poets, most prominently William Wordsworth and Samuel Taylor Coleridge, had a deep and enduring impact which finds voice in his perspective on the positive role of nature as provider and sustenance for some of the most valuable and enduring kinds of happiness. Romantic poetry often takes nature as its subject, and Mill expresses his susceptibility to the pleasures of reading poetry with this focus. His reflections about the effects of encounters with great natural beauty reverberate throughout his writings. Yet his positive appreciation of nature has limits, set out by his basic philosophical commitments to empiricism and to a value theory that takes intrinsic value to be located in states of consciousness. Mill is not anthropocentric, or human-centered, as this term is used in the literature. Both he and Bentham notably extend the circle of moral standing to include those non-human animals capable of experiencing pain and pleasure. But he does not accept the view of radical environmentalism that nature has intrinsic value in itself, apart from human consciousness. Nor does he agree with one radical environmentalist argument that human intervention in the environment ought to be severely limited in order to preserve wilderness. However, he certainly agrees that the intervention ought to be held in check and moderated, and in this regard he parts company with many of his fellow nineteenth-century economic theorists. He does not see the good in destroying the environment in order to pander to the materialism and greed of those who are already wealthy by any reasonable standard. His theory offers a middle way between the anti-environmentalist Lockean perspective that maintains that nature is only a collection of natural resources and the radical environmentalist position that claims untouched nature has intrinsic value. Mill's commitments allow for robust defense of limits to human intervention in the natural environment. Both Mill and John Locke believe that nature does not have intrinsic value. But this leaves room for a broad range of perspectives, some more enlightened and environmentally friendly than others.

In the essay "Nature," Mill expresses clearly the boundaries of his positive attitudes towards the environment. Indeed, if the essay is read on its own, one could conclude that Mill is no advocate for the environment. But the essay is just one piece of the picture, and its context is important. Its expressed purpose is to critique arguments of some specific opponents. The argument is part of one of three essays on religion. His intention is to respond to Natural Law theories of the cosmos, and to counter certain arguments from design used to bolster natural law arguments for the existence of God or intelligent design in the universe. Some of his arguments are quite heated, yet they express his views concerning the place of environmental ethics within the context of his Art of Life, which has the goal of promoting good for sentient beings (including many non-human animals) who are capable of experiences of happiness or suffering. His argument is that nature does not provide a guide to moral conduct for humans, contra the claims of Natural Law theorists. Mill distinguishes two main senses of nature. "In one sense, it means all the powers existing in either the outer or the inner world and everything which takes place by means of those powers. In another sense, it means, not everything which happens, but only what takes place without the agency, or without the voluntary and intentional agency, of man" (CW 10:375).

In *The Subjection of Women*, recall, Mill argues vehemently against the notion of ideas concerning what is "natural" or "unnatural" for women and men. He argues there that notions of the natural are generally cloaks or code for what is merely conventional or customary. In that work, he directs his attack at those who invoke "the natural" to prop up patriarchal ideas about what is or is not suitable for women. In the essay "Nature" he widens the scope of this interrogation of "the natural." He notes that his objective is "to inquire into the truth of the doctrines which make Nature a test of right and wrong, good and evil, or which in any mode or degree attach merit or approval to following, imitating, or obeying Nature" (CW 10:378). He opposes arguments that people should "conform" to Nature. In the first sense above, we cannot avoid doing this, because all action must conform to the laws of nature and it is physically impossible to do otherwise. Nor could anyone reasonably dispute that it is rational to study nature, to understand its properties and how these can promote or obstruct our ends. This is the essence of intelligent action. However, such conformity to physical laws is not what Natural Law theorists have in mind. Natural Law theorists regard the rule to conform to nature as a moral norm, not a prudential norm. They refer to the other sense of Nature, "that in which Nature stands distinguished from Art, and denotes, not the whole course of the phenomena which come under our observation, but only their spontaneous course" (CW 10:380). This is Nature as spontaneous and outside of human intervention. Some environmentalists say that we should not interfere in the spontaneous workings of nature, that we should leave wilderness areas be. This environmental perspective enjoins limiting our intervention, or even leaving zones of wilderness alone, although we obviously must alter other areas of nature in order to meet necessities of life. It is degree of interference that is at issue. The dispute concerning the proper degree of intervention in nature is sprawling and complex. And certainly in some contexts Mill invokes the distinction between the spontaneous and organic and the robotic and machine-like, praising the former and disparaging the latter. In the essay "Nature," however, Mill's immediate concern is with the claim that we should "let nature be our guide" in a very general way. He says that it is patently absurd to claim that we should follow Nature in this general sense.

> If the natural course of things were perfectly right and satisfactory, to act at all would be a gratuitous meddling, which as it could not make things better, must make them worse . . . If the artificial is not better than the natural, to what end are all the arts of life? To dig, to plough, to build, to wear clothes, are direct infringements of the injunction to follow nature. (CW 10:380–81)

This, says Mill, is simply going too far, as we all approve of many triumphs over nature's capacity to cause harm. For example, we approve of draining marshes, using lightning rods to deflect electricity, building embankments to prevent flooding, and so on. Nature is often the antagonist and enemy of humans. "All praise of Civilization, or Art, or Contrivance, is so much dispraise of Nature; an admission of imperfection, which it is man's business, and merit, to be always endeavouring to correct or mitigate" (CW 10:381). The truth is that all action to improve the human condition alters the spontaneous workings of nature. But we cannot maintain human life without such interferences.

So this extreme interpretation will not do. Mill also critiques the related view that we can observe the workings of Providence in the order of Nature. He attacks the notion of the sublime, so prevalent in the nineteenth century, as encouraging "natural prejudices." Certain natural feelings can intrude and interfere with sound judgment. Encounters with nature inspire feelings of astonishment and awe. However, we would err if we were to conclude that the natural phenomena which engender awe based on their vastness or power furnish models of moral conduct for emulation. Impressive natural phenomena such as hurricanes, mountain peaks, vast deserts or oceans, or the solar system inspire feelings of sublimity and wonder in the face of this grandeur.

> But a little interrogation of our own consciousness will suffice to convince us, that what makes these phenomena so impressive is simply their vastness . . . the feeling it inspires is of a totally different character from admiration of excellence. Those in whom awe produces admiration may be aesthetically developed, but they are morally uncultivated. It is one of the endowments of the imaginative part of our mental nature that conceptions of greatness and power, vividly realized, produce a feeling which though in its higher degrees closely bordering on pain, we prefer to most of what are accounted pleasures. But we are quite equally capable of experiencing this feeling towards maleficent power. (CW 10:384)

Nature embodies also the sort of recklessness that would be pronounced criminal in human conduct. Nature exhibits shocking disregard for human life and well-being. Is nature a model for human moral conduct? This cannot be reasonably maintained for "in sober truth, nearly all the things which men are hanged or imprisoned for doing to one another, are nature's every day performances" (CW 10:385). Nature kills in horrific ways, and frequently. Hurricanes, locusts, fires, diseases, and numerous other calamities are nature's regular offerings. Improvements consist of overcoming natural calamities. In sum, "the duty of man is to co-operate with the beneficent powers, not by imitating but by perpetually striving to amend the course of nature" (CW 10:402).

This is one piece of the picture. But we get another and quite different perspective from Mill's reflections on the destructive human penchant for constant growth and endless cycles of "more, more, more" which imprudently and insensitively harm nature and threaten nature's ability to provide the source of some of the most enduring and uplifting joys and human experiences.

In contemporary dialogues on environmental ethics, Mill is often portrayed as a friend of the green movement and an exemplar of enlightened and progressive attitudes towards the natural environment. In his economic writings, he argues against the idea that continual economic growth furnishes good means to promote human well-being. He argues instead that a stationary state of growth in which both economic growth and human population reach a state of equilibrium is better for promoting happiness. Mill had long-standing concerns about overpopulation and participated in activist programs, including campaigns for birth control that had as their goal to contain human population so that the imprint would not engender environmental destruction. He stands out as a positive example for environmentalists, and is often contrasted in this regard with John Locke, whom environmentalists consider to personify the attitudes that have provoked the current environmental crisis. Mill is an early advocate of sustainable development. He advocates forms of sustainable agriculture. He supports individual peasant proprietors and families working in small-scale farming, in many cases in preference to larger-scale entrepreneurial farming businesses.

Mill's conception of human nature grounds his views about economic activity within the Art of Life. C. B. Macpherson explores the history of liberalism and its core notion of individualism. The examination illuminates some of the grounds for Mill's more progressive stance. Mill rejects the notion of possessive individualism which permeates earlier liberal thought from the time of Thomas Hobbes to that of Bentham and James Mill. This earlier notion regards human nature as primarily acquisitive, as concerned with and even addicted to acquiring more and more material possessions. Humans are regarded as being proprietors of their own persons, and thus their persons can be conceived of as commodities. Market relations permeate and infiltrate all human relations. Macpherson argues that the earlier forms of liberalism, beginning with Hobbes, rely upon a model of human nature in which people are essentially "a bundle of appetites demanding satisfaction" (Macpherson 1984, 4). Humans have infinite desires and rational conduct lies in "unlimited individual appropriation, as a means of satisfying unlimited desire for utilities" (5). Locke's famous dictum sums it up. Locke claims that

> every man has a *property* in his own *person* . . . The *labour* of his body, and the *work* of his hands, we may say, are properly his. Whatsoever then he removes out of the state that nature hath provided, and left it in, he hath mixed his *labour* with, and joined to it something that is his own, and thereby makes it his *property*. (Locke [1689] 1980, 19)

Nature in itself, according to Locke, is almost worthless, requiring human labor to add and create value. Human needs are supplied by work and industry, and God has commanded us to labor. "God and his reason commanded him to subdue the earth, i.e. improve it for the benefit of life, and therein lay out something upon it that was his own, his labour" (21). Whatever part of nature we leave untouched by human labor simply lies in waste. The combination of ideas that untouched nature is wasted, that only labor adds value, and that human beings are characterized by limitless desires to appropriate and consume have lethal consequences for the environment. Mill rejects the stance that humans are primarily consumers. "Man is essentially not a consumer and appropriator . . . but an exerter and developer and enjoyer of his capacities" (Macpherson 1980, 48). The human capacity for relationship and connection extends beyond our species. Humans are not atomistic and separate, as the communitarian critique claims liberalism asserts them to be, but they are interconnected with other humans, other animals, and with their environment. They are individuals, but they are also relational and social beings.

In the *Principles of Political Economy*, Mill expresses his distaste for the view of humans as selfish, competitive consumers and appropriators, which is the essence of the model of possessive individualism.

> I confess I am not charmed with the ideal of life held out by those who think that the normal state of human beings is that of struggling to get on; that the trampling, crushing, elbowing, and treading on each other's heels, which form the existing type of social life, are the most desirable lot of human kind . . .
> . . . those who do not accept the present very early stage of human improvement as its ultimate type, may be excused for being comparatively indifferent to the kind of economic progress which excites the congratulations of ordinary politicians; the mere increase of production and accumulation. (CW 3:754–5)

Mill writes a passage which, almost on its own, has made his reputation as an environmentally friendly philosopher. He expresses his skepticism about the benefits of ever-increasing human population. He says that the human species has already reached the level of population needed to secure the benefits accruing from social cooperation and connectivity. He adds that even under conditions in which there is enough food, clothing, and shelter for all, there can still be undesirable crowding of the sort that does not permit solitude. The effect is to cramp the human spirit and to crush the environment.

> It is not good for man to be kept perforce at all times in the presence of his species. A world from which solitude is extirpated, is a very poor ideal. Solitude, in the sense of being often alone, is essential to any depth of

meditation or of character; and solitude in the presence of natural beauty and grandeur, is the cradle of thoughts and aspirations which are not only good for the individual, but which society could ill do without. Nor is there much satisfaction in contemplating the world with nothing left to the spontaneous activity of nature; with every rood of land brought into cultivation, which is capable of growing food for human beings; every flowery waste or natural pasture ploughed up, all quadrupeds or birds which are not domesticated for man's use exterminated as his rivals for food, every hedgerow or superfluous tree rooted out, and scarcely a place left where a wild shrub or flower could grow without being eradicated as a weed in the name of improved agriculture. If the earth must lose that great portion of its pleasantness which it owes to things that the unlimited increase of wealth and population would extirpate from it, for the mere purpose of enabling it to support a larger, but not a better or a happier population, I sincerely hope, for the sake of posterity, that they will be content to be stationary, long before necessity compels them to it. (CW 3:756)

Mill argues that a stationary state of population and economy would not result in stagnating human progress and happiness; quite the reverse. Mental and moral progress and culture would be freed up by the release from being "engrossed by the art of getting on." The Art of Living would thrive and prosper. Economic arts and sciences could be channeled into their progressive forms to "produce their legitimate effect, that of abridging labour." Up to this time, inventions had not in the least reduced the working day or the drudgery of workers, but had only increased the fortunes of the wealthy. "Only when, in addition to just institutions, the increase of mankind shall be under the deliberate guidance of judicious foresight, can the conquests made from the powers of nature by the intellect and energy of scientific discoverers, become the common property of the species, and the means of improving and elevating the universal lot" (CW 3:756–7).

Mill argues that the stationary state would be better for all concerned: better for humans and better for the environment. He cannot accept the rampant materialism of his own society. "I know not why it should be matter of congratulation that persons who are already richer than anyone needs to be, should have doubled their means of consuming things which give little or no pleasure except as representative of wealth" (CW 3:755). What is needed, rather, is a better means of distribution of the wealth already accumulated. Control of the level of human population is a crucial means both for reducing excessive impact on the natural environment and for providing more equitable and adequate wages and resources to all workers. His stance recognizes the connection between reduction of poverty and inequality within human society and control of human destruction and unnecessary intervention into the natural environment. In this insight he agrees with many environmental activists and theorists who argue that inequality and forms of oppression and exploitation that are internal to human societies, such as those based upon gender, class, or race, are often mirrored in human activities which play out in their exploitation and oppression of the natural environment.

Mill and Radical Environmentalism

On balance thus far, Mill appears to be an environmentally friendly philosopher, with some provisos and limits. He argues for preserving the environment when its resources are not needed to supply important human needs. He lambastes materialism and greed as vices that are driving forces behind much environmental destruction. He holds a conception of human nature that rejects possessive individualism and makes generous provision for human respect and appreciation of the environment. However, it is still an open question whether these environmentally friendly elements of his theory satisfy the threshold demands of some current environmental theories which insist that a much stronger basis is needed to respect nature and protect it from human encroachment. Many contemporary environmental theories argue that nature has value in itself and that the recognition of nature as a locus of intrinsic value is necessary in order effectively to preserve it. Something has instrumental value if it is valuable only as means to an intrinsically valuable end. Something which is intrinsically valuable is good in itself, and not merely as a means to a further end or in relation to something else. This environmentalist argument claims that if nature is seen as having merely instrumental value, then the temptation to intervene and deplete it will overpower any arguments to leave it alone. Prudence and enlightened self-interest do not provide sufficiently strong motivation to guarantee conduct that will preserve and respect nature.

Mill is no radical environmentalist. His attitudes are progressive, especially for their time, but he did not make the leap of acknowledging that the natural environment has intrinsic value on its own, apart from any connection to consciousness. Opponents of radical environmentalism can respond that regarding the environment as having only instrumental value is not a recipe for or an invitation to environmental destruction. Adopting attitudes of enlightened prudence and a sense of stewardship towards nature on behalf of future generations would go a long way towards its protection. In addition, much hangs upon the kind of means and ends we have in mind when considering the usefulness of the natural environment. One scenario occurs when we regard the environment as being merely a collection of natural resources which by their very usage are consumed. Intervention and depletion under such a scenario are unavoidable. But there are alternative scenarios. If we regard the natural

Wendy Donner

environment as the source of aesthetic and spiritual experiences which are useful or even irreplaceable for some kinds of cultivation of the excellences, then we will avoid interventions which destroy nature and the possibility of such uplifting and morally regenerative encounters in the future. Mill connects moral and emotional development with opportunities to experience natural beauty which tend to elevate feelings and cultivate imagination. Imagination nurtures sympathy and empathy, which are important abilities for morality and virtue. We will have strong reasons to leave nature untouched, because such experiences are crucial to well-being. These regenerative encounters with the environment can be described as a kind of human use of the environment, but of a different order than those uses which consume it. These are non-consumptive uses of the environment, and they are not destructive of nature, since nature must be preserved for such encounters to occur at all.

Mill clearly is unable to advocate that nature has value in itself, apart from any relation to appreciating consciousness, since he is bound by his theoretical commitments to restrict value to those states of consciousness. However, the form of qualitative hedonism that he maintains has resources to bridge the gap between radical environmentalism and consciousness-based theories of value. These resources are not available to advocates of quantitative hedonism who claim that quantity is the only characteristic of states of consciousness that matters for value. Quality or kind of satisfaction matters in Mill's qualitative theory, and this commitment opens up a further channel to ground respect for nature.

Radical environmentalists maintain that stewardship and enlightened self-interest or prudence will not suffice. The human attitude towards nature under these human-centered accounts induces alienation and separation from nature, when what is needed is interconnection and relation with nature, both for human benefit and nature's integrity. However, Mill's qualitative hedonism does offer means for recognizing value in the significant human relationship with the environment. To inquire into how well this bridges the gap, I turn to environmental philosopher Baird Callicott's projectivist or relational account of value. Mill's theory cannot do as much as Callicott's for deepening the human–nature connection, but Mill's philosophy has the resources to go part of the way with Callicott's. Certainly his theory can do more than quantitative hedonism allows.

Callicott explains a key tenet of his projectivist account of value.

> [T]he *source* of all value is human consciousness, but it by no means follows that the *locus* of all value is consciousness itself or a mode of consciousness like reason, pleasure, or knowledge. In other words, something may be valuable only because someone values it, but it may also be valued for itself, not for the sake of any subjective experience (pleasure, knowledge,

aesthetic satisfaction, and so forth) it may afford the valuer . . . An intrinsic-ally valuable thing on this reading is valuable *for* its own sake, *for* itself, but it is not valuable in itself, that is, completely independently of any con-sciousness, since no value can, in principle . . . be altogether independent of a valuing consciousness. (Callicott 1989, 133–4)

According to this account, it is as though value is projected onto the environment by appreciative consciousness. Although consciousness is necessary for there to be value, on Callicott's view the *locus* of the value is actually in nature, and nature is not valued simply because it provides pleasure to the appreciative consciousness. The object of appreciation, nature, is now valued for itself, and not as a means to anything further. The projection metaphor is somewhat misleading. Perhaps it is more accurate and helpful to say that according to this view value is embedded in the relationship between consciousness and the object of its appre-ciation. According to the radical environmentalist perspective, the degree of value present will depend upon the quality of the relationship between appreciating consciousness and nature. The highest degree of value will be present when the appreciating consciousness is know-ledgeable about the environment and properly emotionally attuned and responsive, and when the environment is relatively untouched by human intervention.

Mill can go part of the way with this relational account. It goes too far, according to his theory, to make nature the locus of value. But con-sideration of the quality of the relationship between consciousness and nature can be built into his qualitative hedonism. Mill argues that kind is a good-making property of happiness. The kind of enjoyment affects the assessment of its value. While the specific discussion of kinds often focuses upon the kinds that consist of the exercise of the human virtues, such as intellectual, aesthetic, or compassionate enjoyments, on closer look Mill actually has a looser notion of kinds. Kinds of satisfaction can be classified by the faculty affected, but kinds can also be classified by the cause of the satisfaction as well as by phenomenal features of the experience. This amplifies the manner in which the human–nature relation can affect value. If a satisfaction is one of connection or engross-ment in natural beauty and untouched nature, then this impacts its value. An authentic, appreciative, and knowledgeable encounter with the environment is a spur to some of the most uplifting, regenerative, and contemplative states of awareness, so much so that in Mill's mind they are the basis for what Romantics experience as transcendental and mystical forms of tranquility, bliss, and awe.

Thus Mill's theory has interesting resources for lifting the value of knowledgeable, sensitively attuned responses to natural beauty. Accord-ing to his theory, the human–nature relation enters into the evaluation

Wendy Donner

of happiness. The relation must be authentic, not fake. If we lack the basics of ecological understanding, then we will not appreciate the difference between the beauty of pristine wilderness and the kitsch of an artificial environment that has been devastated and then reconstructed by human enterprise. If we are knowledgeable about the difference between authentic and artificial nature, the educative process leading to this ecological understanding will likely have engendered know-ledge and appreciation for spontaneous, untrammeled natural beauty. Habituation in the virtues of wisdom and compassion is the best guar-antee of their continued development and exercise. Habituation in the emotional, aesthetic, and imaginative virtues engendered by direct encounters with natural beauty produce similar results.

Mill and Romanticism

Mill's relationship to Romanticism is very complex, and a thorough examination is beyond the scope of this work. My aims here are limited. I explore his relationship with the Romantic poet Wordsworth in order to illustrate some key aspects of this connection as it clarifies his envir-onmental ethics. Mill's ambivalence towards the natural environment parallels his ambivalence towards Wordsworth. In his *Autobiography* Mill documents the important role that Wordsworth and his poetry played in his recovery from the "mental crisis." It is apparent that Mill feels deeply indebted to Wordsworth and his poetry for aiding his recov-ery from depression. Wordsworth's influence played a significant role in Mill's expansion and reweaving of his philosophy in the ensuing period. Mill even goes as far as to describe himself as a "Wordsworthian" during one phase of the reconstruction of his philosophy. Yet despite this Mill draws clear boundaries around the areas of Wordsworth's philosophy that he thinks are reasonable and acceptable; he will not be drawn beyond the limits set by his empiricism and associationist psychology.

Mill describes his time of mental and emotional crisis and recovery in the *Autobiography* as an "important transformation in my opinions and character" (CW 1:137). It began as an episode of depression that he attributed to defects and severe limitations in his own childhood private education. Although he had been thoroughly prepared by his father James Mill to inherit the mantle of utilitarianism, to carry forward the utilitarian philosophy and be a "reformer of the world," he came to realize that this education had been very constricted (CW 1:137). He describes himself at that time as being like "a mere reasoning machine" (CW 1:111). He frequently draws a distinction between living, organic, spontaneous beings and machines and robots. Organic language and metaphors figure prominently in descriptions of the positive personality traits of spontaneity and energy; correspondingly he deflates "machine-like" passivity as unworthy.

He describes the onset of his emotional crisis as being like an awakening from a dream and as resembling "the state . . . in which converts to Methodism usually are, when smitten by their first 'conviction of sin'" (CW 1:137). His deployment of noticeably religious language to describe the process raises interesting questions. He invokes the language of spiritual crisis and regeneration and depicts the process as transformative and involving a conversion. Mill was acutely aware of the effects of the excessive rationalism of his education and the emotional deadness that was its result. He laments that he was left "without any real desire for the ends which I had been so carefully fitted out to work for: no delight in virtue or the general good" (CW 1:143). Although he explains that his crisis was silent and undetectable to those around him, his anguish was severe. He uses lines from "Dejection: an Ode" by Coleridge to describe his state:

> A grief without a pang, void, dark and drear,
> A drowsy, stifled, unimpassioned grief,
> Which finds no natural outlet or relief
> In word, or sigh, or tear.
> (CW 1:139)

The impact of Mill's subsequent realization of the lingering effects of certain aspects of his childhood education, particularly its excessive rationalism and denigration of emotion, reverberate throughout his writing. "I, for the first time, gave its proper place, among the prime necessities of human well-being, to the internal culture of the individual . . . The cultivation of the feelings became one of the cardinal points in my ethical and philosophical creed" (CW 1:147). When he recovered his ability to feel, he recognized that emotional sensibility furnished "some of the material out of which all worth of character, and all capacity for happiness, are made" (CW 1:145). Poetry had provided the resources for his retrieval of feeling, but he subsequently arrived at the conviction that poetry was a universal source of an especially valuable form of enjoyment. Reading poetry also helps in developing sympathetic imagination, which is a core trait of moral development. Natural beauty was the subject of Wordsworth's poetry and Mill believed that this was the key to its success in engaging and engendering emotional sensibility and responsiveness. Wordsworth has meditative inclinations. He has the habit of combining nature and feeling as subjects, and thus each subject reinforces the other. From his poetry "I seemed to draw from a source of inward joy, of sympathetic and imaginative pleasure, which could be shared in by all human beings" (CW 1:151). The source of joy was universal, perennial, and reliable. The poetry was personally therapeutic, but this kind of higher pleasure was general and available to anyone. Those who portray Mill as a prime booster for the high value of intellectual pleasures overlook his strong appreciation of emotional pleasures, especially those with the combined source of poetry and nature as subject. Wordsworth's *Lyrical Ballads* of 1815 furnished exactly what he needed at the time. Primarily, this was because

> these poems addressed themselves powerfully to one of the strongest of my pleasurable susceptibilities, the love of rural objects and natural scenery to which I had been indebted . . . for much of the pleasure of my life . . . What made Wordsworth's poems a medicine for my state of mind, was that they expressed, not mere outward beauty, but states of feeling, and of thought coloured by feeling, under the excitement of beauty. They seemed to be the very culture of the feelings, which I was in quest of . . . I needed to be made to feel that there was real, permanent happiness in tranquil contemplation. (CW 1:151, 153)

Although his portrayal of this process uses religious language of conversion, sin, transformation, and quest, Mill does not interpret his experiences using a religious framework. Instead, he views them entirely within the empiricist framework of thought, feeling, and perception. In so doing, he draws firm boundaries and disdainfully rejects the theological metaphysics which underlies Wordsworth's Romantic poetry. Although his rationalism had been shattered and he lived through a period that he describes as a conversion, he only allowed this process to go so far.

In his period of recovery, Mill discovered that Wordsworth had also suffered through a similar emotional crisis "that he also had felt that the first freshness of youthful enjoyment in life was not lasting" (CW 1:153). In fact, Mill's experience paralleled the Wordsworthian "crisis-autobiography," which can be explored as an example of writing about religious transformation and regeneration. M. H. Abrams argues that Wordsworth regarded himself as adopting the role of the poet-prophet who has undertaken the task of interpreting for his age "the Christian pattern of the fall, the redemption, and the emergence of a new earth which will constitute a restored paradise" (Abrams 1971, 29). This fall occurred because humans became separated and alienated from nature, and redemption will come from reconciliation with nature. Abrams interprets Wordsworth's account of his recovery as resulting from an interaction between mind and nature. Human suffering will be removed and the union of mind and nature will overcome our alienation from nature and restore paradise on earth (113). Wordsworth is commonly regarded as being a "nature mystic" and Mill certainly sees him in this light. In Wordsworth's worldview, nature is not simply an object of beauty. It is also a source of mystical and transcendental experiences and forms of awareness. As well, the transformative processes resulting from encounters with natural beauty have an underlying spiritual dimension. They are not only uplifting, but they can also lead to enlightenment. Wordsworth adopted the two categories of the beautiful and the sublime for classifying experiences and valuations of natural scenes. Abrams explains the categories. "By and large the beautiful is small in scale, orderly and tranquil, effects pleasure in the observer, and is associated with love; while the sublime is vast (hence suggestive of infinity), wild, tumultuous, and awful, is associated with pain, and evokes ambivalent feelings of terror and admiration" (98).

I noted previously Mill's dismissal of the interpretation of "the sublime" as pointing to transcendental or mystical experiences. Mill's attitude towards Wordsworth is ambivalent; he separates Wordsworth the poet from Wordsworth the metaphysician and assesses these two personas very differently. His evaluation of Wordsworth very much reflects his own empiricist commitments.

Mill has strong praise for Wordsworth the poet. On January 30, 1829, Mill took part in a debate on the topic "Wordsworth and Byron" with John Sterling and John Roebuck at the London Debating Society. This event was a turning point (CW 26:434–42). Calling himself a "Wordsworthian," he declared publicly an important change in his way of thinking (CW 1:153). He dissented strongly from Roebuck on the question of the importance of cultivating feeling and he complained that his friend could not acknowledge that development of feeling has value as an aid in character formation. Describing the event in the *Autobiography* Mill says that Roebuck

> wished that his feelings should be deadened rather than quickened . . . He saw little good in any cultivation of the feelings, and none at all in cultivating them through the imagination, which he thought was only cultivating illusions. It was in vain I urged on him that the imaginative emotion which an idea when vividly conceived excites in us, is not an illusion but a fact, as real as any of the other qualities of objects; [and does not imply] anything erroneous and delusive in our mental apprehension of the object. (CW 1:157)

Mill's notes for this speech reveal the depth of the division between himself and Roebuck. Mill invokes his doctrine of self-development and his test based upon competent acquaintance. He draws a clear line between those whom he believes are and are not entitled to claim to be adequately informed on the question under debate. His notes are sharp and pointed.

> Begin . . . by reprehending any attempt to turn Wordsworth into ridicule . . . I am perfectly willing to refer all my ideas on this subject to the verdict of

those among my audience, and no doubt there are many, who are my equals or my superiors in intellectual and moral cultivation. But I cannot consent [*page ripped*] those the judges of it, whom I consider as my inferiors in both. (CW 26:434–5)

In this speech and in several essays on literary criticism, Mill emphasizes Wordsworth's superior talent for describing nature and its effect upon human feelings in such a manner that this indeed aids cultivation and elevation of feeling and imagination. Poetry's ability to evoke tranquility is highly prized. One role of the poet is to cultivate taste in the audience and this task includes educating readers to appreciate emotion. The noble end of poetry is its role in "acting upon the desires and characters of mankind through their emotions, to raise them towards the perfection of their nature" (CW 1:414).

Mill looks to Wordsworth as the guide for learning how to cultivate elevated feeling, but he sets clear boundaries to the counsel he accepts. In his debating speech he says "I have learned from Wordsworth that it is possible by dwelling on certain ideas to keep up a constant freshness in the emotions which objects excite . . . to connect cheerful and joyous states of mind with almost every object" (CW 26:441). It is noteworthy that the variant reading for "dwelling on certain ideas" in the above passage is "a proper regulation of the associations" (CW 26:441). This signals that Mill regards associationist psychology as a key tool for analyzing how poetry works to affect its readers' emotions. He wants to avoid any recourse to unruly metaphysical claims.

Setting limits to the changes and upheavals in his thought, Mill couples his strong praise for Wordsworth the poet with equally strong rejection of Wordsworth the philosopher and metaphysician. According to Mill, there is a difference between describing feelings, for which Wordsworth has superior talent, and being able to analyze them, which he does badly.

If people tell me then of his exaggeration and mystification of this, his talking of holding communion with the great forms of nature . . . I allow that this is nonsense but the introduction of this into the present question is charging Wordsworth the poet with the faults of Wordsworth the metaphysician . . . [T]he tendency of a man who by a long indulgence of particular trains of association, has connected certain feelings with things which excite no such feelings in other men, if he then attempts to explain is very likely to go into mysticism . . . he looks *beyond* them and conceives something spiritual and ideal in them which the mind's eye only can see – witness the mysticism of devotion – communion with God etc. (CW 26:440)

Mill contends that his own associationist psychology is adequate for the task of analyzing the lofty ideas that Wordsworth mistakenly believes have religious sources. John Ruskin also links these lofty ideas to theological origins. Mill examines Ruskin's analysis of the idea of the sublime in order to counter his appeal to religious metaphysics. Mill has a substitute analysis based upon empiricist associationist psychology. Whether the associationist explanation for the lofty ideas of the sublime is convincing is an interesting question to ponder.

Mill sets out his views on associationism in editorial footnotes to the second edition (1869) of his father James Mill's *Analysis of the Phenomena of the Human Mind* (Mill, James, [1869] 1967).[1] In these editorial footnotes, Mill attempts to account for the imposing character and loftiness of the ideas and feelings of the sublime. Ruskin argues in *Modern Painters* that the lofty ideas are "embodied in the universe, and correspond to the various perfections of its Creator" (CW 31:224).[2] According to Mill's way of thinking, this claim is another variant of the ideas that he disputes in the essay "Nature." These ideas of the sublime, Mill admits, are more complex and imposing than our ordinary ideas and feelings. Yet, he says, while Ruskin is quite successful in making out his case, he believes that associationism can provide an alternative analysis of these elevated ideas. Since complex ideas often do not resemble the simpler ideas out of which they are generated through the operations of psychological laws of association, the lofty feelings of supposedly mystical experiences of nature can be perfectly well explained using other ordinary ideas and feelings. Mill offers the general claim that "the things which excite the emotions of beauty or sublimity are always things which have a natural association with certain highly impressive and affecting ideas" (CW 31:224). For example, the idea of infinity, or magnitude without limit, is sufficient to explain the impressiveness of such feelings. Recall Mill's comments that from Wordsworth he learned to generate emotions by "dwelling on certain ideas" or by "a proper regulation of the associations." This method will suffice for explaining the generation of lofty ideas. Mill himself signals his awareness that a strong defense of associationism is required, yet his defense is noticeably less robust than his strongly dismissive conclusion.

"Theism," the last of Mill's three essays on religion, is a companion piece to "Nature." In this essay he argues against the proof of God's existence based upon an argument from consciousness, or the idea that if we can clearly and distinctly conceive of the idea of a God who is perfectly powerful, wise, and good, this idea must correspond to a real object. While this proof which appeals to reason is of a different order from arguments based upon direct experiences of the mystical order of nature, Mill's estimation of it illustrates his reasons for rejecting the metaphysical claims of Wordsworth and nature mystics. Mill says that when

> we are told that all of us are as capable as the prophet of seeing what he sees, feeling what he feels, nay, that we actually do so, and when the

utmost effort of which we are capable fails to make us aware of what we are told we perceive . . . the bearers may fairly be asked to consider whether it is not more likely that they are mistaken as to the origin of an impression in their minds, than that others are ignorant of the very existence of an impression in theirs. (CW 10:444–5)

Mill's argument here is similar to his claim that mystics and those of religious faith are mistaken in their analysis of their experience. Applying the above line of argument to the case of nature mysticism, it appears that he believes that the lofty feelings and thoughts that he has experienced from his encounters with nature are essentially the same as the experiences that Wordsworth and many others have attempted to describe as mystical experiences in their encounters with natural beauty. This is an interesting example of the radical disconnection between the worldview and experience of the religious skeptic and that of the religious devotee and mystic. Many who believe that they have had mystical experiences in nature claim that they cannot doubt the veracity of their experience; skeptics reply that they are indulging in fantasy and confusing imagination and reality.

There is a palpable lack of connection between Mill's experiences of nature, as inspiring and therapeutic as they were for his recovery from depression, and descriptions of mystical experiences in nature. While it is unlikely that the question of the status of transcendental or mystical experiences of nature can be decided with any degree of certainty (and certainly not here), yet it does seem that Mill has not fully appreciated the experiences of transcendence which he condemns as nonsensical. The journals of Mill's walking tours illustrate well both what unites him with and draws him to poets of nature as well as what divides him from them. Nature brings him great pleasure and joy; it charms him and induces feelings of tranquility and harmony. Its beauty uplifts him and is an antidote to depression. But the flashes of the transcendental vision that inspire Wordsworth are absent from Mill's accounts (CW 27:455–636).

The general question is not easily settled. However, it is an interesting question to consider whether Mill's theoretical commitments place him in an awkward position when he dismisses the religious interpretation of mystical experiences out of hand. In the realm of value theory, recall, he propounds qualitative hedonism in which value resides in pleasurable experiences, and certain kinds of satisfying experiences are more valuable than others. His test for measuring value is the preference of competent agents who are acquainted with these satisfying experiences and who are in a position to be knowledgeable judges. He is referring to the educative process of development and self-development. Mill exemplifies the perspective of the religious skeptic. His own test for the value of experiences holds that those competently acquainted with the experiences are the ones "entitled to an opinion" or competent to make the judgment of value, as he argues in his debating speech defending Wordsworth. But Mill's writings do not give any evidence that he has experienced the forms of mystical awareness that Wordsworth, Coleridge, and other Romantics claim to have experienced. Mill sets out elaborate views on the education and nurturing of human capacities. But he disdains spiritual cultivation. He believes that he is entitled to judge and dismiss as nonsensical claims about the reality and value of the sacred, even though he has not undergone a process of spiritual cultivation, including participation in practices such as meditation and contemplation. This is the dilemma of the religious skeptic. While some mystical and other sacred experiences may be experienced spontaneously, many, if not most, arise from the very sort of cultivation and development process that Mill sets out for reason and feeling. Religious skeptics hold back from engagement in the very practices that in many cases provide the training and cultivation which are the background and preconditions for experiencing the sacred. Mill chides Roebuck for doing something similar in dismissing the power of feelings.

There is a radical tension in Mill's views on this question. If he were to follow his procedure for other sorts of cultivation, he would feel it necessary to at least experiment with or try out a religious or spiritual practice before he would accept that he was qualified to judge these experiences. It would be an example of his favored "experiments in living." But it is difficult for one committed to skepticism to follow this program. Although as a skeptic he has not taken part in religious institutions and groups or undergone any of the techniques of prayer or meditation which have been used in many spiritual traditions to make students receptive to the sacred, he feels entitled to judge and dismiss the claims of those who have undergone these processes of development of their spiritual capacities.

Despite his rejection of the religious dimension of the human–nature connection, Mill's arguments for the importance of preserving the natural environment to promote crucial human ends stand out and entitle him to be regarded as an exemplar of progressive human attitudes towards nature.

notes

1 John Stuart Mill's editorial footnotes to this work also appear in CW 31:93–256.
2 Mill's reference is to John Ruskin, *Modern Painters*, 5 vols. (London: Smith, Eider, 1851–60).

further reading

Abrams, M. H., *The Mirror and the Lamp: Romantic Theory and the Critical Tradition* (Oxford: Oxford University Press, 1953).

Macpherson, C. B., *The Political Theory of Possessive Individualism* (Oxford: Oxford University Press, 1962).

Stephens, Piers H. G., "Plural Pluralisms: Towards a More Liberal Green Political Theory," in Iain Hampshire-Monk and Jeffrey Stanyer, eds., *Contemporary Political Studies 1996*, vol. 1 (Oxford Political Studies Association of the UK, 1996), 369–80.

Stephens, Piers H. G., "Green Liberalisms: Nature, Agency, and the Good," *Environmental Politics* 10, no. 3 (2001), 1–22.

Winch, Donald, "Thinking Green, Nineteenth-Century Style: John Stuart Mill and John Ruskin," in Mark Bevir and Frank Trentmann, eds., *Markets in Historical Contexts: Ideas and Politics in the Modern World* (Cambridge: Cambridge University Press, 2004), 105–28.

mill's logic, metaphysics, and epistemology

Richard Fumerton

introduction and background

In some ways it is plausible to think of Mill's metaphysics and epistemology as the culmination of British empiricism and as a natural transition to the logical positivism of the early twentieth century. In saying this, however, I don't want to denigrate the importance of Mill's work. Mill takes ideas planted by philosophers like Berkeley and Hume and works those ideas out with the kind of detail that is necessary to critically evaluate them. This step is crucial even if the end result is often the rejection of the views.

In all of his major works Mill tried to work out carefully a radical foundationalism and an equally radical reductionist program that would allow one to employ inductive reasoning to move from non-inferential knowledge of subjective phenomena to the world of common sense and science. If Mill's metaphysics and epistemology do not have as honored a place in the pantheon of great works by the modern philosophers, it is only because he rarely displays the kind of originality or rhetorical flair that so characterized such figures as Descartes, Berkeley, and Hume. Indeed, it is clear that Mill himself thought that he was largely building on and refining the ideas of others. His restriction of epistemic foundations to mental phenomena (modifications of the mind) of which we are directly aware was a theme that consistently ran though the work of many of his immediate predecessors and contemporaries. His analysis of causation and his insistence that only induction could advance one beyond the phenomenologically given to any genuinely new knowledge were elaborations (albeit often more sophisticated elaborations) of ideas introduced by Hume. Even the reduction of propositions describing the physical world to propositions describing "the permanent possibilities of sensation" was already hinted at (albeit not as explicitly or consistently) by Berkeley. Where Mill is most original, he is often least plausible. His apparent endorsement of induction as the source of even elementary knowledge of arithmetic and geometric truths, for example, isolates him from even his most staunch fellow empiricists.

Still, to characterize Mill only as someone primarily interested in developing the views of others is to radically understate his contributions to metaphysics and epistemology. Although he often did not anticipate many of the critical problems that were to beset the reductionist programs of the positivists, he took the views of the British empiricists to the point at which others could begin to see clearly some of the enormous obstacles those views must surmount. That transition from the sketch of interesting new and original ideas to clearly worked out views whose vulnerability becomes exposed was an enormously important development in the history of philosophy. Nor should one downplay the significance of his role as critic of other philosophers. *An Examination of Sir William Hamilton's Philosophy*, for example, is a work truly impressive not only as a vehicle through which Mill developed his own views, but as a tribute to the often highly sophisticated theories of philosophers who through the many accidents of history have not survived as dominant figures, but whose work is often every bit as sophisticated as that of present-day metaphysicians and epistemologists. *A System of Logic* is far more than a work on logic. It engages a vast array of problems, from issues concerning the foundations of knowledge, the philosophy of language, the metaphysics of causation, and ultimately even to the metaphysical underpinnings of value judgment.

Radical Empiricism

It is often surprisingly difficult to characterize the central tenets of major movements in philosophy. Philosophers are, after all, radically individualistic and there are fundamental disagreements on major issues among philosophers who historically fall within a given camp. Radical empiricism is no exception to this rule. Locke, Berkeley, Hume, and Mill are all classified as empiricists, but they have significantly different views about the nature of mind, physical reality, ethical judgments, and justification and knowledge. If there is one doctrine most commonly associated with empiricism, however, it is the view that all ideas are copies of prior impressions. Everything we can think of, according to the empiricist, results from ideas that come to us as "copies" of the data received "directly" in sense experience.

The view as just stated is obviously implausible. We have ideas of mermaids, unicorns, and centaurs, for example, and we have never run into any such creatures (or, more precisely, have never had experiences of such creatures). There is, however, a relatively quick fix for the fundamental idea behind empiricism. The idea of a unicorn, one might suppose, just is, roughly, the idea of a white horse combined with the idea of a horned head. It is only *simple* ideas that are copies of prior impressions of sense. Our minds can use imagination to mix and match these simple ideas in all sorts of wondrous ways. The complex ideas so formed may or may not "match" or "correspond" to anything that anyone has ever experienced or will ever experience.

It is one thing to claim that all simple ideas are "copies" of what has been presented to us in sense experience. It is another to specify precisely what *is* given to us in sense experience. The radical empiricists denied that physical objects or the non-relational properties of physical objects are *given* to us through the senses. Rather, they claimed, we are *directly* aware only of fleeting and mind-dependent sensations/perceptions/ideas of sense (the terminology varied from philosopher to philosopher). Twentieth-century philosophers often called the perceiver-dependent objects of which we are directly aware in sense experience *sense data*. There were many arguments for this claim, all of them highly controversial. One of the most common was an argument from perceptual relativity. It seems at least initially plausible to claim that the character of what we are immediately aware of in sense experience causally depends as much on the perceiver and various conditions of perception as on any properties that belong to an external object. An object that looks round to a creature with our kind of eye, might look oval to a creature with another kind of eye. An object that looks red to you under one set of conditions (lighting conditions for example), might look yellow or orange under other conditions. Indeed, there seems to be a clear sense in which the apparent shape of an object constantly changes as our perspective on that object changes. But physical objects and their objective properties are, by definition, perceiver-independent. They are supposed to have, as Hume said, an independent and continued existence. What we are aware of in sense experience is perceiver-dependent and fleeting. It is, therefore, not a physical object with its properties.

That there is a "gap" between subjective appearance and external reality, might seem an easy enough claim to accept, but the existence of the gap raises enormous epistemological and metaphysical problems – problems that are still debated vigorously. If all of our simple ideas are ideas of subjective sense impressions, then how do we form the idea of physical objects at all? The logical consequence of this radical empiricism might seem to be the view that Hume so poetically expressed in the *Treatise of Human Nature*:

> Now since nothing is ever present to the mind but perceptions, and since all ideas are deriv'd from something antecedently present to the mind; it follows that 'tis impossible for us so much as to conceive or form an idea of any thing specifically different from ideas and impressions. Let us fix our attention out of ourselves as much as possible: Let us chase our imagination to the utmost limits of the universe; we never really advance a step

beyond ourselves, nor can conceive any kind of existence, but those perceptions, which have appear'd in that narrow compass. This is the universe of the imagination, nor have we any idea but what is there produc'd. (Hume [1739–40] 1888, 67–8)

Radical empiricism with its insistence that all complex ideas must be built out of simple ideas that are copies of prior impressions seems to invite a skepticism about even the *intelligibility* of thought about a world of perceiver-independent physical objects. As we will see, this is a problem with which Mill was centrally concerned.

Even if one concedes the intelligibility of thought about external reality, the same radical empiricism that restricted simple ideas to ideas of prior sense impression also raised enormous epistemological problems. Virtually all of the radical empiricists (and Mill was no exception) were committed foundationalists. All knowledge and justified belief rests ultimately on a "foundation" of truths we know or justifiably believe directly, without inference. If you think about the vast majority of what you think you know and justifiably believe, it probably won't be that hard to convince yourself that you have the relevant knowledge and justified belief only because you can legitimately infer what you believe from something else different that you know or justifiably believe. You probably think that George Washington was the first president of the United States. And if you ask yourself how you know this, you will probably offer as your evidence that you've read various history books that appear to be reliable, or that you've seen relevant monuments, or that your junior high school history teacher told you that he was. Of course, these other purported truths can get you knowledge of Washington's presidency only if you know or justifiably believe them. Garbage in – garbage out. The following principle was virtually taken for granted by the vast majority of epistemologists in the history of philosophy:

> To be justified in believing P by inferring it from E one must be justified in believing E.

The vast majority of empiricists, I would argue, accepted yet a stronger principle, a principle we might call the Principle of Inferential Justification (PIJ):

> (PIJ) One is justified in believing P by inferring it from E only if (a) one is justified in believing E and (b) one is justified in believing that E makes probable P (where E's guaranteeing the truth of P would be the upper limit of E's making probable P).

Insistence on the second clause might again seem part of common sense. If someone claims to have good reason to believe that you will live a long life and offers as his evidence that you have a long "life-line" on the palm of your hand, you would probably challenge his evidential claim by insisting that he has no reason to believe that there is any connection between a long life-line and a long life.

The first clause of PIJ is a premise in a classic argument for foundationalism. The argument goes as follows:

1   If the only way to know or justifiably believe any proposition P is to infer it from something else E1, then from clause (a) of PIJ, one knows or justifiably believes P only if one knows or justifiably believes E1.
2   But if the only way to know or justifiably believe any proposition P is to infer it from something else, then to know or justifiably believe E1 one must infer it from something else E2, which one must infer from something else E3, which one must infer from something else E4, and so on *ad infinitum*.
3   A finite mind cannot complete the infinite regress described in (2), so if the only way to know or justifiably believe anything is through inference, we have no knowledge or justified belief.
4   It's absurd to suppose that we have no knowledge or justified belief (we wouldn't even be able to justifiably believe this).

Therefore,

5   There must be knowledge or justified belief that does not depend on inference, and all knowledge and justified belief must "rest" on such knowledge or justified belief.

With clause (b) of PIJ there is yet another regress that looms. To justifiably believe P on the basis of E1, one must not only justifiably believe E1, but one must justifiably believe that E1 makes likely P. If all justification were inferential, one would need to infer that E1 makes likely P from something else F1, which one would need to infer from F2, and so on. But one would also need to justifiably believe that F1 does make likely that E1 makes likely P and one would need to infer that from something else G1 which one would need to infer from G2, and so on. But one would also need to justifiably believe that G1 makes likely that F1 makes likely that E1 makes likely P, and one would need to infer that . . . Unless there are foundations to knowledge and justified belief, one would need to complete an infinite number of infinitely long chains of reasoning.

It is one thing to claim that there must be direct knowledge or non-inferential justification. It is another to figure out what constitutes such knowledge and what actually can be known in this way. And this brings us to another central tenet of radical empiricism. The same direct acquaintance that yielded the content of simple ideas was also taken to provide us with epistemological foundations. We are non-inferentially justified in believing that we are in pain, for example, because we are directly and immediately aware of the very pain that is the "truthmaker" for our belief. It is precisely because the empiricists thought that we are never directly acquainted with physical objects and their properties that truths about the physical world were rejected for inclusion in the foundations of knowledge. The idea that we don't infer that we are in pain is also, plausibly, just part of common sense. When you hit me on my kneecap with a hammer, it is hardly as if I infer the presence of searing pain from the fact that I am bleeding profusely and appear to be screaming at the top of my lungs. The knowledge is more direct than this. So the most radical of empiricists wanted to restrict all foundational knowledge of *contingent* truth to knowledge of the current contents of one's mind. As we will see Mill adopts a slightly more liberal foundationalism that includes direct knowledge of past experiences revealed through memory.

Contingent truths are truths that describe the world as it happens to be. Necessary truths describe the world as it must be. And most of the radical foundationalists wanted to include in the foundations at least some simple necessary truths – simple truths of arithmetic and geometry and some conceptual (analytic) truths (that bachelors are unmarried, that parents have children, that squares have four sides), and, perhaps, some principles of reasoning (propositions of the form E entails, or, even, makes probable P). More often than not these empiricists tried to locate the truthmakers for even necessary truths "in the mind." So for Hume, necessary truths were made true by "relations between ideas." By locating the truthmakers in mental states the empiricist maintained a continuity between the account they gave of foundationally known necessary truths and foundationally known contingent truths. Both rested on a direct awareness of what goes on within the confines of one's mind.

The problem of skepticism loomed large given the radical empiricist's rather spartan foundations for knowledge and justified belief. The road back to common sense is long and winding once one restricts one's available premises to truths about the contents of one's mind. A great deal depends, of course, on what one takes oneself to know concerning the principles that sanction inferences from the foundations. An argument is deductively valid when its premises entail its conclusion, when, that is, it is absolutely impossible for its premises to be true while its conclusion is false. Even the most radical of skeptics in the history of philosophy typically allowed themselves knowledge and use of deductively valid reasoning as a way of moving beyond available foundations. The difficulty, of course, is that one can't move very far that way. There is a sense in which the conclusion of a deductively valid argument is already implicitly contained in the conjunction of the argument's premises. One can't get from what one seems to remember to anything actually having happened through deduction. One can't get from the world of subjective appearance to the world of objective fact through deduction. While some of the most radical skeptics insisted that the only legitimate form of reasoning was deductively valid reasoning, it was more common for radical empiricists to allow the legitimacy of at least some forms of non-deductive reasoning. And one of the most promising candidates for such reasoning was what is often called enumerative induction.

Inductive reasoning involves two kinds of conclusions. But all inductive arguments move from observed correlations between properties or kinds of events to the relevant conclusions. The more ambitious inductive reasoning will move from the fact that all (most) observed F's have been G to the general conclusion that all (most) F's are G. We observe a finite amount of metal that is heated and that expands and we infer from this that all metal expands when heated. A less dramatic inductive argument moves again from the premise that all (most) observed F's have been G, together with a premise describing something as F, to the conclusion that that thing is also G. Neither sort of argument is deductively valid. The turkey that expects to be fed when called shortly before Thanksgiving quickly discovers that observed correlations aren't guaranteed to continue into the future. But, just like the turkey, we seem to be willing to "bet our lives" on projecting discovered correlations. Every time you take a drink of water expecting it to quench your thirst rather than kill you, you are, arguably, betting your life that an observed correlation will continue into the future.

Mill clearly allowed induction as a legitimate method of expanding knowledge. Indeed, as we shall see, he appeared to argue that so-called deductive reasoning was really a disguised form of inductive reasoning. As we shall also see he seemed to argue (against many of his fellow empiricists) that even mathematical reasoning was fundamentally inductive. Whether or not induction is a legitimate form of reasoning, it isn't easy to see how one can move far beyond the radical empiricist's foundations to the conclusions of common sense using only deductive and inductive reasoning. In particular it is difficult to see how one can get to the external world. Inductive reasoning allows one to project only observed correlations. But if one is never directly aware of anything but sensations or perceptions, then how do we observe the correlations between perceptions and physical objects that must be described in the premises of an inductive argument? The same Hume who argued that our imagination is limited to perception also noted the obvious difficulty in trying to reason our way inductively to the physical world:

> The only conclusion we can draw from the existence of one thing to that
> of another, is by means of the relation of cause and effect, which shews,

that there is a connexion betwixt them, and that the existence of one is dependent on that of the other. The idea of this relation is deriv'd from past experience, by which we find, that two beings are constantly conjoin'd together, and are always present at once to the mind. But as no beings are ever present to the mind but perceptions; it follows that we may observe a conjunction or a relation of cause and effect between different perceptions but can never observe it between perceptions and objects. 'Tis impossible, therefore, that from the existence or any of the qualities of the former, we can ever form any conclusion concerning the existence of the latter, or ever satisfy our reason in this particular. (Hume [1739–40] 1888, 212)

Although the problem is not discussed nearly as much, one must also wonder how inductive reasoning can get one from apparent memory to knowledge of the past. To reason inductively one would need to rely on a premise correlating apparent memory with past events. But to use such a premise one would need (by PIJ) to have reason to believe it. But how could one discover that in the past when we seemed to remember having done something we did it without relying on memory, the very memory reliability of which is to be shown!

Mill was acutely aware of both problems and, as we shall see, tried desperately to solve them, albeit in radically different ways. It is probably no understatement to suggest that throughout his metaphysics, epistemology, and logic, Mill was driven to find a way of reconciling common sense with an appropriate respect for Hume's arguments against it.

further reading

Ayer, A. J., *The Problem of Knowledge* (Edinburgh: Penguin, 1956), chapter 2.
Berkeley, George, *Three Dialogues Between Hylas and Philonous*, ed. Colin M. Turbayne (Indianapolis: Bobbs-Merrill, 1954).
Fumerton, Richard, *Metaphysical and Epistemological Problems of Perception* (Lincoln and London: University of Nebraska Press, 1985), chapter 2.
Wilson, Fred, *Psychological Analysis and the Philosophy of John Stuart Mill* (Toronto: University of Toronto Press, 1990), chapter 1.

logic and epistemology

A s we noted in the last chapter, Mill, like almost all of his predecessors and contemporaries, thought it obvious that some form of foundationalism was true:

> Truths are known to us in two ways: some are known directly, and of themselves; some through the medium of other truths. The former are the subject of Intuition, or Consciousness; the latter, of Inference. The truths known by intuition are the original premises from which all others are inferred. Our assent to the conclusion being grounded on the truth of the premises, we never could arrive at any knowledge by reasoning, unless something could be known antecedently to all reasoning. (CW 7:6–7)

Firmly in the tradition of his fellow British empiricists, Mill also seemed to think that it was simply obvious that the data of which we are directly and immediately aware are the contents of mind – sensations, ideas, sentiments, beliefs, and the like. Propositions describing the occurrence of the "phenomena" are the truths that can be known non-inferentially and that constitute the foundations of all other knowledge. There is but one means of moving beyond knowledge of what we apprehend directly to knowledge of truths describing what is not before consciousness, and that is through inductive reasoning. Since inductive reasoning always requires awareness of correlations among the occurrences of various phenomena, Mill, like Hume before him, was convinced that we could never really reach any conclusions that take us beyond the realm of the phenomenal. Unlike Hume (more like Berkeley), Mill thought that he could reconcile this conclusion with common sense – if we understand properly the content of ordinary everyday beliefs, we'll find that there is a sense in which such beliefs never really *require* us to advance beyond complicated claims about the *kind* of phenomena with which we are directly acquainted. We'll have much more to say later about Mill's attempts to reconstruct the content of ordinary beliefs so as to make them amenable to inductive proof.

Initially, there might seem to be nothing very interesting or original about the truths Mill identifies as foundational. One is, however, immediately taken aback to find that the examples Mill gives of truths known immediately include not only descriptions of *present* conscious states, but also descriptions of *past* conscious states:

> Examples of truths known to us by immediate consciousness, are our own bodily sensations and mental feelings. I know directly, and of my own knowledge, that I was vexed yesterday or that I am hungry to-day. (CW 7:7)

One might initially put this down to carelessness but it seems clear that Mill did not think that one's knowledge of one's own past conscious states through memory was *inferential* knowledge – or, if it was inferential knowledge, it clearly constituted an exception to his otherwise exceptionless principle that all inferential knowledge required inductive reasoning. His most extensive discussion of the epistemic status of phenomenal truths (truths about the qualitative character of experience) presented to us through memory is in a long footnote in *An Examination of Sir William Hamilton's Philosophy* from which I here quote:

> Our belief in the veracity of Memory is evidently ultimate; no reason can be given for it which does not presuppose the belief, and assume it to be well grounded. (EWH 209)

Perhaps to reassure himself that he is not out on a limb here, Mill does claim that all of his predecessors who attempted to secure knowledge from a foundation consisting of truths about sensation, also "gave" themselves memory-based knowledge of their immediate phenomenal past (EWH 210n). But philosophy is one field in which there simply is no safety in numbers, and it is worth exploring the issues raised here in more detail, for they invite questions that threaten to undermine Mill's entire project.

There are, it seems, only two real possibilities. Either (a) Mill thought that through memory one could know directly and immediately at least some truths about the past or (b) he recognized that there is a sense in which truths about the past are implicitly inferred from present memory "experience," but held that the non-deductive principle sanctioning the inference is known directly (through intuition). If (a) is true, Mill is in danger of losing any clear criteria to characterize foundational knowledge; (b), on the other hand, is simply incompatible with the entire thrust of an epistemology that allows only inductive reasoning as a legitimate epistemic tool for advancing knowledge. Let me elaborate.

Although Mill sometimes seems to eschew introspection as a way of determining what can or cannot be known directly, there are a number of passages in which he does seem to identify what is directly known through consciousness with what cannot be doubted or what cannot be believed falsely. He recognizes, of course, that there is enormous debate about such questions as whether we can apprehend directly physical objects and their properties – this is one of the primary themes discussed in connection with Hamilton's philosophy. And he certainly doesn't think that one can decide that issue simply by paying close phenomenological attention to the character (the intentional character) of one's sensory states and the beliefs to which they give rise. But here he is primarily concerned with confusion that is likely to beset the philosopher who has become so accustomed to various associations of phenomena built up from earliest experience that the philosopher cannot separate in thought that which involves inference from that which does not. So consider, for example, your expectation that the drink of cold water will quench your thirst, or that approaching the fire will warm you. While Mill (and almost all of his predecessors and contemporaries) takes it to be virtually uncontroversial that such beliefs can only be inferentially justified (see Chapter 9), he also realizes that one will typically be unaware of any *conscious* inference from available premises to the relevant conclusion. The expectations are, in a sense, spontaneous. They are the product of endless exposure to correlations that have created in us a Pavlovian response to the relevant stimuli. Some contemporary philosophers might even suggest that at least some of the relevant responses to stimuli are now a product of evolution. We are *born* with dispositions to respond to various sensory stimuli with certain beliefs. But in the context of justification, the spontaneous character of a belief does not settle the question of whether one needs other justified belief in order for the belief to be justified. If all this is so, how, then, can one recognize genuine foundational justification?

Mill does seem to think that we can identify that which is *truly* given (non-inferentially) to consciousness with that about which we cannot be mistaken:

> Consciousness, in the sense usually attached to it by philosophers, – consciousness of the mind's own feelings and operations, cannot, as our author [Hamilton] truly says, be disbelieved. (EWH 172)

And again:

> The facts which cannot be doubted are those to which the word consciousness is by most philosophers confined: the facts of internal consciousness; "the mind's own acts and affections." What we feel, we cannot doubt that we feel. It is impossible to us to feel and to think that perhaps we feel not, or to feel not, and think that perhaps we feel. What admits of being doubted, is the revelation which consciousness is supposed to make (and which our author considers as itself consciousness) of an external reality. (EWH 168)

In these passages, Mill certainly seems to be implying that the mark of what is truly presented directly to consciousness (in a way that affords us direct, non-inferential knowledge) is that there is no possibility of doubt concerning its existence. The impossibility of doubt isn't the same thing as the impossibility of error, but again in this context (and the tradition in which this locution is used), one might reasonably infer that for Mill the given in consciousness is the truthmaker for a proposition that can be infallibly believed. The tradition of identifying genuine foundations with indubitability is, of course, most famously associated with Descartes. Descartes sought to identify secure foundations upon which he could build an ideal system of knowledge. And he proposed indubitability as the criterion for inclusion in the foundations. Descartes suggested that we should purge from the foundations any belief if we can conceive of possessing whatever justification we have for the belief while the belief is nevertheless false. As we saw in Chapter 9, the rationalist Descartes, and all of the radical empiricists, rejected as foundational any belief about the physical world. The best evidence we could have in support of some claim about the physical world is the "testimony" of our senses when the object is supposed to be in front of us in broad daylight. But no matter how vivid our sensations, it seems that we have little difficulty imagining that those sensations occur in the context of a vivid dream or a hallucination. Mill like Descartes sometimes seems to embrace the very strong Cartesian requirements for foundational knowledge.

But here one must wonder how Mill can possibly recover in the *foundations* of knowledge his experiential *past*. Philosophers have worked hard through fanciful thought experiments involving illusion, hallucination, dreams, and the like, to convince us that sensory experience is never an infallible source of knowledge about the external world, but it takes almost no effort at all to convince even the most philosophically unsophisticated that apparent memory, even apparent memory of what seems to be the relatively immediate past, is fallible. To be sure, there is a use of the expression "I remember that . . ." which makes it "factive" (in the use of that term made by Williamson 2000). There are a host of expressions describing intentional states (psychological states that have an "aboutness") whose correct use implies that what the state is about obtains. So "I know that P," "I see that P," "I remember that P," "I realized that P," and many similar locutions, all imply that P is the case – these expressions are used factively. Others, like "I fear that P," "I hope that P," "I believe that P," are obviously used in such a way that the state described can obtain whether or not P is the case – these verbs are not used factively. So there is almost certainly a use of "I remember that P" that can express a truth only if P. But it seems equally obvious that we can have a "non-veridical" counterpart of memory and that, consequently, we need a more neutral expression that can describe that state that we often confuse with veridical memory. Let us say that S *seems to remember* that P when we want to leave open the question of whether or not what S seems to remember actually occurs. And it seems just obvious (particularly to those of us who are getting a bit long in the tooth) that one can seem to remember that P, indeed, that one can *vividly* seem to remember that P, even when P never happened. If Mill allows in the foundations of empirical knowledge truths about one's experiential past, he has allowed into the foundations of knowledge beliefs that are fallibly believed (beliefs whose justification does not guarantee the truth of what is believed).

Once we allow in the foundations of knowledge *one* sort of fallible belief – belief in the past prompted by present memory – it's hard to see how one can maintain a *principled* objection to those philosophers who claim to know directly certain truths about the physical world where the occasion of such knowledge is the occurrence of sensory states that give rise to (fallible) beliefs about the external world. To be sure a sensory state can occur in the absence of the physical object we take to be its cause, but then an apparent memory experience "of" a past sensory state S can occur in the absence of the sensory state S we take to be its cause.

In contemporary epistemology there is an increasingly popular view called externalism. Many externalists divorce completely the idea of a non-inferentially justified belief from the idea of an infallible belief. So, for example, the reliabilist suggests that a belief is non-inferentially justified if it is reliably produced where the "input" of the belief-producing process is something other than a justified belief. We may well have evolved in such a way that we now respond to sensory stimuli or apparent memory with beliefs about the external world and the past respectively. And if these beliefs are true more often than not, then they are reliably produced. A crude reliabilist will take these reliably produced beliefs to be not only justified, but non-inferentially justified. Given the passages quoted earlier, however, it is hard to imagine that Mill was a tentative forerunner of externalist epistemology.

If including beliefs about the past in the foundations of knowledge threatens to open the floodgates to spurious claims of direct knowledge, option (b) discussed above threatens to open the floodgates to unwanted non-deductive principles of reasoning that go well beyond Mill's treasured principle of induction. Within the framework of traditional foundationalism Mill is, of course, right in suggesting that there is no possibility of *reasoning* to the conclusion that memory is generally reliable.[1] Any such argument must appeal to evidence, and in the passing of a moment, that evidence will be "lost" to the past. Its "recovery" will involve relying on memory. It is particularly obvious that an *inductive* justification of the reliability of memory is a non-starter. It is the essence of inductive reasoning that the person who employs it reaches a conclusion based on *past* observed correlations among phenomena. But to get that knowledge of past correlations, one cannot avoid relying on memory.

It is to Mill's great credit that he realizes the enormity of the problem here and that he doesn't try to hide it.[2] But understanding that one faces a problem and having a solution to that problem consistent with the system of philosophy one defends are not the same. In the end, Mill seems resigned to arguing that we simply have no choice but to concede that memory gives us knowledge of the past. We *need* to make such an assumption if we are to have any chance of knowing anything beyond the momentary, fleeting, contents of our minds. But skeptics have never been much impressed with the philosopher's plaintive appeals to what is needed in order to get the knowledge we would *like* to have. Descartes *needed* knowledge of a non-deceiving God, Berkeley may have *needed* a God to keep in existence a world unperceived by finite minds, and Mill *needed* knowledge of past experiences. But what has philosophical need got to do with what one is philosophically entitled to claim? Mill knows perfectly well that there are all kinds of philosophers convinced that his attempts to regain knowledge of the external world by performing inductions on experiential phenomena will itself be doomed to failure. If he were to conclude that he does so fail, would he also give himself whatever epistemic principles were needed to convert beliefs in material objects prompted by sensory states into knowledge?

Mill on Our Knowledge of the External World

Even if one does give oneself unproblematic access to past experience, an epistemologist restricted to the foundations Mill recognizes faces formidable difficulties securing knowledge or even justified belief about the physical world. How does Mill rescue justified belief in the physical world from a stark foundation that consists solely of knowledge of present and past experiential states and a view of reasoning that recognizes only induction as a means of projecting past correlations among phenomena into the future? How does he solve Hume's problem? You will recall from Chapter 9 that Hume argued that if all we know directly are truths about perceptions, we can use induction only to make predictions about perceptions. While we can correlate sensations with sensations, we can't correlate sensations with anything other than sensations.

The solution, Mill argues, is to understand clearly the *content* of beliefs about the physical world. Such beliefs should be understood as beliefs in "the permanent possibility of sensations." Some earlier representative realists wanted to construe the secondary qualities of objects as "in" the objects only as powers to produce certain sensations under certain conditions. So to take a fairly plausible example, one might suppose that the sourness of a lemon is "in" the lemon only as its power to produce in normal people that familiar sour taste sensation. The reluctance to put the sourness of the lemon "out there" in the lemon had something to do with the realization that the way a thing tastes obviously depends on the subject tasting that thing. If you have a really bad cold and bite into a lemon, it won't taste sour. Just as some would argue that beauty is in the eye of the beholder, so many contemporaries of Mill would argue that the sourness of the lemon is in the taste buds of the beholder. But once one begins down this path it is difficult to stop. Apparent color just as obviously depends on the perceiver and the conditions of perception. Artists are particularly sensitive to the changes in apparent color as the light gradually changes throughout the day. And anyone who has worn sunglasses realizes that what color things seem to have depends very much upon the medium through which the light waves travel. Indeed, if we look at a colored object under high magnification the color either disappears or changes radically. So color often went the way of taste. And one can see how shape might soon follow if our reluctance to postulate a reality corresponding to appearance is a function of our realization that the appearance is clearly dependent on the perceiver and on the conditions of perception. Like Berkeley and Hume before him, Mill thinks that there is no principled way to separate the secondary qualities from the so-called primary qualities (qualities that exist not only in the world of subjective appearance but in the object). Mill's solution was to reduce *all* claims about the physical world to claims about the existence of permanent powers to affect sentient beings in certain ways under certain conditions. Physical objects, he said, are the permanent possibilities of sensation. As we will see in some detail in the next chapter, Mill's view admits of different possible interpretations. For now, however, we will note only that Mill's solution to the epistemological problems of perception stands or falls with his account of what we mean when describing the physical world, and we will examine and evaluate that analysis in some detail in the next chapter.

Mill on Our Knowledge of "Necessary" Truths

Not content with attempting to establish that observed correlations among phenomena allow one to inductively establish truths about the physical world, Mill also infamously seemed to claim that induction was the source of even general knowledge of the most basic axioms of arithmetic and geometry. Always distrustful of claims to know through "intuition," Mill argued that we reach such conclusions as that "no space can be enclosed by two straight lines" inductively (CW 7:231–3). After examining indefinitely many pairs of straight lines, none of which enclose a space, we arrive at the conclusion that no two straight lines enclose a space. As such the inference is no different in principle from an inference from what we observe happening to individual pieces of metal when heated to the conclusion that all metal expands when heated.[3]

Mill is well aware that his position on this matter will be rejected by most philosophers and again, to his credit, he carefully considers and attempts to reply to objections. The first such objection centers on the plausible observation that there is a crucial difference between discoveries of fundamental arithmetic and geometrical truths, and discoveries of empirical regularities. The former can be known without relying on sense experience, solely by employing *thought* experiments. The latter cannot. We cannot discover that a stone thrown in water sinks, Mill concedes, just by thinking about stones and water (CW 7:233). We can discover that $2 + 2 = 4$, or that equilateral triangles are equiangular triangles, just by thinking about the subject matter of these claims.

Such an objection, Mill argues, misses its mark for while it does point to a crucial difference between the kind of inductive evidence available in support of "necessary" truths in contrast to the kind of inductive evidence in support of empirical truths, the *reasoning* in both cases is still inductive. We need not leave the confines of our minds to discover the axioms of geometry because the mental pictures we form there exemplify the very properties we are trying to correlate in the premises of our inductive argument. Mental pictures of straight lines contain real straight lines in a way that mental pictures of stones in water do not contain either stones or water. The distinction between so-called *a priori* knowledge of generalizations and *a posteriori* knowledge of generalizations is simply a distinction between inductive generalizations processing correlations of phenomena that can occur in the mind as opposed to correlations of phenomena that exist outside the mind (as permanent possibilities of sensations).

Even if the initial objection can be met this way, it will soon be followed by the complaint that Mill's account of the relevant reasoning fails to distinguish generalizations which are necessarily true, and *known* to be necessarily true, from those that just happen to be true (CW 7:236–8). We know not only that no two straight lines enclose a space, but also that it is *impossible* for two straight lines to enclose a space. We may know on the basis of inductive evidence that metal expands when heated, but there is surely a clear sense in which we also realize that this generalization is not necessarily true. No matter how many pieces of metal we heat and observe expand, we understand clearly that it is always possible, if exceedingly unlikely, that the very next piece of metal will contract or disappear *in nihilo* when heated. If we inductively establish both the generalizations we regard as necessarily true and those we regard only as contingently true, then what accounts for our radically different view of the nature of the two kinds of truths?

This objection surely is ultimately devastating to Mill's position. He attempts to reply to it but it is difficult to see how the reply is even *prima facie* credible. His reply begins by arguing that claims about truths being necessary are only claims about what is or is not conceivable. To assert that it is necessarily true that no two straight lines enclose a space is only to claim that we cannot conceive of two lines enclosing a space. But our inability to conceive the negation of a so-called necessary truth, Mill seems to argue, can be traced to the fact that the relevant invariable associations that confirm such truths have been found to hold from the earliest moments of our consciousness. Even our *imagination* never produces anything but two straight lines that fail to enclose a space. But such a reply seems to miss the point. The effects of the earth's gravitational field have been experienced from our earliest moments as well, but we have no difficulty conceiving of a body not falling to the surface of the earth when released. Even if all of the pairs of lines (external and internal) we have examined fail to enclose a space, why can't we *conceive* of two lines which do? Mill's critic is not claiming that the falsehood of necessary truths is inconceivable in the sense that it is causally impossible for us, or difficult for us, to conceive of a world in which they are false. The critic is claiming that, is impossible in a stronger sense for us to conceive of a world in which they would be false. We can't conceive of two straight lines enclosing a space because it is in the nature of straight lines that such a possibility is precluded. And no inductive evidence seems relevant to establishing *that* conclusion.

Although Mill is well known for his claims that so-called necessary truths are knowable only through inductive reasoning, it is worth noting that his subsequent discussion of the issue in *A System of Logic*, at the very least, muddies the waters. In his later discussion of inductive reasoning, Mill characterizes a kind of reasoning that is *improperly* called inductive and gives as an example the way in which we conclude after looking at a single triangle that all triangles have angles adding up to 180 degrees. He suggests that it is better to call this induction "by parity of reasoning" (CW 7:290). Shortly thereafter he characterizes Newton's discovery of the binomial theorem as *a priori*. These admissions seem starkly inconsistent with his earlier vehement and unqualified insistence that inductive reasoning is the only source of knowledge available for the discovery of mathematical truths.

Mill's "Reduction" of Deductive Reasoning to Inductive Reasoning

Mill's *A System of Logic* is not nearly as valuable today as a work in logic as it is as a work in metaphysics and epistemology. Modern predicate logic has supplanted Mill's now outdated categorizations of argument kinds. Still, the work contains many intriguing suggestions. The most startling is that *all* genuine reasoning is inductive reasoning. What's more, Mill seems to argue that all inductive reasoning is itself inference from particulars to particulars (CW 7:193). When we conclude that all metal expands when heated after observing individual pieces of metal expand when heated, the universal conclusion is just our way of marking the fact that for any *particular* metal we heat next, it will expand. Of course, one needs only to state the thesis clearly in order to see that it is in danger of becoming merely verbal. One hasn't avoided a universal conclusion by thinking of the conclusion sanctioned by the inductive evidence as one about *all* particular unexamined and future pieces of metal that have been heated. There is good reason to think that Mill believed that universal generalizations were themselves just conjunctions of particular propositions. That all men are mortal is equivalent to that Jones is a man and is mortal, and that Smith is a man and is mortal, and . . . And so on until we have named *all* of the men. Of course the fact that we need to add this last part with the italicized "all" indicates why the proposed translation must fail (as a meaning analysis). But in any event, if Mill believed that general propositions were themselves conjunctions of particular propositions, his claim that all reasoning is from particulars to particulars immediately becomes less mysterious.

If Mill's claim that inductive reasoning always takes one from particulars to particulars is itself at best misleading, his further thesis that syllogistic reasoning is not genuine reasoning at all, is even more puzzling. When we conclude that John is mortal based on the premises that all men are mortal and that John is a man, it certainly looks as if we are engaged in genuine deductive (not inductive) reasoning. Mill, however, tries to convince us that the general proposition in the syllogism is just a kind of reminder that you have, or at least have had, at your disposal an array of particular propositions which would allow one to inductively infer that John is mortal. The conclusion about John is a conclusion based on "forgotten facts" about particular men dying (CW 7:193).

Now construed literally as an attempt to reduce deductive reasoning to inductive reasoning the above seems just wrong. There is a relation of entailment between the premises of a syllogism and its conclusion which we can "see" and which we can use to draw out of a universal claim various consequences. Deductively valid arguments are simply not disguised inductive arguments. But Mill is probably not really trying

Richard Fumerton

to make a point of *logic*. His concern is better construed as one of *episte-mology*. If one is to know something about John's dying, Mill is arguing, no argument whose premises describe universal truths about the mortality of man will capture the structure of the *evidence* upon which one bases one's conclusion. One's justification for believing the conclusion of an argument based on its premises is never any better than one's justification for believing the premises, and the epistemologist's task is to lay bare the structure of the evidence upon which one relies in reaching a conclusion. In this context Mill's claim becomes relatively straightforward. If he's right, one's evidence for believing that all men are mortal is itself observations of correlations between particular individuals being men and those men eventually dying. Knowledge of those particulars allows one in a sense to infer the universal proposition that all men are mortal, but if Mill's earlier claim is also true, then the intermediate universal conclusion is just our way of reminding ourselves that whatever particular conclusion we next draw about the mortality of some particular man will be inductively supported. We can now see how Mill might argue that it would be more *perspicuous* to represent the relevant *reasoning* as an inductive argument that proceeds directly from observed men dying to the conclusion about John's mortality. Furthermore, if Mill's views discussed in the previous section were correct (they are not) and there is no way of knowing *any* general truth other than through inductive reasoning, then this reconstruction of all reasoning as moving inductively from evidence describing correlations among particulars to conclusions projecting those correlations in the case of new particulars would seem quite plausible.

Mill on the Ground of Inductive Reasoning

We have discussed at some length the fundamental role that inductive reasoning plays in Mill's epistemology. As we have seen, Mill seems almost obsessed with construing *all* reasoning as implicit inductive reasoning. But why should one suppose that inductive reasoning itself is legitimate? What grounds do we have for supposing that the premises of an inductive argument make probable its conclusion? Why should we assume that just because we have always found F's followed by G's the next F we find will also likely be G? Mill is sensitive to the fact that this question needs to be answered, but it is not at all easy to make sense of the answer (or answers) he gives.

On the face of it, Mill seems to offer the straightforward, if counter-intuitive, suggestion that we justify our reliance on induction by *inductively* establishing that induction is reliable. But he gets off to a bad start by first putting the point in terms of an assumption or axiom that inductive reasoning requires. Mill claims that whenever we reason inductively, we take as an axiom that the future will resemble the past in relevant respects, or that nature is *uniform* in relevant respects (CW 7:306–7). At one point, he even seems to suggest that if we take this assumption as an implicit premise we can transform inductive arguments into syllogistic deductively valid arguments. Instead of reasoning from observations of F's which have been G's to the conclusion that the next F will be G, we can make explicit the premise that if observed F's have all been G's that indicates that there is uniformity in nature with respect to F's being G's. That premise with our observation of F's which are G's will allow us to *deduce* that the next F we observe is a G.

You will recall from the previous section, however, that Mill believes that it is a kind of illusion to suppose that we can really advance our knowledge through any sort of syllogistic reasoning, and so it is not surprising that he later (CW 7:572) makes clear that one isn't really getting anywhere by trying to transform inductive arguments into deductively valid syllogisms. The major premise does no epistemic work – the argument is only as good as is the inference from observed F's being G's to particular conclusions about unobserved F's being G's.

The whole discussion is complicated by the fact that Mill sometimes seems to run together the question of how we justify our belief that inductive reasoning is legitimate with the quite different question of how we can justify our belief in the law of causality, the principle that everything that happens has a cause, where causation is understood in terms of Humean constant conjunction. The principle that the universe is deterministic is a contingent proposition that *can* plausibly be regarded as itself the conclusion of an inductive argument. Mill's famous methods of discovering causal connections sometimes seem to presuppose the principle of determinism. So, for example, if we discover that the only common denominator to events preceding an event of kind B is an event of kind A, then we can deduce from the principle that everything has a cause and a crude regularity theory of causation, that A is the cause of B. But that reasoning is only as strong as is the conclusion that everything has a cause. Mill construes the inductive reasoning that supports the law of causation as a relatively straightforward, if ultimately implausible, argument from success. As we examine carefully one kind of phenomenon after another, Mill argues, we find again and again (through induction) that we can subsume the phenomenon under universal laws. We simply project such success in the cases in which we have yet failed to look, or look hard enough, to find the exceptionless regularities. It is interesting to speculate as to how Mill would react to the relatively sanguine reaction of most contemporary physicists to the conclusion that there exists fundamental indeterminacy at the quantum level.

However we evaluate Mill's claim that the thesis of determinism is inductively confirmed, we are still left without an answer as to how we could establish that inductive reasoning is legitimate. The relevant truth we need to know is that the premises of an inductive argument do indeed make probable its conclusion. How can we use induction to confirm that proposition? It is tempting to suggest that in a confused way Mill's discussion of this issue was a harbinger of contemporary internalism/externalism disputes in epistemology. Contemporary externalists such as reliabilists argue that a method of forming beliefs results in justified beliefs if as a matter of contingent fact the belief-forming process is reliable when it comes to producing true beliefs (conditionally, if the belief-forming process is belief-dependent, i.e. takes as input beliefs; unconditionally, if the belief-forming process is belief-independent, i.e. takes as input stimuli other than beliefs).[4]

I have argued elsewhere[5] that if one accepts something like a reliabilist account of justified belief, there is no objection in principle to using a reliable belief-forming process in order to discover that that very process is indeed reliable. If inductive reasoning is generally reliable then its output beliefs are justified. If one wants to find out whether or not inductive reasoning is reliable one can simply remember (assuming that memory is reliable) past successful uses of inductive reasoning in order to inductively conclude that induction is reliable. This suggestion would, of course, strike someone like Hume as being almost comical. The idea that one could use a method of reasoning to ascertain whether or not it was reliable seems pathetically question-begging. But Hume wasn't an externalist about justification. Hume wanted some sort of direct and immediate access to the legitimacy of inductive reasoning, and without such access he was convinced that we would be unable to satisfy the philosophical demands of reason with respect to grounding appropriately our reliance on induction.

For some reason Mill didn't seem bothered by the idea that there is no viable alternative to using inductive reasoning to establish its own legitimacy. He couldn't bring himself to introduce a faculty of "intuition" the purpose of which was to allow us to see that inductive reasoning was reliable. And it is perhaps small wonder that a philosopher who couldn't convince himself that we can just see by the light of reason that $2 + 2 = 4$, wouldn't be able to convince himself that we can just "see" the truth of the far more complicated principle of induction. But if anyone should have been sensitive to the charge that he was begging the question in using induction to ground induction it should have been Mill. Such a charge lay at the heart of his complaint that syllogistic reasoning could hardly be thought of as a (non-question-begging) way of increasing our knowledge. In the end, though, perhaps all we can do is speculate that one of the pivotal philosophical figures closing out the nineteenth century would have been far more comfortable in the company of late twentieth-century epistemologists who, through their externalist analyses of epistemic concepts, took a radical naturalistic turn in epistemology. Coming full circle to the issues raised at the start of this chapter, Mill could take fundamental belief-forming processes such as memory and induction to need no further "ground" than that provided by a *nature* that cooperates so as to insure that the beliefs produced in this way are usually true. On the other hand, if Mill were vulnerable to the seduction of contemporary naturalistic approaches to epistemology, it is not clear what would motivate him to labor so hard in an effort to restrict available legitimate belief-forming processes to just introspection, memory, and induction.

Mill's Methods

In the preceding discussion we have focused heavily on the way in which Mill thought one could employ enumerative induction to justify beliefs about the world, and even about mathematical truths. No discussion of Mill's epistemology would be complete, however, without examination of his famous methods for discovering causal connections. The methods go beyond enumerative induction, and derive, in part, from his metaphysical views about the nature of causal connection. We'll critically evaluate that account in more detail in the next chapter, but for now it suffices to note that Mill, like Hume before him, supported a version of the so-called regularity of causation. Mill says:

> To certain facts, certain facts always do, and, as we believe, will continue to, succeed. The invariable antecedent is termed the cause; the invariable consequent, the effect. And the universality of the law of causation consists in this, that every consequent is connected in this manner with some particular antecedent or set of antecedents. (CW 7:327)

He goes on to note that:

> It is seldom, if ever, between a consequent and a single antecedent that this invariable sequence subsists. It is usually between a consequent and the sum of several antecedents; the concurrence of all of them being requisite to produce, that is to be certain of being followed by, the consequent. In such cases it is very common to single out one only of the antecedents under the denomination of Cause, calling the others merely Conditions. (CW 7:327)

So, for example, I might well describe a dropped match as the cause of the fire in my basement despite the fact that I know full well that it is only the dropped match in the presence of oxygen, flammable material, the absence of a sprinkler system, and so on that would have been followed by the fire.

The regularity theory of causation faces enormous difficulties as an account of the meaning of causal claims. We'll briefly discuss some of those problems in the next chapter when we evaluate this fundamental metaphysical claim. But for now, it is important that we see Mill's Methods against the backdrop of his idea that causality is all about regularities in nature. While Mill unquestionably endorsed the idea that causation is nothing but regularity, it might be more plausible to suppose that his famous methods presuppose only what we might call a *generality* theory of causation. Like the regularity theorist, the generality theorist insists that particular causal claims presuppose regularities between kinds of events. Unlike the regularity theorist, a generality theorist leaves open that the relevant laws might themselves invoke some strong notion of necessary connection.

With the presupposition that causal connection is underwritten by regularities, or at the very least generalities, in nature, Mill introduces his methods for discovering the cause of some phenomenon we are investigating – methods that do seem undeniably to capture certain commonsense considerations we take into account in investigating causes. Again, the methods are not altogether new. Some of them get at least inspiration from Hume's "Rules by which to judge of causes and effects" in *A Treatise of Human Nature*. But Mill's statement of the methods is perhaps the clearest, most comprehensive, and, certainly, most influential of the early attempts to set out the epistemology of causal knowledge.

The first of Mill's Methods he calls the *Method of Agreement*. And he states it this way:

Method of Agreement

If two or more instances of the phenomenon under investigation have only one circumstance in common, the circumstance in which alone all the instances agree is the cause (or effect) of the given phenomenon. (CW 7:390)

The basic idea is simple and familiar. Suppose that my television occasionally has a distorted picture and I'm trying to figure out what causes the interference. I started paying attention to various conditions that immediately precede the problem when it occurs. On Monday, I notice that the interference was preceded by my wife's using her hairdryer, the stereo's playing in the living room, strong winds outside, and my neighbor's mowing of her lawn. On Wednesday the interference begins again. The stereo is playing, my neighbor is mowing her lawn, and there are strong winds, but my wife isn't using the hairdryer. On Friday when the interference begins, the stereo is playing, but my wife isn't using the hairdryer, my neighbor isn't mowing her lawn and there are no strong winds. I'm now in a position to conclude (tentatively) that it is the stereo playing havoc with my television.

As Mill himself concedes (CW 7:390), employment of the method carries with it a number of often highly problematic assumptions. Perhaps, most obviously, we are presupposing that we have isolated from among the indefinitely many antecedent conditions those that are candidates for the cause. Many more things were happening prior to the problem with the television than we enumerated in our example. Indeed, there were certain kinds of events that occurred every time the disturbance occurred, kinds of events that we are confident had nothing to do with the interference. As we'll see this confidence is often underwritten by use of other methods. But we are also presupposing that the cause of the interference on Monday was the same kind of condition that caused that interference on Wednesday and Friday, and that we weren't dealing with a case of causal overdetermination. It is possible, for example, that the hairdryer in conjunction with some other unobserved condition was the cause of the interference on Monday, while the strong winds in conjunction with yet other conditions was the cause on Friday. Or it might be that the hairdryer or the high winds were each independently causally sufficient for the distortion on the television screen. It may be that if we make specific *all* of the background assumptions employed in our reasoning, we really have a case of enthymematic deductive reasoning.

Enthymematic reasoning is reasoning that relies on unstated, and perhaps not even consciously entertained, premises justified belief in which is nevertheless necessary to justifiably infer a given conclusion. So, for example, when I come home and find my window broken and my valuables missing, I'll immediately infer that I've been robbed. But there probably is no legitimate reasoning that takes us directly from those premises to that conclusion. I know that windows don't spontaneously break every so often and I know that it is not an acceptable custom in our society for people to borrow valuables when random window breakings occur. I know that valuables don't disappear into thin air as a result of window breakings. I know all this and much more, and, arguably, if I didn't have that background knowledge (or at least background justified belief), I wouldn't be entitled to infer that I'd been robbed.

In like fashion, I'm suggesting that the use of Mill's Methods might often be best seen as deductively valid reasoning from the observations described in the method supplemented by background premises which if justified allow us to deduce the conclusion in question.

We noted that the method of agreement can go wrong in all sorts of ways. Our background assumptions may fail to be true or even warranted.

Use of the second method, the *Method of Difference*, can help lessen the possibility of error:

Method of Difference

If an instance in which the phenomenon under investigation occurs, and an instance in which it does not occur, have every circumstance in common save one, that one occurring only in the former; the circumstance in which alone the two instances differ is the effect, or the cause, or an indispensable part of the cause, of the phenomenon. (CW 7:391)

So in our example of the distortion of the television picture, if we find that there are four factors, A, B, C, and D, which are always followed by distortion, but then find that when we remove D, the distortion disappears, we then tentatively conclude that D was the culprit. The method of difference is particularly useful when the candidates for cause are easy to manipulate. So I can yell at my wife to stop using the hairdryer and see whether the interference stops. And I can get up and turn off the stereo to see whether that makes a difference (hence "method of difference"). If we knew in advance that the cause was one of A through D, then we could, of course, deduce that none of A through C is the cause, at least the full cause, once we have those conditions and we don't have the interference. The full cause of a kind of event X, you will recall, is that kind of condition or set of conditions which is *invariably* followed by events like X. Once we don't have the distortion even as we have A, B, and C, we have eliminated A, B, and C as the full cause.

Once again, it is important to emphasize that we are describing the use of a method against idealized and often problematic background assumptions. As Mill would be the first to point out, we are unlikely to have isolated all of the relevant candidates for the full cause. We typically have very little idea of what the full cause of even familiar phenomena is. I turn the light switch and the light goes on. Is the turning of the switch the full cause? Hardly. I know it has something to do with wires hooked up to still more wires that eventually connect to a generating plant somewhere, but the truth is I don't know much about electrical power or how it works. So when I get up to turn off the stereo and find that the interference stops, I might easily overlook the possibility that it is actually the hairdryer with the stereo that is causing the interference. Neither by itself is causally sufficient – they only produce the effect when operating in conjunction.

There is, of course, nothing to prevent one from using both the method of agreement and the method of difference together. And with that in mind Mill (somewhat arbitrarily) gives a separate label to the joint use of the above methods (arbitrarily, because, of course, one could give a separate label for the joint use of any number of different methods):

Joint Method of Agreement and Difference

If two or more instances in which the phenomenon occurs have only one circumstance in common, while two or more instances in which it does not occur have nothing in common save the absence of that circumstance: the circumstance in which alone the two sets of instances differ, is the effect, or cause, or an indispensable part of the cause, of the phenomenon. (CW 7:396)

Since as the name implies, the joint method is nothing more than the use of both the method of agreement and the method of difference, there is no reason to discuss it in any more detail. It obviously combines whatever virtues each method has individually.

The *Method of Residues* is a prescription for how to identify causes against a background of prior causal knowledge. Mill states it as follows:

Method of Residues

Subduct from any phenomenon such part as is known by previous inductions to be the effect of certain antecedents, and the residue of the phenomenon is the effect of the remaining antecedents. (CW 7:398)

So *if* (and of course this is a big if) you find that A, B, and C are followed by X, Y, and Z, and you have already established that A is the cause of X, and that B is the cause of Y, then you can justifiably start speculating that C (the residue, that which is left over) is the cause of Z. So suppose I drink red wine, with a hot dog, and also eat (perhaps for the first time) fried squid. I know that drinking red wine gives me heartburn, and eating hot dogs gives me a stomach ache. Sure enough, I have the heartburn and the stomach ache, but this time I also begin to vomit. I may well begin to suspect that the fried squid has something to do with this unanticipated result. Again, it seems obvious that the reasoning is highly enthymematic. As Mill himself would emphasize, you would have to antecedently know not just that A and B are the cause of X and Y respectively, you would also have to know that C is the only other antecedent condition that is a plausible candidate for the cause of Z. As we have already had occasion to note in discussing the method of agreement, there are always indefinitely many other circumstances that occur along with the occurrence of A, B, and C, any one of which might be the cause of Z. Unless one combines the method of residues with one or both of the methods of agreement and disagreement, it's hard to see how one can get very far with this "process of elimination."

The Method of Concomitant Variations

> Whatever phenomenon varies in any manner whenever another phenomenon varies in some particular manner, is either a cause or an effect of that phenomenon, or is connected with it through some fact of causation. (CW 7:401)

When I began to suspect that the stereo had something to do with the interference with my television picture, I might have investigated further by moving the stereo closer and farther from the set. Suppose that as I move the stereo closer, the picture gets worse, and as I move it farther away, the picture gets better. Common sense would certainly suggest that I have gained more evidence for the conclusion that the stereo is indeed the culprit.

It is not entirely clear to me that the method of concomitant variation is distinct from the method of difference. The various forms of picture distortion are, after all, distinct events, each requiring a causal explanation (on the supposition that there is a cause of the phenomenon). I suspect that the proximity of the stereo is a cause of that severe picture distortion. I then remove the stereo from that place and *that* distortion no longer occurs. Another less severe problem still exists with the picture and I might suspect that problem has as its cause the new location of the stereo. As I move it again, I see that the difference in location results again in a difference in the picture. The method, then, might be construed as repeated application of the method of difference, together with, perhaps, reliance on an inductive principle that where we find a certain kind of cause responsible for a certain kind of effect, and we have another presumed effect similar to the first kind of effect, we should look for a similar sort of cause. The principle probably does have significant (enumerative) inductive support. So, for example, if we find that a given disease is often carried from one person to another by insects, and we are searching for the causal explanation of how another different disease gets transmitted from one person to another, we would probably be well advised to search for some sort of organism that moves from person to person.

notes

1 As we will see later, in connection with Mill's inductive justification of induction, certain externalist approaches to knowledge of reliable belief-forming processes might actually allow one to use the very process one is investigating in order to certify its reliability.

2 The same cannot be said for a great many of Mill's predecessors and contemporaries. Often it seemed that either they didn't realize the threat of skepticism with respect to the past, or they realized it and chose to ignore it.

3   As we'll see in the next section, it may be misleading to describe the conclu-
    sion of an inductive argument as a generalization. In a sense we must explain,
    Mill seems to hold that all inference is from particulars to particulars.
4   The best and clearest statement of such a view is still, arguably, Goldman
    1979. Although he flirted with importantly different variations on the origi-
    nal theme, I think it is fair to suggest that Goldman eventually returned to the
    heart of the views defended in this classic piece (for at least one fundamental
    concept of justification).
5   The theme runs through much of Fumerton 1995, but is developed most thor-
    oughly in Chapter 6.

further reading

Copi, Irving, *Introduction to Logic*, 2nd edn. (New York: Macmillan, 1961), chap-
    ter 12.
Mackie, J. L., "Mill's Methods of Induction," in P. Edwards, ed., *The Ency-
    clopedia of Philosophy*, vol. 5, pp. 324–32 (New York: Macmillan, 1967).
Russell, Bertrand, *The Problems of Philosophy* (Oxford: Oxford University Press,
    1959), chapters 6–7.
Ryan, Alan, *The Philosophy of John Stuart Mill* (London: Macmillan, 1970),
    chapters 2–5.
Wilson, Fred, *Psychological Analysis and the Philosophy of John Stuart Mill*
    (Toronto: University of Toronto Press, 1990), chapters 2–5.
Wilson, Fred, "John Stuart Mill," sections 3–5, in *Stanford Encyclopedia of
    Philosophy*, 2002, http://plato.stanford.edu/entries/mill/.

metaphysics

Physical Objects as the Permanent Possibility of Sensations

In Chapter 10, we discovered that Mill seems committed to a meager foundation for knowledge consisting of what we can know directly about present and past experience. Furthermore, he allowed himself only induction as a means of moving beyond those foundations. In Chapter 9, we noted that radical empiricists working within such a framework face enormous difficulties avoiding radical skepticism. In particular, it is difficult to see how one can justify belief in propositions describing the physical world. Indeed, given the radical empiricist's claim that all simple ideas are copies of what is given to one in sense experience, it is difficult to see how one can even find *intelligible* thought about a world of mind-independent, enduring physical objects. As we noted briefly in the last chapter, Mill's solution to both problems is to construe claims about the physical world as equivalent in meaning to complex claims about experience.

As I argued in Chapter 10, one can get a feel for the view by looking first at a more modest claim accepted by most empiricists and, probably, even most rationalists. At the time Mill wrote, almost everyone accepted a so-called primary/secondary quality distinction. One of the most common philosophical views about our relation to physical objects through perception was a view called *representative realism*. The representative realist rejected what Hume called the view of the vulgar, a view that has more recently been called naive realism, or, more politely, direct realism. The direct realist claims that in perception we are directly and immediately aware of physical objects and at least some of their properties. Relying heavily on facts about the way in which our perceptual experience is affected by our environment and our sense organs, the representative realist argues that experience cannot give us direct knowledge of a perceiver-independent world. Rather, we must think of physical objects as entities that affect us in various ways. They leave their mark, their image on the mind, and we must infer their presence from that mark or image. The expression "impression of sense" was often used and it conveys the idea nicely. Just as a signet ring leaves its impression on the wax, so also, physical objects leave their "impression" on our mind through the senses. Just as one can "read off" certain characteristics, e.g. the shape of the ring's surface, by looking at the impression it made on the wax, so also, one can read off certain characteristics of physical objects by paying attention to the "impressions" they make on the mind. But while one can, perhaps, discover the *shape* of the ring by looking at the wax impression, there are other characteristics of the ring that are not revealed through the wax impression. And indeed, there are properties of the impression that are not necessarily properties of the ring. The wax might be red, for example, while the ring is silver. And that's the idea behind the primary/secondary quality distinction made by most representative realists. Some of the properties exemplified by the mental ideas or impressions are also in the physical object that caused them. But others are not, at least they are not in the object in the way in which they are in the mental representation of the object. Let me explain further.

Start with a relatively easy example. We say of sugar that it is sweet and lemons that they are sour. In what does the sourness of a lemon consist? What makes it true that a lemon is sour? It surely has *something* to do with that familiar sour taste sensation that one gets when one bites into a lemon. But is the sourness of the taste sensation "in" the lemon? Can one even make sense of *that* idea? To be sure, along with our physical constitution, there are properties of the lemon that cause it to taste a certain way to us. It is also obvious that we do describe lemons as being sour. But is there any more to the sourness of the lemon than the fact that it would cause in us under certain conditions that familiar sour taste sensation?

Just as many representative realists became convinced that the sourness of the lemon was nothing more than the lemon's power to produce in "normal" humans under "standard" conditions a sour taste sensation, so also many were convinced that the color of objects was nothing more than the causal power certain objects have to produce in "normal" people under "standard" conditions certain color sensations. It is probably no accident that the view became popular around the time people were discovering more and more powerful ways to magnify the appearance of objects. One can't help but notice that the colors one associated with the object often change or disappear as one examines the object under magnification. But long before high-powered magnification, all of us have always known that the colors that appear to us vary dramatically depending on the conditions of perception. If you paint landscapes for any length of time, you'll start noticing that the way things look varies dramatically depending on the time of day and year, the cloud cover, and neighboring objects. Most of us have put on various sorts of sunglasses and have noticed the often dramatic change in the apparent color of what we see. It is really hard to figure out what the "real" color of the object is given that it presents so many different appearances under so many different conditions. Indeed, it seemed to the representative realist that it was better to let color go the way of sourness. We say of objects that they have a given color, but all that we could mean is that the object would cause under certain conditions a certain color sensation. A physical object is blue if it would "appear blue" to a normal person under standard conditions.

In his *Three Dialogues Between Hylas and Philonous*, Berkeley relentlessly exploits the arguments for thinking that the secondary qualities of objects are only in the object as powers, to conclude that there is no principled distinction between them and the so-called primary qualities – qualities that were supposed to be properties both of the ideas or images and also of the object that caused them. The shapes, textures, motion, and so on that appear to one directly, he argued, are no less perceiver-dependent than taste and color. Whatever one says about the latter, one should say about the former. And this is precisely the suggestion that Mill is following in trying to understand our assertions about the physical world so that such assertions are both intelligible and epistemically accessible. Just as a great many earlier philosophers conceded that the taste of an object is nothing but a power to produce a taste sensation, so Mill wants to argue that the physical object itself is nothing but a permanent possibility of sensation.

Now the above crude sketch of Mill's view still suggests two importantly different, though closely related, theories. On the one view, as Mill describes it:

> External things exist, and have an inmost nature, but their inmost nature is inaccessible to our faculties. We know it not, and can assert nothing of it with a meaning. Of the ultimate Realities, as such, we know the existence, and nothing more. But the impressions which these Realities make on us – the sensations they excite, the similitudes, groupings, and successions of those sensations, or, to sum up all this in a common though improper expression, the *representations* generated in our minds by the action of the Things themselves – these we may know, and these are all that we can know respecting them. (EWH 9–10)

This is essentially the last attempt Hylas (Berkeley's foil in his *Three Dialogues*) makes in an effort to rescue an intelligible concept of material objects before his complete capitulation to Philonous's (Berkeley's protagonist) idealism (the view that there exists nothing but minds and their ideas). Such a view would certainly have a claim to being one according to which the concept of a physical object just is the concept of a permanent possibility or power of producing sensations of various sorts. In the language of contemporary predicate logic, claims about the existence of physical objects are existential claims whose variables range over objects other than sensations, but whose predicate expressions are exhausted by causal descriptions of the ways in which those objects affect sentient beings. So on such a view to assert that there exists something rectangular and brown might be to assert that there exists that which could (lawfully) cause in a subject the visual sensation of seeming to see something rectangular and brown, and is such that if it were causing such a sensation and the subject were to have the kinesthetic sensation of initiating a certain grasping motion, and if conditions of perception were normal then it would also produce the tactile sensation of seeming to feel something rectangular, and . . . The analysis trails off in this way to indicate that there is an indefinitely complex array of possible sensations that could and would be produced under the relevant conditions.

It is important to recognize that Mill has no principled objection to the intelligibility of the above view. It is, however, probably not the understanding he wanted of permanent possibilities of sensations. In *An Examination of Sir William Hamilton's Philosophy* Mill describes a version of what he calls the doctrine of the Relativity of Knowledge with which he is clearly sympathetic:

> the sensations which, in common parlance, we are said to receive from objects, are not only all that we can possibly know of the objects, but are all that we have any ground for believing to exist. What we term an object is but a complex conception made up by the laws of association, out of the ideas of various sensations which we are accustomed to receive simultaneously. There is nothing real in the process but these sensations. They do not, indeed, accompany or succeed one another at random; they are held together by a law, that is, they occur in fixed groups, and a fixed order of succession; but we have no evidence of anything which, not being itself a sensation, is a substratum or hidden cause of sensations. (EWH 8)

If Mill is endorsing *this* view, then his identification of material (physical) objects with the permanent possibilities of sensations is his attempt to formulate one of the earliest and clearest versions of reductive *phenomenalism*. Reductive phenomenalism is best understood as the view that assertions about the physical world are equivalent in meaning to indefinitely complex subjunctive conditionals that make assertions about what sensations *would* follow others.[1] That Mill can most naturally be read as a phenomenalist is evidenced by passages such as this:

> I believe that Calcutta exists, though I do not perceive it, and that it would still exist if every percipient inhabitant were suddenly to leave the place,

Richard Fumerton

or be struck dead. But when I analyze the belief, all I find in it is, that were these events to take place, the Permanent Possibility of Sensation which I call Calcutta would still remain; that if I were suddenly transported to the banks of the Hoogly, I should still have the sensations which, if now present, would lead me to affirm that Calcutta exists here and now. (EWH 253)

The idea Mill is putting forth is strikingly similar to at least one passage in Berkeley's *Dialogues*. Berkeley (through his spokesman in the dialogue, Philonous) has convinced Hylas that there exists nothing but minds and sensations. But he also tries to convince us that this view is in perfect accord with common sense and implies no sort of skepticism. Hylas is bewildered by that suggestion and raises a number of objections. Among others, he complains that this sort of "idealism" is incompatible with the commonsense view that the world has existed long before people walked its face (long before creation). When explaining how he can make sense of objects coming into existence before sentient beings, Philonous says the following:

> Why I imagine that if I had been present at the creation, I should have seen things produced into being; that is become perceptible, in the order described by the sacred historian. (Berkeley [1713] 1954, 245)

But while Berkeley clearly toyed with Mill's idea of understanding objects in terms of possibilities of sensation, more often than not he seemed to retreat to ideas in the mind of God to secure for objects their independence of human sentient beings.

As I indicated above, there are two ways in which one might naturally understand Mill's idea that physical objects are permanent possibilities of sensation. They are (a) physical objects should be understood as potential causes (unknown as to their non-relational character) of various sensations, and (b) physical object claims should be understood as complex conditional claims about what sensations a subject would have were he to have certain others. The two views are strikingly similar. Both rely crucially on subjunctive or counterfactual conditionals describing the sensations a subject would have under certain conditions. However, (a) commits the theorist to the existence of something other than sensations; (b) does not. But it is precisely for that reason that despite the valiant efforts of twentieth-century positivists, reductive phenomenalism wilted before devastating objections.

The first and most obvious problem for phenomenalism, the one labeled by R. M. Chisholm (1948) as the problem of perceptual relativity, virtually cries out to be noticed in Mill's various characterizations of the permanent possibilities. For the reductive analysis to work, for Mill to secure a meaning for physical object claims that allows one to establish such claims *solely* through correlations discovered among sensations, the antecedents and consequents of the subjunctive conditionals must make reference to nothing other than sensations. And here the phenomenalist's critic simply waits patiently for the phenomenalistic analysis to be offered. Mill's crude analysis of his belief about Calcutta clearly fails the test of a successful phenomenal translation. If he were transported to the banks of the Hoogly he would have various sensations. Perhaps he would, but our *translation* of what we believe into phenomenal language must replace reference to the *physical* location, the banks of the Hoogly, with a purely phenomenal description of experience. But how would that translation proceed? If I were to have the sensations of floating through the air and have the sensations of seeming to see a river and if I were to have the tactile sensations of ground beneath me then I would have . . . But this isn't going to work. There are indefinitely many real and imaginable places that are visually indistinguishable from various places along the banks of the Hoogly. Moreover, as Chisholm pointed out, what sensations a subject would have even if one could "fix" the subject's relevant "location" (again, something the phenomenalist must do without referring to *physical* space or *physical* spatial relations) depends on the state of the subject's *physical* organs of sense. Blind people wouldn't have any visual sensations were they on the banks of the Hoogly. A person whose entire body had been anesthetized would have no kinesthetic or tactile sensations. And one can't revise one's conditionals so as to take account of the absence of these physical conditions without violating the phenomenalist's commitment to fully reducing talk about the physical world to complex talk of phenomena.

Wilfred Sellars (1963) presented an argument against phenomenalism which in many ways was quite similar to Chisholm's. Sellars stressed that subjunctives of the sort used in a phenomenalist's analysis of the meaning of physical object claims assert *lawful* connections between their antecedents and their consequents. To be sure, the antecedent might be only a non-redundant part of some complex condition that is lawfully sufficient for the antecedent, but given the phenomenalist's *ontological* commitments the other conditions presupposed must themselves be purely phenomenal. But, Sellars argued, there simply are no laws of nature correlating sensations. As we noted earlier, Mill was a Humean about laws of nature. Laws assert only exceptionless correlations between phenomena.[2] But ask yourself whether you can describe any universal truths describing sequences of sensations. Is it true that whenever anyone seems to see a table and seems to reach out and touch it that person seems to feel one? No it isn't. Dreams, illusions, hallucinations, and people with anesthetized hands testify to the fact that there is no genuinely lawful connection between these sensations. Can't we "save" the regularity by making the relevant description of the

Richard Fumerton

related sensations complicated enough? Do it, the phenomenalist's critic insists. There are too many causally relevant *physical* conditions of perception to allow one to construct genuine lawful regularities in the world of phenomena, and for that reason the antecedents of subjunctive conditionals used by the phenomenalist must make reference to normal or standard conditions of perception where such reference can only be construed as implicit acknowledgment of a world different from, but causally relevant to, sensation.

Given the limits of space, I won't try to defend Mill against these enormously powerful objections. I would, however, argue that he might have been better off had he construed the permanent possibility of sensations in the first of the two ways identified earlier. Provided that he could come up with an inductive argument for the principle that everything has a cause (something he claims he can do – *A System of Logic*, Book III, Chapter 5) he wouldn't necessarily encounter insurmountable epistemological problems by allowing in to his metaphysics entities whose sole function was to plug nomological holes in "gappy" correlations among sensations. Furthermore, he would have had a much more natural way of attempting to secure meaning for "bare" existential claims about physical objects, claims which provide no "setting" for the actual and possible sensations described by the relevant counterfactuals. How would a phenomenalist, for example, understand the bare existential claim that there exists *something somewhere* in the universe that is brown? If a subject were to have the visual experiences we would associate with canvassing the entire infinite universe that subject would eventually have the visual experience of seeming to see something brown? Hardly. How would one successfully distinguish *phenomenologically* covering the universe from moving around in slow circles in empty space? With Hylas's model of matter as the thing unknowable in itself but the potential cause of sensations, one has a solution, at least, to *this* problem. The analysis of what is clearly a non-hypothetical claim begins with the existential claim that there does exist some x which (lawfully) could produce the relevant sensations and which would produce certain others under normal (perhaps statistically defined) conditions.[3]

Mill's Metaphysics of Causation

In Chapter 10 we discussed Mill's Methods and noted that they seemed to be underwritten, at least in part, by his analysis of causation. Mill was clearly a regularity theorist and was following closely in the footsteps of Hume. The regularity theory of causation was one of the most dramatic (and strikingly original) results of trying to follow rigorously the empiricist's injunction that we recognize as legitimate only ideas that are either copies of prior impressions, or built up out of ideas that are copies of prior impressions. Hume famously sought in vain for that impression which gives rise to the idea of causal necessary connection. Because his paradigm of causal connection was action and reaction, Hume tried to find the source of his idea of causation in the experience of one billiard ball striking another and causing it to move. But all he found focusing on the particular sequence of events was one billiard ball's coming into physical contact (he called this spatial contiguity) with another just prior to (temporal contiguity) the other billiard ball's movement. In his dismissal of any interest in the metaphysician's idea of an insensible necessary connection, Mill seems equally confident that there is nothing more to be found in experience. Almost all of the rationalists who preceded Hume thought of causation as "powers" that reside in the objects that are causes, but they had very little to say about just exactly what these powers were or how we were supposed to get an idea of them. Both Hume and Mill were convinced that you would look in vain for causal connection focusing on some sequence of *particular* events. You will never find your idea of causal connection until you start thinking about sequences of events of the same kind, and find in nature the patterns or regularities that, according to them, define the existence of causal connection.[4] The idea of causal connection just is the idea of regularity.

While the basic idea behind the regularity theory seems clear enough, it is not that easy to refine it. For one thing, one needs to find a way of specifying more clearly the idea of regularity that is the heart of the theory. In Hume's classic statement of the (objective) regularity theory (see note 4), he says, in effect, that one "object" X causes another "object" Y when all objects *resembling* X stand in relations of spatial and temporal contiguity to objects resembling Y. But it is odd to talk of objects as the relata of causal connection. And the notion of resembling to which Hume appeals is hopelessly vague. Every two things resemble each other in infinitely many ways and are different in infinitely many ways. Should we not conclude that the one billiard ball caused the other to move because when I throw a pea at a boulder the boulder doesn't move?

In an interesting comment in his "rules" by which to judge of causes and effects, Hume suggests that when different objects cause the same effect it is by means of common properties the objects have. And reference to properties will be enormously helpful to the regularity theorist. An object doesn't cause anything. Rather it is an object's having a certain property, an object's undergoing a certain change, standing in certain relations to other objects that is, properly speaking, the cause of another object's acquiring a property, changing, standing in new relations to other objects. Once we have reference to properties in the perspicuous formulation of a causal claim, we have a relatively straightforward way of specifying the relevant regularity that the regularity theorists view as the truthmaker

Richard Fumerton

for the causal claim. Crudely put, a's being F just prior to a's being G is the (full) cause of a's being G when it is true that whenever something is F it is immediately afterwards G. When other objects are involved the analysis gets a bit more complicated. We can say that a's being F under conditions C1 and standing in relations R to b which is G under conditions C2 causes b to be H when it is true that whenever one thing is F under conditions C and stands in relations R to another different thing which is G under conditions C2, that other thing then becomes H.

Again, as we noted in our earlier discussion of Mill's Methods, Mill would be the first to admit that we often succeed only in identifying a part of the complete cause of some phenomenon. In claiming that that part is "the" cause, we are, presumably, claiming that there is some more complex condition of which it is a (non-redundant) part, where the relevant regularity obtains between the occurrence of that kind of complex condition and the occurrence of the kind of phenomenon we take to be the effect.

It is perhaps a tribute to the lingering force of radical empiricism that the regularity theory is still probably the received view among contemporary philosophers despite what appear to be devastating objections to the view. Probably the most well-known problem the view faces is that of distinguishing between genuinely *lawful* regularities of the sort that might seem to generate causal connections, and *accidental* regularities which clearly do not. I have a certain unique pattern of fingerprints, call it alpha pattern of fingerprints. My grandmother also has a certain unique pattern of fingerprints – call it beta pattern. As it turns out I meet my grandmother only once just as she is about to die. The second before she dies I reach out and touch her hand. Did my touching her hand cause her to die? Surely, we are not *forced* to that conclusion. But given the hypothetical situation the following general claim is true: whenever a person with alpha pattern of fingerprints touches the hand of a person with beta pattern of fingerprints the person with beta pattern of fingerprints dies. One might be tempted to suppose that one can deal with the problem by stipulating that the relevant regularities must have a certain number of instances, but it won't be difficult to come up with artificially contrived situations in which the non-lawful regularity has a great many instances, and it won't be difficult to come up with genuine laws that have few or no instances (think of Newton's first law of motion).

Even if one finds a solution to the problem of distinguishing genuine laws from spurious laws, a daunting task, one still faces problems involved in distinguishing genuinely *causal* laws from non-accidental, but non-causal regularities. So to take a well-known example, we know that the rapid fall of a barometer under certain conditions precedes stormy weather. The regularity exists, but we don't think of the barometer's fall as the cause of the storm.

The above is intended to give the reader only a feel for the kinds of problems that beset a regularity theory. And I'm not suggesting, of course, that there are no solutions to the problems. It is fair to suggest, however, that neither Mill, nor Hume before him, seemed to fully appreciate the extent of the problems, nor did they seem to have much to say by way of solving those problems.

In discussing Mill's Methods, I suggested that at least some of those methods could best be seen as involving enthymematic reasoning that presupposed Mill's account of causation. More carefully, however, I suggested that they need only presuppose what I called a generality theory of causation. Like the regularity theory, the generality theory argues that the truthmaker for a causal claim is a law of nature. Unlike the regularity theorist, however, the generality theorist will often deny that one can understand laws as mere regularities. The philosopher who identifies only with a generality theory is more likely to be sympathetic to the idea that there are those "mysterious" metaphysical ties in nature eschewed by both Hume and Mill. Even the generality theory is not without its critics, however. It has become commonplace to view the microworld as governed by indeterministic laws. There simply are no universal regularities governing, say, the time it will take a radioactive element to decay. And some philosophers will claim that an indeterministic universe is still compatible with the existence of causal connections between particular events. So consider again the example of partial causation and let's use an example once put forth by Carl Hempel (1966) (though in the context of developing an account of what he called probabilistic explanation). Jim was playing with Sally who had a bad cold, and shortly thereafter Jim got a cold. Probably, most of us would not argue with the supposition that the cause of Jim's getting the cold was his contact with Sally. Is it a law of nature that whenever anyone comes into contact with someone who has a cold, they also get infected? Hardly. It isn't even true that people usually get a cold when they come into contact with an infected person. So far, though, there is no real problem for Mill. He will treat this as a case of partial causation. Strictly speaking the full cause of infection is a much more complicated condition that includes not just the contact but the precise nature of the contact and countless conditions and relations that obtained at the time of the contact. Here we will (and must) find the relevant regularity if our causal claim is true. But suppose (perhaps implausibly) that the world of disease is just as indeterministic as the world of quantum particles. There simply are no universal laws to be discovered. The phenomena are "governed" only by various statistical claims about the percentage of people who become infected under the relevant conditions. If this were the way of things, would we take this to entail that there was no causal connection in the case described? If the answer is "No," then even a generality theory is suspect.

There may be a solution to the problem that one can employ within the spirit of regularity/generality theories of the sort endorsed by Mill. Some, for example, would argue that the key is to find the right statistical regularity that can underwrite a causal claim. But so-called statistical-relevance models themselves face a host of problems, discussion of which would take us too far afield.

Mill as Direct Reference Theorist

In recent years there has been a marked surge in references to Mill, but primarily on a subject about which Mill wrote relatively little, philosophy of language. So-called direct reference theorists often refer approvingly to the doctrine Mill appears to defend in *A System of Logic* that the meaning of a proper name is the referent of that name.

First a bit of background. There was enormous controversy for a very long time concerning the meaning of names, both names for kinds of things (common nouns) but also names for particular objects (proper names). One natural view was that a proper name, unlike a description of a thing, is a mere *label* for the thing named. That view, however, created all sorts of puzzles – puzzles that often led philosophers to exotic metaphysical commitments. Consider, for example, such commonplace assertions as the following:

1   Pegasus doesn't exist.

If the meaning of a name is the thing the name refers to, then either "Pegasus" is meaningless or (1) is not only false, but, arguably, necessarily false. But "Pegasus" is clearly not a meaningless expression, and (1) is true. In the grips of the theory that names are mere labels, some philosophers suggested that perhaps we should acknowledge that there *are* things (like Pegasus) that don't *exist*, but it is perhaps understandable that many found it a bit disconcerting that the universe is populated by such shadowy entities as "beings" that don't exist.

Or consider another familiar datum that puzzled philosophers for a very long time. We can make interesting and informative identity claims using proper names. None of the following seem trivial:

2   Hesperus is Phosphorus (where "Hesperus" was used to refer to the morning "star" – actually the planet Venus – and "Phosphorus" was used to refer to the evening "star" – also the planet Venus).
3   Mark Twain is Samuel Clemens.
4   Deep Throat is W. Mark Felt.

If the *meaning* of a name is just the referent of the name, then anyone who *understands* (2)–(4) should immediately just see that they are true. But it was an important scientific discovery that Hesperus is Phosphorus, a fact not known to some that Mark Twain is Samuel Clemens, and a discovery of great political interest that Deep Throat and Mark Felt are the same man.

In his classic "On Denoting" Bertrand Russell proposed a solution to these (and other) puzzles. Russell in effect claimed that even proper names were "disguised" descriptions – *definite* descriptions. A definite description is a noun phrase that begins with the definite article – e.g. "the tallest man in America," or "the author of *Tom Sawyer*." Russell in turn suggested that we can understand definite descriptions as equivalent to general claims about existence. The assertion that the F is G is just the claim that there is one and only one thing that is F and that thing is also G.[5] "Pegasus" in (1) has the meaning of just such a description – perhaps something like "the winged horse that Perseus captured and rode" and the claim that Pegasus doesn't exist is just the claim that it is not the case that there is one and only one thing that is a winged horse that Perseus captured and rode. "Hesperus" had some such meaning as "the brightest light appearing in a certain region of the morning sky." "Phosphorus" meant something like "the brightest light appearing in a certain region of the evening sky." And, of course, it was a matter of considerable interest that it turns out that the one and only brightest object in the morning sky is also the one and only brightest object in the evening sky. One can easily see how a similar story could be told to explain the informative character of (3) and (4).

Despite its enormous appeal and power to solve puzzles, Russell's theory has come upon hard times. Largely due to the influence of Saul Kripke's *Naming and Necessity* (1980), many contemporary philosophers became convinced that we should return to the so-called direct reference theory. While their arguments are complicated, one can get a feel for them by considering the difficulty in actually coming up with plausible definite descriptions with which we can identify the *meaning* of names. In some cases, we have relatively little difficulty in thinking of definite descriptions that we believe pick out the item named. So, to take a much-used example, I believe that Aristotle is the philosophical teacher of Alexander. But if "Aristotle" means "the teacher of Alexander" then I couldn't even make sense of someone's claiming to have discovered that Aristotle did not, in fact, teach Alexander. That claim would be equivalent to the claim that the teacher of Alexander didn't teach Alexander – a clear contradiction. But I *can* make sense of the claim, and thus I clearly don't really regard "Aristotle" and "the teacher of Alexander" as synonymous. Alternatively, there are other names I use successfully to refer even though I would be hard-pressed to

Richard Fumerton

come up with any definite descriptions that I even believe pick out the person named. So, for example, I might tell someone that Scattergood is a private school, but I seem to have no particular definite description in mind when I use the name "Scattergood." I don't even think of it as the school named "Scattergood" as I suspect that there may be more than one school with that name.

While I don't in fact think that the above arguments give good reasons for abandoning Russell's approach (see Fumerton 1989), many philosophers have been persuaded that one should think more carefully before abandoning the slogan that the meaning of a name is its referent. Many of those also think that the meaning of certain general terms like "man" or "gold" is the class of things to which those expressions refer. And at least for the idea that a proper name has as its meaning its referent, some claim to find their inspiration in remarks made by Mill.

Mill begins his discussion of names by apparently repudiating what he takes to be Hobbes's suggestion that names signify ideas (CW 7:24–5). He goes on to make a distinction between concrete names and abstract names, where the former signify objects, and the latter attributes or properties (CW 7:29). This is followed in turn by a distinction between names that are connotative and names that are non-connotative. A non-connotative term denotes (refers) directly. A connotative term also denotes, but "implies" an attribute (CW 7:30–31). If we look at his examples, the connotative terms denote what they do through reference to a property that all of the things picked out by the term have. So, for example, "man" is a common noun that picks out all sorts of individual men. It picks out those men (it denotes the class of men) by its implicit reference to the property of being a man that all those men share. About proper names (Caesar, Washington, etc.), Mill says that they are non-connotative, that they "denote the individuals who are called by them; but they do not imply any attributes as belonging to those individuals" (CW 7:33). This does seem to be in stark contrast to the Russellian idea that names are disguised definite *descriptions*. As we saw above, if Russell is correct, then when I use the name "Caesar" I am (if successfully referring) picking some individual out but only as the unique bearer of certain attributes (properties). So if one focuses on these passages, one can see how contemporary direct reference theorists might view Mill as the historical model of the philosopher who holds that the meaning of a proper name is its referent – that one cannot distinguish between the sense of a name and the thing named.

The above, however, barely scratches the surface of Mill's extensive discussion of kinds of names and kinds of propositions. And the discussion is particularly difficult for contemporary philosophers given the arcane terminology Mill brings to his various distinctions. Careful contemporary direct reference theorists will often shy away from unequivocally attributing to Mill something like their view. And they are probably well-advised to use such caution. First, we must remember Mill's controversial analysis of claims about the physical world. As we saw, *all* talk of physical objects is translatable into talk about the permanent possibilities of sensations. And if the interpretation offered earlier is correct, talk about the permanent possibilities of sensations is equivalent in meaning to complex subjunctive conditionals *describing* the experiences one would have were one to have certain others. It is not at all clear how one can directly "name" the fact that is the truthmaker for the subjunctive conditional. Indeed the physical object as an entity referred to in the subject term of a claim seems to "disappear" on Mill's understanding of the claim. Consider an analogy. Suppose I decide to give the name "Fred" to the average man. I want the name to refer directly (to be non-connotative in Mill's sense). But there is an obvious problem. It takes but a little reflection to realize that claims about, say, the height of the average man are complex claims about the results of certain mathematical operations performed on the heights of individual men. We'll "translate" away any apparent reference to an average man, and with our translation we'll be left without any obvious candidate for the "directly referring" name "Fred" to denote. As far as I can see that's what happens to most candidates for the referents of most names on Mill's phenomenalistic analysis. To be sure, it is not uncommon for philosophers to "bracket" some of their philosophical views in discussing other issues. And, indeed, it seems relatively clear to me that in *A System of Logic* Mill didn't want to presuppose his controversial metaphysical views. Nevertheless, if we put together a view that is consistent with *all* of what he has to say, the theory of proper names as mere labels for the thing named does not sit well.

There are still other passages that present difficulties for the interpretation of Mill on names. We noted earlier that Mill seems to reject Hobbes's suggestion that names refer to ideas rather than things to which the ideas correspond. And in keeping with this thought, he suggests (CW 7:35) that "When we impose a proper name, we perform an operation in some degree analogous to what the robber intended in chalking the house [a robber who marks a house with chalk to remind himself that that's the house he is going to rob]." So far, so good. But then he adds:

> We put a mark, not indeed upon the object itself, but, so to speak, upon the idea of the object. A proper name is but an unmeaning mark which we connect in our minds with the idea of the object, in order that whenever the mark meets our eyes or occurs to our thoughts, we may think of that individual object. (CW 7:35)

And this idea seems to be the *antithesis* of the direct reference theorist who didn't want anything in the mind of the person using the name to be the vehicle through which reference was achieved.

It may be, of course, that Mill did not have a consistent view. And even if he were a direct reference theorist it is not clear how he would have handled the problems which the descriptivist tries to solve. But this would not be peculiar to Mill. While many direct reference theorists articulate at some lengths their criticisms of Russell, they often struggle mightily to explain the various puzzles to which Russell's theory was a solution. There are at least some signs that Mill may have been seduced by his view of names into thinking that there are things that don't exist. He does say that "all names are names of something, real or imaginary" (CW 7:27). And later in discussing our thoughts of a loaf of bread eaten yesterday, a flower about to bloom tomorrow, and a hobgoblin, he says:

> But the hobgoblin which never existed is not the same thing with my idea of a hobgoblin, any more than the loaf which once existed is the same thing with my idea of a loaf, or the flower which does not yet exist, but which will exist is the same with my idea of a flower. They are all, not thoughts, but objects of thought; though at the present time all the objects are alike non-existent. (CW 7:51–2)

It would be more than a little ironic if the empiricist's empiricist, the philosopher who sought to avoid commitment to a mysterious matter as the unknown cause of our ideas, ended up committed to a universe populated by entities that have being but no existence.

Before ending this brief discussion, it will be good to remind the reader once again how much of a very brief and broad-stroke overview it has been. The general theory of names, language, ideas, and truth that Mill addresses in *A System of Logic* cannot be treated in any but a cursory way in this brief space, and there is a great deal to be said by way of alternative readings of most of what Mill says about these matters.

Mill's Metaethics

It is perhaps fitting that this book ends by coming full circle. It is doubtless true that Mill will be better known in centuries to come for his views in ethics and political philosophy than his views in epistemology and metaphysics. But for a radical empiricist who was clearly interested in reducing talk of problematic entities and their properties to descriptions of the "phenomenal" data of which he thought we had a clearer grasp, there is surprisingly little *direct* discussion by Mill of how to *understand* ethical claims (the subject matter of what philosophers sometimes call metaethics). To be sure, one can infer from the way he presents his utilitarianism that he thinks that the concept of being intrinsically good or desirable as an end is more fundamental than the concepts of right and wrong action. He seems to take the claim that the only thing desirable as an end is pleasure and freedom from pain to be simply an alternative way of stating the greatest happiness principle (the principle that actions are right in proportion as they tend to produce happiness). And the most obvious explanation for this is that he simply takes for granted a version of consequentialism. The consequentialist is convinced that we can *define* talk about right and wrong in terms of talk about the way in which actions produce intrinsically good and bad consequences. To be sure, there remain controversies over whether Mill was an act- or a rule-utilitarian. But his discussion of the role rules play in reaching ethical conclusions, and his account of how we come by these "corollaries" to the principle of utility seem to me to leave little doubt that he is, at heart, an act-utilitarian. He doesn't think rightness and wrongness are *defined* by rules. Rather, he thinks that rightness and wrongness are a function of long-term consequences of individual acts in particular settings. There are further issues facing any consequentialist concerning the questions of whether it is actual, or probable or possible consequences of an act whose value defines rightness and wrongness. If one does move to possible consequences one needs a way of adjusting value that takes into account probability before one "sums" values of consequences (where the standard way of doing this is to multiply value by probability).

If we assume that Mill did think that one could find conceptual connections between right and wrong, and good and bad, that would still leave open this critical metaethical question: what does it mean to say of something that it is intrinsically good? There are passages in *Utilitarianism* that are at least suggestive of Mill's position. But there is another striking passage in *A System of Logic* that suggests that he may have held a more surprising view still.

In *Utilitarianism*, the first hint of a metaethical position concerning the analysis of intrinsic desirability comes in the context of his discussion of the way in which intellectual pleasures are superior to bodily pleasures. He doesn't spend a great deal of time explaining precisely what the distinction is between the two sorts of pleasures. The bodily pleasures presumably include those associated with food, drink, and sex. But food, drink, and sex all surely have associated with them an aesthetic component, and one might suppose that aesthetic enjoyment falls on the intellectual side of pleasure. Operationally, we might suppose that the physical pleasures are those "lower" animals are capable of experiencing, while the intellectual pleasures are those that only persons can experience. In any event, he seems to think that it is pretty obvious that intellectual pleasures are superior to physical pleasures both in quantity and quality. I take it that when he talks about their *quantitative* superiority he means to be suggesting that the activity that yields the intellectual pleasure, yields more net pleasure (a greater balance of pleasure over pain) than the activities associated with the physical pleasures. Why? It seems that Mill thinks that intellectual pleasures last longer, are less costly, and have less of a downside in terms of accompanying pain. Sexual gratification, he probably thinks, is short-lived. The indulgences of a libertine exact a long-term price on the body and the mind. The pleasures involved in enjoying stimulating intellectual discussion, literature, and art are lasting in the sense that we can return to them in imagination at will. Furthermore, they involve relatively little cost or risk. That's the idea. But, of course, the real world is more complicated. Van Gogh's relentless pursuit of artistic perfection may have cost him both his sanity and his ear. The frustration one feels when one fails to achieve philosophical understanding is real and, often, unpleasant. But none of this is all that relevant to uncovering Mill's metaethical position. It is his discussion of the alleged qualitative superiority of intellectual pleasures over bodily pleasures that gives us a clue. In one of the few places that Mill uses the expression "means" in discussing an ethical judgment he says the following:

> If I am asked what I mean by difference of quality in pleasures, or what makes one pleasure more valuable than another, merely as a pleasure, except its being greater in amount, there is but one possible answer. Of two pleasures, if there be one to which all or almost all who have experience of both give a decided preference, irrespective of any feeling of moral obligation to prefer it, that is the more desirable pleasure. (CW 10:211)

There is a great deal of debate concerning just how to interpret this "competent judge" test of intrinsic superiority. In particular, one can wonder whether Mill meant to claim that all or almost all of those competent will always in all circumstances choose an intellectual pleasure over a physical pleasure – a wildly implausible claim – or whether he meant only that if we were forced to choose between a life containing only one of the two sorts of pleasures, we'd all choose a life with the intellectual pleasures. But for our purposes here it doesn't matter. The point is that he appears willing to define the comparative notion of being intrinsically better than. Specifically, he seems willing to define the relevant concept in psychological terms. But if he is willing to define the comparative "better than" in terms of being preferred to or desired more than, then one might surmise that he would be willing to define the non-comparative "good in itself" in terms of being desired for its own sake. Such an approach still leaves open the question of precisely whose desires define the critical concept. Shall we define intrinsic desirability in terms of what most experienced people desire for its own sake? Or shall we relativize desirability to individuals – X is desirable as an end for S when S desires X as an end?

In seeking to reduce morality to psychology, Mill might seem to be following once again in the footsteps of Hume. Hume famously suggested that we will never find the subject matter of our moral judgments until we turn our attention inward "and find a sentiment of disapprobation, which arises in you towards this action." (Hume [1739–40] 1888, 469). He went on to suggest:

> So that when you pronounce any character or action to be vicious, you *mean* [my emphasis] nothing, but that from the constitution of your nature you have a feeling or sentiment of blame from the contemplation of it. (469)

He went on to compare talk about value with talk about so-called secondary qualities of things, where a secondary quality of an object (see earlier discussion) is that object's disposition to produce in you a certain subjective response – the sourness of the lemon is allegedly nothing but the capacity of that lemon to produce in a normal person a sour taste sensation (469).

That Mill may have been a Humean on matters metaethical might further be implied by his famous (infamous) proof for the principle of utility. While one is warned by Mill himself not to make too much of its status as "proof," Mill does clearly try to move from psychological facts about what people desire as an end to conclusions about what is in fact desirable as an end. Relying on the inference, he concludes first that since each person desires as an end his or her happiness, that person's happiness is desirable as an end to him or her. He then somehow tries to get to the conclusion that the general happiness is desirable as an end to the aggregate (though I've never run across anything even remotely plausible as a defense of this problematic move).

More controversially still, one might wonder if one can't detect yet another Humean influence on Mill's metaethical views. In his *Treatise*, Hume is said to have introduced the claim that there is an is/ought gap. He complains about philosophers who go on and on describing how things are and all of a sudden start talking about how things ought to be, and he demands a reason for "what seems altogether inconceivable, how this new relation can be a deduction from others, which are entirely different from it" (Hume [1739–40] 1888, 469). In *A System of Logic* Mill says something strikingly similar. While describing the subject of morality as art, Mill contrasts science with morality. He says the following:

> It is customary, however, to include under the term Moral Knowledge, and even (though improperly) under that of Moral Science, an inquiry the results of which do not express themselves in the indicative mood, or in periphrases equivalent to it; what is called the knowledge of duties, practical ethics, or morality. (CW 7:943)

He goes on to say:

> Now the imperative mood is the characteristic of art, as distinguished from science. Whatever speaks in rules or precepts, not in assertions respecting matters of fact, is art; and ethics or morality is properly a portion of the art corresponding to the sciences of human nature and society. (CW 7:943)

Earlier I speculated about Hume's influence on Mill's metaethics. While Hume himself sometimes seems willing to view moral claims as equivalent in meaning to psychological claims, there are other passages in which Hume seems to be suggesting that moral judgments have no truth value. If one emphasizes these passages, Hume might be construed as the forerunner of twentieth-century non-cognitivists – philosophers who modeled ethical statements on meaningful discourse that is not descriptive. So emotivists, for example, suggested that ethical statements should be thought of as expressing attitudes rather than describing them (much the way that "Ouch" expresses but does not describe pain). Prescriptivists, by contrast, wanted to model the meaning of ethical statements on the kind of meaning imperatives have. To claim that abortion is morally wrong is to issue the imperative "Stop abortion." (Notice how little difference it would make to her message whether the pro-life demonstrator put on her sign "Stop abortion" rather than "Abortion is wrong.") In the passage quoted above, one might wonder whether Mill is at least toying with a view very much like twentieth-century prescriptivism.

Of course, all these speculations are based on very little textual evidence. And one must wonder why, if Mill held either of the views discussed above, he didn't straightforwardly say so, particularly in his most important ethical work *Utilitarianism*. While it may not be the most charitable interpretative stance, one might wonder if Mill didn't realize at some level that the metaethical views to which he was inclined don't obviously sit well with the normative ethical theory he was determined to defend. If one is trying to base morality on psychology, for example, it seems almost preposterous to suppose that people are impartial in the way that Mill's utilitarianism demands. And if they are not, it is unclear why they would describe or prescribe as right all and only actions that lead to the general happiness.

notes

1 This sort of phenomenalism had its heyday in the early part of the twentieth century. See Ayer 1952 for a youthful and exuberant (if not very careful) defense of the view, and C. I. Lewis 1946 for one of the clearest and most sophisticated presentations and defenses of phenomenalism.

2 Of course, they don't really assert only exceptionless correlations among phenomena. To this day, regularity theorists like Mill are plagued by the problem of distinguishing lawful from accidental regularities. In the few places where Mill addresses this problem, he simply turns to the subjunctive conditional in explaining the difference. The fundamental problem for a regularity theorist, however, is to specify the truth conditions for contingent subjunctive conditionals without invoking the concept of law we are trying to analyze using subjunctives. We'll say more about this shortly in our brief discussion of Mill's metaphysics of causation.

3 For a full defense of this sort of view, see Fumerton 1985, chapters 4–6.

4 Hume's view was actually a bit more complicated. Hume famously gave his readers a choice between two different definitions of cause. One we might call subjective; the other, objective. On the subjective definition (and paraphrasing liberally), X causes Y when X is temporally and spatially contiguous with Y (he later expressed doubts about the necessity of spatial contiguity) when the idea of X gives rise to the idea of Y and the experience of X gives rise to the expectation of Y. The objective definition that parallels Mill's more closely defines causation in terms of regularity – and is the inspiration for the so-called regularity theory of causation. On this definition, X causes Y when the relative contiguity exists and when all events (objects Hume calls them) resembling X stand in like relations of contiguity to objects resembling Y. Obviously, much has to be done explaining the relevant notion of resemblance. I'll talk about this more in connection with Mill.

5 The claim is essentially general because the assertion that there is one and only one thing that is F is, on Russell's view, equivalent to the claim that there is something x that is F and that all things y are such that if they are F they are identical with x.

further reading

Armstrong, D. M., *What is a Law of Nature?* part 1 (Cambridge: Cambridge University Press, 1983).

Chisholm, R. M., "The Problem of Empiricism," *Journal of Philosophy* 45 (1948), 512–17.

Richard Fumerton

Firth, Roderick, "Radical Empiricism and Perceptual Relativity," *Philosophical Review* 59 (1950), 164–83, 319–31.

Fumerton, Richard, *Metaphysical and Epistemological Problems of Perception* (Lincoln and London: University of Nebraska Press, 1985), chapters 5–6.

Russell, Bertrand, "On Denoting," *Mind* 14 (1905), 479–93.

Ryan, Alan, *The Philosophy of John Stuart Mill* (London: Macmillan, 1970), chapter 6.

Wilson, Fred, *Psychological Analysis and the Philosophy of John Stuart Mill* (Toronto: University of Toronto Press, 1990), chapter 5.

Wilson, Fred, "John Stuart Mill," section 8, in *Stanford Encyclopedia of Philosophy*, 2002, http://plato.stanford.edu/entries/mill/.

bibliography

Abrams, M. H. (1953) *The Mirror and the Lamp: Romantic Theory and the Critical Tradition* (Oxford: Oxford University Press).

Abrams, M. H. (1971) *Natural Supernaturalism: Tradition and Revolution in Romantic Literature* (New York: W. W. Norton and Company).

Anderson, Elizabeth (1991) "John Stuart Mill and Experiments in Living," *Ethics* 102, 4–26.

Annas, Julia (1977) "Mill and the Subjection of Women," *Philosophy* 52, 179–94.

Appiah, Kwame Anthony (2005) *The Ethics of Identity* (Princeton: Princeton University Press).

Ayer, A. J. (1952) *Language, Truth and Logic* (New York: Dover).

Bailey, James Wood (1997) *Utilitarianism, Institutions, and Justice* (New York: Oxford University Press).

Baum, Bruce (1997) "Feminism, Liberalism, and Cultural Pluralism: J. S. Mill on Mormon Polygamy," *Journal of Political Philosophy* 5, 230–53.

Baum, Bruce (2000) *Rereading Power and Freedom in J. S. Mill* (Toronto: University of Toronto Press).

Baum, Bruce (2003) "Millian Radical Democracy: Education for Freedom and Dilemmas of Liberal Equality," *Political Studies* 51, 404–28.

Bentham, Jeremy (1961–) *The Collected Works of Jeremy Bentham*, ed. J. H. Burns (1961–79), J. R. Dinwiddy (1977–83), Fred Rosen (1983–94), Fred Rosen and Philip Schofield (1995–2003), Philip Schofield (2003–) (London and Oxford).

Bentham, Jeremy (1970) *The Collected Works of Jeremy Bentham: An Introduction to the Principles of Morals and Legislation*, ed. J. H. Burns and H. L. A. Hart (London: Athlone Press).

Berger, Fred (1984) *Happiness, Justice, and Freedom: The Moral and Political Philosophy of John Stuart Mill* (Berkeley: University of California Press).

Berkeley, George ([1713] 1954) *Three Dialogues Between Hylas and Philonous*, ed. Colin Turbayne (Indianapolis: Bobbs-Merrill).

Berkowitz, Peter (1999) *Virtue and the Making of Modern Liberalism* (Princeton: Princeton University Press).

Berlin, Isaiah (1969) *Four Essays on Liberty* (Oxford: Oxford University Press).

Bradley, F. H. (1962) *Ethical Studies*, 2nd edn. (London: Oxford University Press).

Brandt, R. B. (1967) "Some Merits of One Form of Rule-Utilitarianism," *University of Colorado, Series in Philosophy, no. 3: The Concept of Morality* (Boulder: University of Colorado Press), 57–8.

Brink, David O. (1992) "Mill's Deliberative Utilitarianism," *Philosophy and Public Affairs* 21, no. 1, 67–103.

Bronaugh, Richard (1974) "The Utility of Quality: An Understanding of Mill," *Canadian Journal of Philosophy* 4, 317–25.

Brown, D. G. (1973) "What is Mill's Principle of Utility?" *Canadian Journal of Philosophy* 3, 1–12.

Brown, D. G. (1974) "Mill's Act-Utilitarianism," *Philosophical Quarterly* 24, 67–8.

Brown, D. G. (1982) "Mill's Criterion of Wrong Conduct," *Dialogue* 21, 27–44.

Callicott, J. Baird (1989) *In Defense of the Land Ethic: Essays in Environmental Philosophy* (Albany: State University of New York Press).

Capaldi, Nicholas (2004) *John Stuart Mill: A Biography* (Cambridge: Cambridge University Press).

Carlisle, Janice (1991) *John Stuart Mill and the Writing of Character* (Athens: University of Georgia Press).

Chisholm, Roderick M. (1948) "The Problem of Empiricism," *Journal of Philosophy* 45, 512–17.

Cooper, Wesley E., Kai Nielsen, and Steven C. Patten, eds. (1979) *New Essays on John Stuart Mill and Utilitarianism, Canadian Journal of Philosophy, Supplementary Vol. 5*, 1–19.

Copp, David (1979) "The Iterated-Utilitarianism of J. S. Mill," in *New Essays on John Stuart Mill and Utilitarianism*, ed. Wesley E. Cooper, Kai Nielsen, and Steven C. Patten, *Canadian Journal of Philosophy, Supplementary Vol. 5*, 75–98.

Crisp, Roger (1997) *Mill on Utilitarianism* (London: Routledge).

Crisp, Roger, ed. (2003) *How Should One Live?* (Oxford: Oxford University Press).

Crisp, Roger, and Michael Slote, eds. (1997) *Virtue Ethics* (Oxford: Oxford University Press).

Cupples, Brian (1972) "A Defence of the Received Interpretation of J. S. Mill," *Australasian Journal of Philosophy* 50, 131–7.

Descartes, Rene (1960) *Discourse on Method and Meditations*, trans. Laurence LaFleur (Indianapolis: Bobbs-Merrill).

Devlin, Patrick (1965) *The Enforcement of Morals* (London: Oxford University Press).

Di Stefano, Christine (1991) "John Stuart Mill: The Heart of Liberalism," in *Configurations of Masculinity: A Feminist Perspective on Modern Political Theory*, ed. Christine Di Stefano (Ithaca: Cornell University Press), 144–86.

Donner, Wendy (1991) *The Liberal Self: John Stuart Mill's Moral and Political Philosophy* (Ithaca: Cornell University Press).

Donner, Wendy (1993) "John Stuart Mill's Liberal Feminism," *Philosophical Studies* 69, 155–66.

Donner, Wendy (1998) "Mill's Utilitarianism," in *The Cambridge Companion to Mill*, ed. John Skorupski (Cambridge: Cambridge University Press), 255–92.

Donner, Wendy (1999) "A Millian Perspective on the Relations between Persons and their Bodies," in *Persons and their Bodies: Rights, Responsibilities, Relationships*, ed. Mark J. Cherry and Thomas J. Bole III (Dordrecht: Kluwer Academic Publishers), 57–72.

Donner, Wendy (2006) "Mill's Theory of Value," in *The Blackwell Guide to Mill's Utilitarianism*, ed. Henry West (Oxford: Blackwell), 117–38.

Donner, Wendy (2007) "John Stuart Mill on Education and Democracy," in *John Stuart Mill's Political Thought: A Bicentennial Re-Assessment*, ed. Nadia Urbinati and Alex Zakaras (Cambridge: Cambridge University Press), 250–74.

Donner, Wendy (2009, in press) "Autonomy, Tradition, and the Enforcement of Morality," in *Mill's "On Liberty": A Critical Guide*, ed. C. L. Ten (Cambridge: Cambridge University Press).

Donner, Wendy, and Michele Green (1995) "John Stuart Mill and the Environment," *Prometeo* 13, no. 50, 6–17. In Italian translation (as "John Stuart Mill e L'ambiente").

Donner, Wendy, and Richard Fumerton (2000) "John Stuart Mill," in *The Blackwell Guide to the Modern Philosophers*, ed. Steven M. Emmanuel (Oxford: Blackwell), 343–69.

Donner, Wendy, Amy Schmitter, and Nathan Tarcov (2003) "Enlightenment Liberalism," in *The Blackwell Companion to Philosophy of Education*, ed. Randall Curran (Oxford: Blackwell), 73–93.

Duncan, G. (1973) *Marx and Mill: Two Views of Social Conflict and Social Harmony* (Cambridge: Cambridge University Press).

Dworkin, Ronald (1977) *Taking Rights Seriously* (Cambridge, MA: Harvard University Press).

Edwards, Rem (1979) *Pleasures and Pains: A Theory of Qualitative Hedonism* (Ithaca: Cornell University Press).

Eggleston, Ben, and Dale E. Miller (2007) "India House Utilitarianism: A First Look," *Southwest Philosophy Review* 23, no. 1, 39–47.

Eisenach, Eldon J. (1998) *Mill and the Moral Character of Liberalism* (University Park: Pennsylvania State University Press).

Eisenstein, Zillah (1981) *The Radical Future of Liberal Feminism* (New York: Longman).

Feinberg, Joel (1983) "The Child's Right to an Open Future," in *Ethical Principles for Social Policy*, ed. J. Howie (Carbondale: Southern Illinois University Press), 97–122.

Fuchs, Alan E. (2006) "Mill's Theory of Morally Correct Action," in *The Blackwell Guide to Mill's Utilitarianism*, ed. Henry R. West (Oxford: Blackwell), 139–58.

Fumerton, Richard (1985) *Metaphysical and Epistemological Problems of Perception* (Lincoln: University of Nebraska Press).

Fumerton, Richard (1989) "Russelling Causal Theories of Reference," in *Rereading Russell*, ed. Wade Savage and C. Anthony Anderson (Minneapolis: University of Minnesota Press).

Fumerton, Richard (1995) *Metaepistemology and Skepticism* (Lanham, MD: Rowman and Littlefield).

Garforth, F. W. (1979) *John Stuart Mill's Theory of Education* (Oxford: Martin Robertson).

Garforth, F. W. (1980) *Educative Democracy: John Stuart Mill on Education in Society* (New York: Oxford University Press).

Gaus, Gerald (1980) "Mill's Theory of Moral Rules," *Australasian Journal of Philosophy* 58, 265–79.

Goldman, Alvin (1979) "What is Justified Belief?" in *Justification and Knowledge*, ed. George Pappas (Dordrecht: Reidel), 1–23.

Gray, John (1983) *Mill on Liberty: A Defence* (London: Routledge).

Green, Michele (1989) "Sympathy and Self-Interest: The Crisis in Mill's Mental History," *Utilitas* 1, no. 2, 259–77.

Green, Michele (1994) "Conflicting Principles or Completing Counterparts? J. S. Mill on Political Economy and the Equality of Women," *Utilitas* 6, no. 2, 267–85.

Griffin, James (1986) *Well-Being: Its Meaning, Measurement, and Moral Importance* (Oxford: Clarendon Press).

Gutmann, Amy (1980) *Liberal Equality* (Cambridge: Cambridge University Press).

Gutmann, Amy (1987) *Democratic Education* (Princeton: Princeton University Press).

Gutmann, Amy, and Dennis Thompson (1996) *Democracy and Disagreement* (Cambridge, MA: Harvard University Press).

Habibi, Don A. (2007) *John Stuart Mill and the Ethic of Human Growth* (Dordrecht: Kluwer Academic Publishers).

Halevy, E. (1934) *The Growth of Philosophic Radicalism* (London: Faber and Faber).

Hare, R. M. (1981) *Moral Thinking: Its Levels, Method, and Point* (Oxford: Clarendon Press).

Harrison, Jonathan (1952–3) "Utilitarianism, Universalisation, and Our Duty to Be Just," *Proceedings of the Aristotelian Society* n.s. 53, 105–34.

Harrod, R. F. (1936) "Utilitarianism Revised," *Mind* 45, 137–56.

Hart, H. L. A. (1963) *Law, Liberty, and Morality* (Stanford: Stanford University Press).

Hempel, Carl (1966) *Philosophy of Natural Science* (Englewood Cliffs, NJ: Prentice-Hall).

Heydt, Colin (2006) *Rethinking Mill's Ethics: Character and Aesthetic Education* (London: Continuum).

Hoag, Robert W. (1986) "Happiness and Freedom: Recent Work on John Stuart Mill," *Philosophy and Public Affairs* 15, no. 2, 188–99.

Hoag, Robert W. (1992) "J. S. Mill's Language of Pleasures," *Utilitas* 4, no. 2, 247–78.

Hollander, S. (1985) *The Economics of John Stuart Mill*, 2 vols. (Toronto: University of Toronto Press).

Holmes, Stephen (1995) *Passions and Constraints: On the Theory of Liberal Democracy* (Chicago: University of Chicago Press).

Hooker, Brad (1995) "Rule-Consequentialism, Incoherence, Fairness," *Proceedings of the Aristotelian Society* 95, 19–35.

Hume, David ([1739–40] 1888) *A Treatise of Human Nature*, ed. L. A. Selby-Bigge (London: Oxford University Press).

Johnston, David (1994) *The Idea of a Liberal Theory: A Critique and Reconstruction* (Princeton: Princeton University Press).

Kinzer, Bruce L., Ann P. Robson, and John M. Robson (1992) *A Moralist In and Out of Parliament: John Stuart Mill at Westminster, 1865–1868* (Toronto: University of Toronto Press).

Kripke, Saul (1980) *Naming and Necessity* (Cambridge, MA: Harvard University Press).

Kübler-Ross, Elisabeth (1997) *The Wheel of Life: A Memoir of Living and Dying* (New York: Scribner).

Kymlicka, Will (2002) *Contemporary Political Philosophy: An Introduction*, 2nd edn. (Oxford: Clarendon Press).

Laine, Michael, ed. (1991) *A Cultivated Mind: Essays on J. S. Mill Presented to John Robson* (Toronto: University of Toronto Press).

Lewis, C. I. (1946) *An Analysis of Knowledge and Valuation* (La Salle, IL: Open Court).

Locke, John ([1690] 1959) *An Essay Concerning Human Understanding*, ed. A. C. Fraser (New York: Dover).

Locke, John ([1689] 1980) *Second Treatise of Government*, ed. C. B. Macpherson (Indianapolis: Hackett Publishing Company, Inc.).

Long, Roderick T. (1992) "Mill's Higher Pleasures and the Choice of Character," *Utilitas* 4, no. 2, 279–97.

Lyons, David (1965) *Forms and Limits of Utilitarianism* (Oxford: Oxford University Press).

Lyons, David (1994) *Rights, Welfare, and Mill's Moral Theory* (Oxford: Clarendon Press).

Lyons, David, ed. (1997) *Mill's Utilitarianism: Critical Essays* (Lanham, MD: Rowman and Littlefield).

Mabbott, J. D. (1956) "Interpretations of Mill's *Utilitarianism*," *Philosophical Quarterly* 6, 115–20.

Macedo, Stephen (1990) *Liberal Virtues: Citizenship, Virtue, and Community* (Oxford: Oxford University Press).

McCloskey, H. J. (1957) "An Examination of Restricted Utilitarianism," *Philosophical Review* 66, 466–85.

Macpherson, C. B. (1962) *The Political Theory of Possessive Individualism* (Oxford: Oxford University Press).

Macpherson, C. B. (1980) *The Life and Times of Liberal Democracy* (Oxford: Oxford University Press).

Macpherson, C. B. (1984) *Democratic Theory: Essays in Retrieval* (Oxford: Clarendon Press).

Makus, Ingrid (1996) *Women, Politics and Reproduction: The Liberal Legacy* (Toronto: University of Toronto Press).

Mill, James ([1869] 1967) *An Analysis of the Phenomena of the Human Mind*, 2nd edn., ed. John Stuart Mill, 2 vols. (Reprinted New York: Augustus M. Kelly).

Mill, John Stuart (1889) *An Examination of Sir William Hamilton's Philosophy* (London: Longmans, Green, and Company).

Mill, John Stuart (1906) *A System of Logic* (London: Longmans, Green, and Company).

Mill, John Stuart (1963–91) *The Collected Works of John Stuart Mill*, ed. John M. Robson, 33 vols. (Toronto: University of Toronto Press).

Mill, John Stuart, Harriet Taylor Mill, and Helen Taylor (1994) *Sexual Equality*, ed. Ann P. Robson and John M. Robson (Toronto: University of Toronto Press).

Miller, Harlan B., and William H. Williams, eds. (1982) *The Limits of Utilitarianism* (Minneapolis: University of Minnesota Press).

Morales, Maria (1996) *Perfect Equality: John Stuart Mill on Well-Constituted Communities* (Lanham, MD: Rowman and Littlefield).

Morales, Maria (2007) "Rational Freedom in John Stuart Mill's Feminism," in *J. S. Mill's Political Thought: A Bicentennial Reassessment*, ed. Nadia Urbinati and Alex Zakaris (Cambridge: Cambridge University Press), 43–65.

Morales, Maria, ed. (2005) *Mill's "The Subjection of Women": Critical Essays* (Lanham, MD: Rowman and Littlefield).

Nussbaum, Martha (1999) *Sex and Social Justice* (Oxford: Oxford University Press).

Nussbaum, Martha (2001) *Upheavals of Thought: The Intelligence of Emotions* (Cambridge: Cambridge University Press).

Nussbaum, Martha (2004) "Mill Between Aristotle and Bentham," *Daedalus* 133, no. 2, 60–68.

Okin, Susan Moller (1979) *Women in Western Political Thought* (Princeton: Princeton University Press).

Okin, Susan Moller (1989) *Justice, Gender, and the Family* (New York: Basic Books).

Okin, Susan Moller (2003) "Feminism, Moral Development, and the Virtues," in *How Should One Live?* ed. Roger Crisp (Oxford: Oxford University Press), 211–229.

O'Rourke, Kevin C. (2001) *John Stuart Mill and Freedom of Expression: The Genesis of a Theory* (Lanham, MD: Routledge).

Packe, M. St John (1954) *The Life of John Stuart Mill* (London: Secker and Warburg).

Pateman, Carole (1970) *Participation and Democratic Theory* (Cambridge: Cambridge University Press).

Pateman, Carole (1988) *The Sexual Contract* (Stanford: Stanford University Press).

Rawls, John (1955) "Two Concepts of Rules," *Philosophical Review* 64, 3–32.

Rawls, John (2002) *Political Liberalism* (New York: Columbia University Press).

Rees, J. C. (1960) "A Re-reading of Mill on Liberty," *Political Studies* 8, 113–29.

Riley, Jonathan (1988) *Liberal Utilitarianism: Social Choice Theory and J. S. Mill's Philosophy* (Cambridge: Cambridge University Press).

Riley, Jonathan (1993) "On Quantities and Qualities of Pleasure," *Utilitas* 5, no. 2, 291–300.

Riley, Jonathan (1998) *Mill on Liberty* (London: Routledge).

Riley, Jonathan (2007) "Mill's Neo-Athenian Model of Liberal Democracy," in *J. S. Mill's Political Thought: A Bicentennial Reassessment*, ed. Nadia Urbinati and Alex Zakaris (Cambridge: Cambridge University Press), 221–49.

Robson, John M. (1968) *The Improvement of Mankind* (Toronto: University of Toronto Press).

Rose, Phyllis (1984) *Parallel Lives: Five Victorian Marriages* (New York: Vintage Books).

Rosen, Frederick (2003) *Classical Utilitarianism from Hume to Mill* (London and New York: Routledge).

Rossi, Alice (1970) "Sentiment and Intellect: The Story of John Stuart Mill and Harriet Taylor Mill," in *Essays on Sex Equality*, ed. Alice Rossi (Chicago: University of Chicago Press), 3–63.

Russell, Bertrand (1905) "On Denoting," *Mind* 14, 479–93.

Ryan, Alan (1988) *The Philosophy of John Stuart Mill*, 2nd edn. (New York: Macmillan).

Sarvasy, Wendy (1984) "J. S. Mill's Theory of Democracy for a Period of Transition Between Capitalism and Socialism," *Polity* 16, no. 4, 567–87.

Scarre, Geoffrey (1997) "Donner and Riley on Qualitative Hedonism," *Utilitas* 9, no. 3, 351–60.

Schneewind, J. B., ed. (1968) *Mill: A Collection of Critical Essays* (Garden City, NY: Doubleday and Company).

Schwartz, Pedro (1972) *The New Political Economy of J. S. Mill* (Durham, NC: Duke University Press).

Sellars, Wilfred (1963) "Phenomenalism," in *Science, Perception and Reality* (London: Routledge).

Semmel, Bernard (1984) *John Stuart Mill and the Pursuit of Virtue* (New Haven: Yale University Press).

Sen, Amartya, and Bernard Williams, eds. (1982) *Utilitarianism and Beyond* (Cambridge: Cambridge University Press).

Shanley, Mary Lyndon (1998) "The Subjection of Women," in *The Cambridge Companion to Mill*, ed. John Skorupski (Cambridge: Cambridge University Press), 396–422.

Shanley, Mary Lyndon, and Carole Pateman, eds. (1991) *Feminist Interpretations and Political Theory* (University Park: Pennsylvania State University Press).

Sharpless, F. Parvin (1967) *The Literary Criticism of John Stuart Mill* (The Hague: Mouton).

Skorupski, John (1989) *John Stuart Mill* (London: Routledge).

Skorupski, John, ed. (1998) *The Cambridge Companion to Mill* (Cambridge: Cambridge University Press).

Skorupski, John (2005) "The Place of Utilitarianism in Mill's Philosophy," in *The Blackwell Guide to Mill's Utilitarianism*, ed. Henry West (Oxford: Blackwell), 45–59.

Skorupski, John (2006) *Why Read Mill Today?* (London: Routledge).

Slote, Michael (2003) "Virtue Ethics, Utilitarianism, and Symmetry," in *How Should One Live?* ed. Roger Crisp (Oxford: Oxford University Press), 99–110.

Smart, J. J. C. (1956) "Extreme and Restricted Utilitarianism," *Philosophical Quarterly* 4, 344–54.

Smart, J. J. C., and Bernard Williams, eds. (1982) *Utilitarianism: For and Against* (Cambridge: Cambridge University Press).

Sneddon, Andrew (2003) "Feeling Utilitarian," *Utilitas* 15, no. 3, 330–52.

Sosa, Ernest (1969) "Mill's Utilitarianism," in *Mill's Utilitarianism*, ed. James M. Smith and Ernest Sosa (Belmont, CA: Wadsworth), 154–72.

Souffrant, Eddy M. (2000) *Formal Transgression: John Stuart Mill's Philosophy of International Affairs* (Lanham, MD: Rowman and Littlefield).

Stafford, William (1998) *John Stuart Mill* (New York: St Martin's Press).

Stephens, Piers H. G. (1996) "Plural Pluralisms: Towards a More Liberal Green Political Theory," in *Contemporary Political Studies 1996*, ed. Iain Hampshire-Monk and Jeffrey Stanyer (Oxford: Political Studies Association of the UK), vol. 1, 369–80.

Stephens, Piers H. G. (1998) "Green Liberalisms: Nature, Agency and the Good," *Environmental Politics* 10, no. 3, 1998, 1–22.

Stocker, Michael (2003) "How Emotions Reveal Value and Help Cure the Schizophrenia of Modern Ethical Theories," in *How Should One Live?* ed. Roger Crisp (Oxford: Oxford University Press), 173–190.

Stout, A. K. (1954) "But Suppose Everyone Did the Same," *Australasian Journal of Philosophy* 32, 1–29.

Sumner, L. W. (1979) "The Good and the Right," in *New Essays on John Stuart Mill and Utilitarianism*, ed. Wesley E. Cooper, Kai Nielsen, and Steven C. Patten, *Canadian Journal of Philosophy, Supplementary Vol. 5*, 99–114.

Sumner, L. W. (1992) "Welfare, Happiness, and Pleasure," *Utilitas* 4, no. 2, 199–206.

Sumner, L. W. (1997) *The Moral Foundation of Rights* (Oxford: Clarendon Press).

Ten, C. L. (1980) *Mill on Liberty* (Oxford: Oxford University Press).

Ten, C. L. (1998) "Democracy, Socialism and the Working Classes," in *The Cambridge Companion to Mill*, ed. John Skorupski (Cambridge: Cambridge University Press), 372–95.

Ten, C. L. ed. (2009, in press) *Mill's "On Liberty": A Critical Guide* (Cambridge: Cambridge University Press).

Thomas, David Wayne (2003) *Cultivating Victorians: Liberal Culture and the Aesthetic* (Philadelphia: University of Pennsylvania Press).

Thompson, Dennis (1976) *John Stuart Mill and Representative Government* (Princeton: Princeton University Press).

Tulloch, Gail (1989) *Mill and Sexual Equality* (Hemel Hempstead: Harvester Wheatsheaf).

Urbinati, Nadia (2002) *Mill on Democracy: From the Athenian Polis to Representative Government* (Chicago: University of Chicago Press).

Urbinati, Nadia, and Alex Zakaris, eds. (2007) *J. S. Mill's Political Thought: A Bicentennial Reassessment* (Cambridge: Cambridge University Press).

Urmson, J. O. (1953) "The Interpretation of the Moral Philosophy of J. S. Mill," *Philosophical Quarterly* 3, 33–9.

Varouxakis, Georgios (2002) *Mill on Nationality* (London: Routledge).

Vernon, Richard (1998) "Beyond the Harm Principle: Mill and Censorship," in *Mill and the Moral Character of Liberalism*, ed. Eldon J. Eisenach (University Park: Pennsylvania State University Press), 115–29.

Vogler, Candace (2001) *John Stuart Mill's Deliberative Landscape: An Essay in Moral Psychology* (New York: Garland Publishing).

Weinstein, David (2007) *Utilitarianism and the New Liberalism* (Cambridge: Cambridge University Press).

Weinstock, Daniel (1996) "Making Sense of Mill," *Dialogue* 35, no. 4, 791–804.

West, Henry (1972) "Reconstructing Mill's 'Proof' of the Principle of Utility," *Mind* 81, 256–7.

West, Henry (1976) "Mill's Qualitative Hedonism," *Philosophy* 51, 101–5.

West, Henry (1982) "Mill's 'Proof' of the Principle of Utility," *The Limits of Utilitarianism*, ed. Harlan B. Miller and William H. Williams (Minneapolis: University of Minnesota Press).

West, Henry (2004) *An Introduction to Mill's Utilitarian Ethics* (Cambridge: Cambridge University Press).

West, Henry, ed. (2006) *The Blackwell Guide to Mill's Utilitarianism* (Oxford: Blackwell).

Williamson, Timothy (2000) *Knowledge and Its Limits* (London: Oxford).

Wilson, Fred (1990) *Psychological Analysis and the Philosophy of John Stuart Mill* (Toronto: University of Toronto Press).

Winch, Donald (2004) "Thinking Green, Nineteenth-Century Style: John Stuart Mill and John Ruskin," in *Markets in Historical Contexts: Ideas and Politics in the Modern World*, ed. Mark Bevir and Frank Trentmann (Cambridge: Cambridge University Press), 105–28.

index